Gender Issues

Poornima Jain
Departmet of Sociology and Political Science
Dayalbagh Educational Institute (Deemed University)
Agra – 282 110

2018

Studium Press (India) Pvt. Ltd.

Gender Issues

ISBN: 978-93-85046-25-4

Published by:

Studium Press (India) Pvt. Ltd.
4735/22, 2nd Floor, Prakash Deep Building
(Near Delhi Medical Association),
Ansari Road, Darya Ganj, New Delhi-110 002
Tel.: + 91-11-43240200-15 (15 lines); Fax: 91-11-43240215
E-mail: pubdir@studiumpress.in
Website: http://www.studiumpress.in

Printed at India

Foreword

There are important domains which occupy concerns of gender issues having a variety of regional, and locational concerns. An important concern in this regard is the health care of women. It is necessary that the notion of health care is appropriately appreciated and formulated with orientation towards resolution of overall health care of women. Generally, in India as in many developing countries health care is given a secondary thought. India being a complex society, the domains of concerns in regard to gender justice go beyond education, employment, and distributive concerns. These issues are embedded in to a variety of orientations based on the complexity of Indian society. Indian society is a highly differentiated social structure, ranging from tribal, regional, and familial varieties of concerns. Gender health care occupies in this regard significant concerns with regard to justice, religious, and ethnic differentiation in which primarily issues of justice occupy the most important place. Gender justice and ethnic concerns in the Indian context are deeply embedded in dependence of women in regard to economic and religious spheres. One significant area in this regard is ethnicity. Ethnic issues are differentiated on the basis of religion, caste, and gender itself.

The essence in this collection of papers highlights the relevance and importance of 'Gender Issues'. These concern normal aspects of health issues, gender justice, women empowerment, position of transgender, and reform movements.

I am sure the articles in this volume will receive very wide attention of national and international social scientists, social activists, policy makers, and social reformers. I am sure this volume will be widely accepted, read, and debated.

Dated: 9.12.17

Yogendra Singh
(Emeritus Professor)
JNU, New Delhi

About the Editor

Poornima Jain is presently holding the position of Professor and Head, Dept. of Sociology and Political Science and Life Long Learning and Extension Activities, Faculty of Social Sciences, DEI (Deemed University), Agra. She has served two terms as the Dean, Faculty of Social Sciences, from year 2002-2004 and 2009-2012.

Prof. Jain has held many offices like:

- Member: Zonal Advisory Board, LIC of India
- Regional Level Sexual exploitation and Mental Torture Grievance Committee.
- Sexual Harassment Committee, LIC of India
- Selection Committee of Universities
- Member, Indian Sociological Society
- Member, Indian Social Science Association
- Member Board of Studies
- Chief Guest outside the Institute
- Judge at various functions outside the Institute
- Resource person in various national and international seminars
- Delivered talks various organizations including media

She has actively organized Seminars/Workshops/Extension Lectures. Published two books and one book is under publication on the topic, "Gender Justice and Inclusion", and 22 research papers and book chapters.

***Awards and Honours*:** Received **Gold Medal** for securing First position in MA.

Prof. Poornima Jain was conferred **Prof. L.P. Vidyarthy Memorial** Award on 5th October 2014 by the Indian Social Science Association.

Honoured by Jain Samaj for significant contribution to uplift of weaker sections of society on the occasion of 'Panch Kalyanak Mahotsav', in 2017.

Preface

With the process of globalization, the notion of gender is gaining wider attention. By enlarge, the notion of gender remains confined to women and their economic conditions. This volume on "Gender Issues" cuts across narrow boundary of the understanding of gender issues as it covers various important dimensions related to gender such as reproductive health, women's health as a right, transgenders and their identity crisis, feminist movements in the United states and in India, gender equality in Islam, gender and law, globalizing the feminine as a practice, methodology of feminist, gender justice, and social reforms

Prominent social scientists and feminists from India and abroad have contributed to bring this volume on "Gender Issues".

This book covers different dimensions of gender issues from sociological, political, historical, and feminist perspectives. I am thankful to all of them for making the book multidisciplinary and trans-disciplinary in orientation.

I specially thankful to my teacher Professor Yogendra Singh who has written the Foreword of the book. I am thankful to all those who have contributed in giving the shape and substance to the book. I am thankful to Dr. Deepti Priya Mehrotra for helping me in many ways. No work can be accomplished without the support of the top administration. I am grateful to Prof. P.K.Kalra, Director, DEI, for continuously boosting my morale to achieve difficult tasks.

I am indebted to Mr. Rajesh Sharma, my husband for supporting me and sacrificing his time for my academic pursuits. I also thank my son, Mr. Gaurav Sharma, Ms. Ishita Sharma Bhatnagar, my daughter, Mr. A.S. Bhatnagar, my son-in-law, and my grand-children, Suraj and Gull for keeping my mood fresh.

Over and above all, I am thankful to Revered Prof. P.S. Satsangi Sahab, Chairman, Advisory Committee on Education, DEI, without Whose Mercy and Grace I cannot achieve my targets.

Editor

Table of Contents

INTRODUCTION

Gender is a complex term in social science parlance. In terms of understanding, transformation, power, justice, inequality, marginalization, movements and so on, it has remained a subject of discussions, debates, and research by enlarge. Gender is a ubiquitous construct determining the important spheres of life of individuals in most societies. It is a set of learned behaviors and practices which segregate society on the basis of division of labour set forth by strict or flexible gender roles which are assigned to individuals of the two sexes. Thus, males are subjected to masculine gender roles and are called men, while females are subjected to feminine gender roles and are called women. However, there are certain universally accepted norms about the gender roles but certain roles differ from society to society.

These roles were assigned on the basis of ancient occupation of men and women; for example hunting is for men and gathering is for women; and many other social processes which saw the potential of men and women in different things. These roles were established through a power structure which was predominantly in the hold of men due to patriarchal social construct and thus resulted in gradation of roles as greater as or smaller than others. Gender roles of men deemed higher value and that of women were side-lined and thus, women from the very beginning felt oppressed and disadvantaged. The privileges which were given to men were denied to women and binary sets which were believed as two equal halves became disproportionate. Traditionally set gender roles were congruent to a certain extent to their times, however, in 21st century there is no visible difference between genders roles of men and women as gender equality is the norm. This equality was pushed throughout the history by the agents of humanity who foresaw the world where men and women comprehend and support each other as a unit where nobody is less or more.

The role of feminist movements is immense in uplifting the status of women in society. The most important move which gave the women the right to vote changed the perspective of the government towards them as they were seen as a potential vote bank and their opinions suddenly started to matter. Feminist movements tried to unite the women folk around the world through their doctrine which focused on enlightening the women about their rights and provided a unite force for safeguarding them. The movements were quite popular amongst the educated folks and western world but their reach was limited in the third world countries where the fight for basic necessities of life outweighed the thought of equal rights for men and women. The thread of traditional mind-set about gender roles and duties was so much tangled that is was not easy to introduce western ideology. Although, things have changed in the circles of third world as well but there are still instances of gender inequalities in the form of female foeticide/infanticide, child marriage, dowry, etc. that shows that the journey of gender equality has a lot of miles to cover.

Gender issues are mainly in perspective of the oppressed gender. And thus women issues dominate the area of gender studies. Women's issues are not only social obligations but there are several health related issues which are connected with the poor facilities and lack of family support. A woman bears an additional responsibility of childbirth and childcare which is too demanding in itself as body requires good nutrition and proper medical help. In absence of these essentials, there is always a risk to the foetus as well as to the mother. In traditional Indian households multiple parities are there with minimum gap period, sometimes in the lieu of a male child, several children are born to a mother which make her weak physically and mentally. Women's reproductive rights are not being considered as they are always made realised that it is their duty to produce offspring. Health related issues also involve chronic malnourishment in poverty stricken areas which results in deficiency diseases among women. In terms of healthcare focusing on women, the Janani Suraksha Yojana (JSY) and National Health Mission are vital to the policy landscape. The JSY has improved maternal healthcare in India through the emphasis on institutional deliveries. Increase of 22 per cent in deliveries in government hospitals, was mirrored by an 8 per cent decline in childbirth at private hospitals and a 16 per cent decline in childbirth at home.

Women are perceived as divine and almost all religions profession to give them special treatment and due respect as they have the power to give birth, but interestingly there have been instances where religious fundamentalists were responsible for estranging women from their rights. Whether it was *sati* in the 19th century or the emerging problem of *triple talaq* in 21st century, all are the religious ways to curtail basic human rights of women.

Education is one sure measure which have made the women aware of their rights and made them united for safeguarding the same. However even in modern times women are being kept away from education because of malpractice of child marriage, to keep them as household labours, and because of a general belief that if they are educated they get spoiled. In the sections where education is reached the exploitation of women was checked as they were aware of their rights.

Forty-two years have passed since the United Nations first decided to commemorate March 8th as International Women's Day, marking a historical transition in the feminist movement. Gender remains a critically important and largely ignored lens to view development issues across the world. In 2016, India ranked 130 out of 146 in the Gender Inequality Index released by the UNDP. It is evident that a stronger turn in political discourse is required, taking into consideration both public and private spaces.

Gender studies are made synonymous with the women studies. However, it literally meant to be different. Men also have their sets of problems and prejudices as they are also expected to behave in a certain way and thus, are under serious pressures of violating the norms knowingly or unknowingly. People tend to have a more indulgent outlook on girls acting like tomboys. However, the opposite is not true for boys. There is a stigma attached to a boy being effeminate. That is the reason why society has a tendency to doubt the masculinity of men who design clothes for women, or male make-up artists, or men who follow any profession that breaks away from the straight and narrow. Somehow, men who don't hold nine to five jobs with a salary cheque that puts food on the table are not deemed manly enough. Thus, opting for professions typically assigned to women make them susceptible to ridicule among the peers. While most people believe that gender bias favors men, men have their own cross to bear. Even in these so-called liberated times, men are expected to go out and earn their bread and butter. The option of staying at home and looking after the children, while the wife goes out to work is not open to them. Thus, the choices are very limited for men. There are innumerable stories of divorcees who have found that they are clueless about their finances and how to manage them without their husbands. It is not that women are incapable. It is just that they have given up the choice to participate.

Gender studies also focus on few other gender categories which do not fall in the binary array of men and women; masculine or feminine. These categories are called as gender non-conformers or more popularly as LGBTs, where L and G represents homosexuals, who are attracted towards the individuals of same sex; B represent bisexuals, who are the individuals which are attracted towards the individuals of either sex. And the most interesting T which represents transgenders, who see their physical bodies as mismatched to their gender identity and dress and act like the opposite gender. These gender non-conformers were present throughout the history and their presence is documented in many historical readings.

These are the gender minorities which are marginalized as they are believed as the violators of stereotypically assigned norms and are pushed to margins by the society through the agency of ridicule and unacceptability. The rights of the transgenders are recognized to a certain extent in India and they were being recognized and enumerated in the census of 2011. However, the truth is it is just a government initiative and they are far from assimilation with general folks which see them as misfits and are amused by their transvestite appearance. The rights of homosexuals are largely missing as their pairing is deemed unnatural by the Honorable Supreme Court of India and is a punishable offence under section 377 of the Indian Penal Code.

The rights of LGBTs are a matter of contemporary debate where one groups assumes them to be a condition which is a function of some psychological disorder and the other group argues that no matter what they are, it is a fact that they exist and they should also possess the equal human rights concerning whom to pair with, what to wear, and to portray the characteristics of men, women or either of the two, and also neither of the two.

Chapter 1

Reproductive Health in India: An Overview Through Feminist Lens

Nadiya Muzaffar and Mohammad Akram

Everyone has a right to life and a right to live with dignity. Being healthy depends on a number of factors that include biological, social, environmental, cultural, economical, as well as political. Across all these factors, gender has emerged as a significant factor in determining health of a man or a woman. However, the health of woman remains of distinguished concern because of the discrimination faced by the women due to several socio-cultural factors present in many societies. Some of the socio-cultural factors that prevent women and girls to gain from quality health services and attaining the best possible level of health include imbalanced power relationships between men and women, social and cultural norms that do not allow women to have proper access to education, employment, healthcare, food etc, the physical, sexual and emotional violence that the women face and an exclusive focus on women's reproductive roles. All these issues become well noticeable in the areas of reproductive and sexual health and hence an attempt to understand the reproductive health approach is necessary.

Sexual and reproductive health and rights can be understood as the right for all, whether young or old, women, men or transgender, heterosexual, gay, lesbian or bisexual, HIV positive or negative, to make choices regarding their own sexuality and reproduction, providing they respect the rights of others to bodily integrity (IDS, 2006). However, conventional interpretations of sexual and reproductive rights often have a heterosexist bias they may favor men and not women and especially the marginalized women which for feminists is a matter of grave concern. According to the UN agencies, sexual health refers to a state of physical, emotional, mental and social well-being in relation to sexuality – and is not merely the absence of disease, dysfunction or infirmity. Sexual health requires a positive and respectful approach to sexuality and sexual relationships, as well as the possibility of having pleasurable and safe sexual experiences, free of coercion, discrimination and violence. For sexual health to be attained and maintained, the sexual rights of all people must be respected, protected and fulfilled (Washington and Tallis, 2012).

Reproductive health implies that people are able to have a satisfying and safe sex life (linking to sexual rights) and that they have the capability to reproduce and the freedom to decide if, when and how often to do so. Implicit in this last condition are the right of men and women to be informed and to have access to safe, effective, affordable and acceptable methods of family planning of their choice, as well as other methods of their choice for regulation of fertility, which are not against the law, and the right of access to appropriate healthcare services that will enable women to go safely through pregnancy and childbirth and provide couples with the best chance of having a healthy infant. The International Conference on Population and Development in Cairo in 1994 placed reproductive health at the centre of the demographic objective instead of fertility reduction. The Cairo Conference recognized women's rights as individual reproductive rights. Gender equity and equality was accepted as a goal for sustained and substantial development (UNFPA, 1995). Gender equity and equality; infant, child and maternal mortality reduction; and the provision of universal access to reproductive health services, including family planning services are some of the areas achieving gender equity which are necessary to reduce the threat to women's reproductive health.

The discourse on sexual and reproductive health first emerged in the mid-1980s as a result of feminist struggles against rape, domestic violence, and access to safe and effective contraceptives and safe motherhood. The feminist movement has had a long history of activism around women's sexuality and all that it entails. It is evident that feminist movements globally led the sexual and reproductive health and rights discourses to get integrated to varying extents within many social justice movements and increasingly incorporated into global and national policy frameworks, especially those relating to gender equality and health. Examples of these include national health programmes, national AIDS plans and women's health programmes (Washington and Tallis, 2012).

In order to understand and comprehend the issues and intricacies of health of woman, one has to include the feminist perspective on health and discuss the feminist perspective at length.

FEMINIST PERSPECTIVE ON HEALTH

Feminism is commonly understood in terms of equal rights for women but this is not as simple as it appears, rather it is very much complicated. Feminism isn't just about equal rights for women. Feminism looks at all the facets of life to recognize those elements that might be oppressive and recommend alternatives. Feminism as a critical project would look especially at what is being thought about women: what social roles are they expected to take, what are their liberties or privileges in relation to men, and similar sorts of inquiries (Scholz, 2011).

Feminism means different things to different people, the meaning varies from a desire to change and challenge the whole existing order of things to the aspiration to bring about a more balanced and reasonable equality between the sexes and achieve a decent individual liberty for women with their natural instincts and characteristics intact. Most conservative standards of feminism perceive the area of marriage as one of the fundamental areas where this equality matters. The female labelling as a sex object is fervently opposed. Women who were distressed by sexism within the family or their personal lives were attracted to feminism (Tandon, 2008). Feminism as a movement might have initiated in the West but in India, the decline in the status of women and the successive endeavors made during the freedom struggle to pave the way for equal access to education and equal status, gave rise to the need for feminist studies.

According to the Oxford English Dictionary, the term 'Feminism' was first coined by the French dramatist Alexander Dumas in 1872. Since then feminism has been used and interpreted in multiple ways. The meaning of the term has gradually transformed and now as per the Merriam Webster Dictionary, it means a 'theory of the political, economic and social equalities of the sexes'. Barbara Berg, in the introduction to "The Remembered Gate: Origins of American Feminism", (as cited in Tandon, 2008) defines feminism as a broad movement embracing numerous phases of women's emancipation. According to her, feminism gives the freedom to decide her own destiny; freedom from sex-determined role; freedom from society's oppressive restrictions, freedom to express her thoughts fully and convert them freely to actions.

According to Tandon (2008), the third world feminists define feminism as an awareness of women's oppression and exploitation within the family, at work and in society, and conscious action by women and men to change this situation. In a seminar on feminist ideology held in Bangkok in 1979 feminism was defined in terms of two long-term goals:

1. Right of women to freedom of choice and power to control their own lives in and outside home, and have control over their bodies; and
2. Creation of more just, social and economic orders naturally and internationally.

Thus, for most, feminism is an ideology which seeks not only to understand the world but to change it to the advantage of women. Though it is an accepted fact that there exist biological differences between male and female, but women in general and feminists in particular no longer accept the conception that woman is inferior to man.

DIFFERENT SCHOOLS OF FEMINIST THOUGHT

"Feminism constitutes the political expression of the concerns and interests of women from different regions, classes, nationalities and ethnic backgrounds... there is and must be a diversity of feminisms responsive to the different needs and concerns of different women and defined by them for themselves" (Cagatay, Grown and Santiago, 1986).

Depending upon the various ways of manifestations of the dislike of patriarchal hierarchization and openness in recognizing the various paths feminist take in order to contest patriarchy, there are different approaches to feminism. These different approaches to feminism will suggest different analysis of the causes and nature of this oppression and thus of the possible solutions (Tandon, 2008). According to Maggie Humm, as cited in Tandon, the elementary goal of feminist perspectives "to understand women's oppression in terms of race, gender, class and sexual preference and how to change it".

Liberal Feminism

Liberal feminism, as the name suggests, adopts the liberal conceptions of human nature and human freedom and tries to copy the liberal principles of justice, liberty and equality to women, without questioning male power (Tandon, 2008). Liberal feminists recognize that it is the lack of legal rights and equal opportunities accorded to women which is the root cause of the oppression of women (Scholz, 2011). Sexism is seen as dysfunctional by the liberal feminists because it divests society of one-half of its creative work force. Mary Wollstonecraft, John Stuart Mill, Betty Friedan, Harriet Taylor belong to this school. Mary Wollstonecraft's 'A Vindication of the Rights of Women' remains a classic of feminist theory. Its central argument is that women remain imprisoned because of a corrupt process of socialization which arrests their intellect and instructs them that their proper purpose in life is to serve men. Wollstonecraft believes that proper education, proper training in critical thinking, is the most important single item on the feminist agenda. She rejects Rousseau's idea that men and women think differently. She establishes a central liberal feminist position: reason is the same in all persons. When women do reason differently or incorrectly; it is due to lack of training (Josephine, 1996).

Radical Feminism

This approach is primarily concerned with the issues arising out of pornography, prostitution, sexual harassment, rape and woman battering. Radical feminists lay down a strategy to create an exclusively female sexuality through celibacy, auto-eroticism, or lesbianism, in order to be liberated from the sexual oppression. They are not in favor of heterosexuality and traditional roles of women as faithful housewives and child bearing machines. Shulamith Firestone, a radical feminist who has written 'The Dialectic of Sex', argues that women can be liberated by a biological revolution. Kate Millet claims that the roots of women's oppression are deeply buried in gender system of patriarchy (Tandon, 2008). Patriarchy is a whole network or system of control of women and women's bodies by men. It is a power structure that recognizes women on the basis of their biological sex and, in particular, their reproductive abilities. Radical feminist believe that it is the sex based childbearing and childrearing roles and the identification of woman with their sexualized bodies which is the root of female oppression. Since women can bear children they have been downgraded to the private sphere of family or domestic life, they are held accountable for reproduction and men are excused from reproductive activities (Scholz, 2011). Further, according to Tandon, they see marriage as a primary formalization of the subjugation of women; they consider rejection of this institution of marriage, both in theory and in practice. The feminist also attacked love as an institution that promotes vulnerability, dependence, possessiveness, susceptibility to pain and prevents the full development of woman's human potential. Radical feminism, according to Daly, is a process or voyage of "women becoming". It is both discovery and creation of a world other than patriarchy. For Scholz, radical feminists also suggest a number of other possible solutions to this oppression and most are, well, quite radical. For example, one way out is to replace biological reproduction with technological reproduction. This would free women from the oppression of reproductive biology. Some radical feminists argue that women must give up the unfair power relationships that develop within the biological family where as a result of the weakness caused by childbearing women become dependent on men for physical survival. According to radical feminists, women cannot be free until they are free to make their own decisions about their bodies and especially their reproductive abilities.

Marxist (Socialist) Feminism

The Marxist feminism advocates that it is the material conditions of life, rather than legal barriers that hinder women's freedom. While the liberal feminists recognize legal, social and intellectual inequality as the causes of oppression of women, Marxist feminists argue that capitalism causes women's oppression in society. As their name suggests, Marxist feminists rely on and build on Marxist theory; class oppression, for Marxists, is the foundation of all other forms of oppression and the most pervasive as well. The first and most important Marxist feminist was Karl Marx's long time intellectual partner Friedrich Engels. In 'The Origin of the Family, Private Property and the State', Friedrich Engels maps out the emergence of the oppression of women and argues that we can see how women's power in the family changed. Men became possessors of the means of production and women's social status decreased considerably. It advocates the economic independence of women. It challenges the power relations in patriarchal capitalist system and argues that as long as there are fundamental differences in wealth, privilege and power, equality of opportunity can never be possible in society. Thus socialist feminist resist both against patriarchy and capitalism. One of the most important contemporary Marxist feminist arguments is over wages for housework. Capitalism depends on a class of people doing reproductive labor that goes unrecognized and unpaid; this includes the childbearing and raising children to making lunches, doing household chores and caring for the elderly (Scholz, 2011). According to Tandon (2008), Marxist feminists have variously argued that this work done in the reproductive sphere must be appreciated as productive and rewarded or be socialized so that women are not relegated to this unpaid workforce. Women must be part of the productive sphere or part of public industry. Moreover, Engels argued that family as an economic unit must be abolished. Restoring a balance within individuals and within social sphere requires an end to the sexual division of labor within the family.

Postmodern Feminism

According to Tandon, Postmodern feminism is the most complex theory and difficult to describe precisely because of the nature of postmodernism. Postmodernism rejects grand narratives or more or less comprehensive explanatory theories. Postmodern feminism must not be thought of as a theory but as a collection of ideas. It is also known as 'French feminism'. It has its origins in the work of De Beauvoir's 'The Second Sex'. The writings of postmodern critics like Helen Cixous, Luce Irigarary and Julia Kristevago beyond the boundaries of feminism and offer to women freedom from oppressive thought. But for Scholz, what makes postmodern feminism different is the refusal to look for a single explanation for the oppression of women. Three ideas that figure prominently in postmodern feminist thought are phallologocentrism, psychoanalysis and sexual difference.

Scholz also states that phallologocentrism literally means centrality of the phallus which is the symbolic representation of the penis. Postmodern feminism looks to the structure of consciousness to see that thought and language are masculine-centered, hence phallogocentrism. Helene Cixous challenged women to engage in feminine writing and contrast it with masculine writing. Whereas masculine writing is singular, feminine writing, like women's sexual experience, is multiple, varied and pleasure filled according to Cixous. Psychoanalysis gets us to look back into our childhood or even our infantile state to find therein the roots of our current way of thinking. The postmodern feminists hold that sexual difference is socially constructed not biologically based. The postmodernists say that sex is socially and linguistically determined rather than any sort of natural fact.

Cultural Feminism

Cultural feminists, as per Scholz, focus on gender as the root of oppression. That is, the root of women's oppression is the devaluation of feminine characteristics in any given society. It recommends that there are elementary differences between men and women and that women's differences are special and should be. It wants to overcome sexism by celebrating women's special qualities, women's way and women's experiences. But, according to Tandon, it believes that woman's way is the better way. Fundamental to this theory was a matriarchal vision- the idea of a society of strong women guided by essentially female concerns and values. These included, most importantly, pacifism, co-operation, non-violent settlement of differences and a harmonious regulation of public life.

In most countries, caring or nurturing capacities are unappreciated, unacknowledged or excluded from politics and morality generally. To devalue care is to devalue the women who do the caring. The caring work that they do is not adequately appreciated and acknowledged and yet society relies on it and often criticizes women who fail to fulfill it. According to cultural feminists oppression is understood as a failure to appreciate care and nurturing as central to human existence. Cultural feminists claim for valuing the work that women do in the family and to facilitate more compassion throughout every sphere of social existence (Scholz, 2011).

Cultural feminists today believe that the traditional realm of women provides the basis for the articulation of a human world view, one which can operate to change the destructive masculine ideologies that govern the public world. Contemporary cultural feminists therefore hold that women's political value system may be derived from traditional women's culture and applied to the public realm. Cultural feminists today bypass the nature versus nurture question by assuming that revolution is a matter of transforming ideology, and that all humans are ultimately educable (Tandon, 2008).

Eco- Feminism

Eco-feminism, according to Tandon, is based on the basic principle that patriarchal ways are detrimental to women, children and other living things. Eco-feminism states that patriarchal society is relatively new which developed over the last 2000 years whereas the matriarchal society was the first society. Eisler's book 'The Chalice and The Blade' is often considered the 'Bible' of eco-feminism. One of the main theoretical projects of eco-feminism is to generate new ways of thinking about the relationship between humans and nature, including animals, replacing the dualistic, objectifying mode, characteristic of Western science. There is much to be worked out in eco-feminist theory. However, it serves to distinguish the direction in which feminist theory is heading away from the traditional conceptualizations of liberal, atomistic theory toward a more comprehensive view that recognized the interrelationships among all living beings and the right of all to exist.

Central to all feminisms is the understanding that patriarchy benefit men by taking the male body as the 'standard' and attaching with it a range of valued characteristics (such as good health, mastery, reason and so on) and presenting the female body as deficient, associated with illness, with lack of control and with intuitive rather than reasoned action. In relating 'deficiencies' of the female body with women's reproductive capacity, patriarchy fuses biological sex and social gender. The broad task of feminism has been to question this elision by showing that gender is socially constructed. Through this we can identify the social processes that construct the female body as inferior and that discriminate against women (and favor men). At the most general level, then, feminist theories of health, illness and health care have the same task in common: the attempt to show that women's experience of health is socially constructed rather than built directly upon biology or the materiality of the body (Annandale and Clark, 1996).

Liberal feminists argue that there is no inherent relationship between sex/biology and gender. Emphasis is placed on women's access to positively valued 'male roles' and male experiences which are associated with good health. As a consequence of focusing on rational behavior, the body is mute and passive (Jaggar, 1983; Scott and Morgan, 1993). Radical feminism takes a contrasting approach which endorses a strong connection between sex and gender. It attempts to undermine patriarchal privilege by positively valuing what is distinctive about the female, rather than the male body. The body is central to, and for some radical feminists effectively determinate of, women's experience. Control over the body is also central to Marxist feminism, although many writers in this tradition are critical of what is seen as radical feminism's essentialism, arguing that while the 'biological base' is important, it is modified in different social contexts according to women's historical relationship to the means of production under patriarchy (Allen, 1983; Barrett, 1980) .

REPRODUCTIVE HEALTH IN INDIA AND MISSING GENDER PRIORITIES

The National Population Policy 2000, the National AIDS Prevention and Control Policy 2002, the National Youth Policy 2003, and the National Adolescent Reproductive and Sexual Health Strategy are key examples of the recognition that the sexual and reproductive health needs and rights of young people require urgent attention (Jejeebhoy and Santhya, 2011). Millennium Development Goal 2 aims to stop and then beginning to reverse the spread of HIV and AIDS by 2015. Millennium Development Goal number 3 aims to promote gender equality and empower women and Millennium Development Goal number 5 focuses substantially on reducing the maternal mortality rate. The second part of the goal is to achieve universal access to health care in general, including ensuring that more women access antenatal care, reducing inequalities in pregnancy care, and expanding access to, and use of, different contraceptives for women (MDG-ICR, 2011).

Despite all the efforts made to enhance the reproductive health, there have been many shortcomings which are reflected well in the society. Reducing maternal mortality to acquire gender equity was one of the key areas of reproductive health approach but the reality is quite different. The maternal reached alarming rates. Human history, all the way through has witnessed death and disability both among women and neonatal due to pregnancy and childbearing. Losing a woman during pregnancy or at the time of giving birth or during the postpartum period does not cause death of a single role. Not only with her dies a mother but also a life partner, a society contributor and the best nurse for the child she gives birth to. This can be avoided if during pregnancy and at the time of childbirth the woman has access to quick treatment, better health facility and financial. Further the women always have faced a disadvantage to men in terms of their access to those resources which promote health. This is apparent from the fact that in a country like India woman eats less food because she eats after every male member finishes eating to their fill. This is coupled with less access to the economic and social capital of the household. Also a woman has the least say in the family planning or contraceptive rights therefore she faces unplanned and unwanted pregnancies. Globally it is estimated that up to half of all pregnancies are unplanned and a quarter of all pregnancies are unwanted. These unwanted and unplanned pregnancies lead to illegal abortions under unhygienic conditions which aggravate the risks of death among them. Providing attention towards the health needs of a woman not only gives an opportunity to that woman to live a healthy life but along with her the next generation which she has to bear and raise (Muzaffar, 2016). Although simple, safe and effective interventions exist, 21.6 million unsafe abortions occur globally every year. Unsafe abortion continues to constitute a major mortality and morbidity burden especially in the developing world (WHO, 2015).

Another important area of focus of reproductive health approach was the right to take decisions on family planning and conception. This freedom to make decisions about their bodies especially about their reproductive abilities was thought by radical feminists as a key to women's freedom. A woman's ability to choose if and when to become pregnant has a direct impact on her health and well-being. However, the data from NFHS-3 (IIPS, 2007), shows that a majority of men think that husband and wife should make decisions jointly but that the husband should have the final word. This has implications for the health-seeking behavior of women, who may be dependent on their husband's permission to access health services. Only 27 percent of currently married women make decisions about their own health care mainly by themselves. In the case of decisions about how many children to have, the vast majority of men (89 percent) say that such decisions should be made jointly and most of the remainder say that the husband should have the greater say. Overall, 2 percent of men say that the wife should be the main decision maker regarding the number of children the couple should have.

Violence against women is a major public health and human rights concern, with intimate partner violence and sexual violence among the most pervasive forms of violence against women. With one in three women has been a victim of physical or sexual violence by an intimate partner at some point in her lifetime, the global plan of action provides a strong mandate to address violence against women and girls as a global and urgent public health problem. The plan provides guidance for Ministries of Health to accelerate the implementation of the health sector's contribution within multi-sectoral efforts to end violence against women and girls. Violence against women and girls is an important risk factor for HIV, other sexually transmitted diseases, unwanted pregnancies and other reproductive health problems. For example, women who have experienced intimate partner violence have a 16% greater chance of having a low birth weight baby and are more than twice as likely to have an induced abortion. In certain regions of the world, women who have experienced intimate partner violence are 1.5 times more likely to acquire HIV and 1.6 times more likely to have syphilis (WHO, 2011). Violence against women and children have also been strongly linked to many other adverse health outcomes affecting the brain and nervous system, gastrointestinal and genitourinary systems, and immune and endocrine function (Black, 2011; Leeb *et.al.*, 2011).

Radical feminists struggled to have discourses on reproductive health in order to overcome the rape and domestic violence, a kind of gender-based violence which has an impact on women's reproductive health. Feminist theorists present several diverse perspectives on how best to increase and protect women's rights. Several feminist scholars have pointed out that woman's low socio-economic status leaves them with few choices for decision making with respect to several aspects of the reproductive process: intercourse, contraception, and gestation. Marxist feminists see the root to women's oppression in the unequal power distribution across gender. This unequal distribution of power across gender resulting in gender inequality and undesirable constraints over social and economic opportunities influences the level of reproductive rights (Pillai and Gupta, 2011). In India, there is a substantial gender gap in the literacy rate, with 54 percent of females and 76 percent of males being literate in 2001. Forty-three percent of women age 15-49 are employed, compared with 87 percent of men in the same age group (NFHS-3).Women have also been shown to experience sexual violence in the form of marital rape during pregnancy (Chhabra, 2008). There is also an association between domestic violence and unintended pregnancy. A study based on data from the NFHS show that women who had experienced physical violence from their husbands were 47 percent more likely to report an unintended pregnancy (Begum *et al.*, 2010). More than a third (34 percent) of women age 15-49 have experienced physical violence, and 9 percent have experienced sexual violence. In all, 35 percent of women age 15-49 in India have experienced physical or sexual violence. Thirty-seven percent of ever-married women have experienced spousal physical or sexual violence and 16 percent have experienced spousal emotional violence. Spousal violence, if it occurs, starts early in marriage: 62 percent of ever-married women who report having experienced spousal physical or sexual violence started experiencing such violence within two years of marriage. Among all ever-married women who reported ever experiencing physical or sexual violence, 36 percent report cuts, bruises, or aches, 9 percent report eye injuries, sprains, dislocations or burns, 7 percent report deep wounds, broken bones, broken teeth, or other serious injury, and 2 percent report severe burns (IIPS, 2007).

Since the independence, the government of India has passed many laws to protect the rights of women. In general, however, implementation of many of these laws is weak. National health surveys have shown that high levels of under-nutrition and anaemia in adolescents and women are exacerbated by early marriage, early childbearing and inadequate spacing between births. Data show that more than half of women in India (55 percent) are anaemic, with 63 percent of lactating women and 59 percent of pregnant women suffering from the condition. If we are to achieve truly voluntary fertility control that respects human rights and advances health, our agenda must include not only improved quality of family planning services, but also expanded approaches that encompass the multiple dimensions of sexual and reproductive health for both women and men — sexuality and gender education, STD prevention and treatment, safe abortion, pregnancy and delivery services, postpartum and gynaecologic care, and child health.

WAY FORWARD

According to World Health Organization (WHO) of all health statistics, the maternal mortality statistics between the developing and developed countries display the greatest difference. More than 99 percent of maternal deaths occur in poor countries; this is due to the risk of dying from pregnancy related complications which are 250 times higher than women in developed countries. Each year 210 million women become pregnant, out of which 30 million develop complications which are deadly in 1.7 percent cases leading to 529,000 maternal deaths per year. Further, almost 4 million infants do not survive childbirth or the immediate postnatal period and millions more are disabled because of inefficiently managed pregnancies and births. This situation has remained almost unchanged for many years (Muzaffar and Akram, 2015).

Given that women bear the primary burdens of reproduction and STDs, that resources and political will to provide reproductive and sexual health centres are limited, and that policy development, institution building, and attitudinal changes cannot be immediately achieved, it is essential that representatives of the women to be served are included in all levels and aspects of decision making. Three priority areas for program investment and development include women's health services, programs for men, and education on sexuality and gender. A major reorientation of research priorities and process is needed to pursue critical technological gaps: woman-controlled methods that will protect against infection, with or without protection against pregnancy; abortifacients; and male methods. Simpler, less-expensive diagnostic techniques and treatments for conventional STDs are urgently needed (Wasserheit and Holmes, 1992).

Other beliefs and practices regarding women's bodies and sexuality also have important health consequences. Beliefs that not know about sexuality can result in high risk of STDs, unwanted pregnancy, and inability or reluctance to seek health care. Gender differentials in access to healthcare put girls and women in unnecessary jeopardy. Women, more than men, have to overcome economic and cultural barriers to seeking and receiving information and care. Social constructions of "proper" female behavior and sexuality deter women from using S T D clinics for fear of being regarded as promiscuous or defiled (Dixon-Mueller and Germain, 1993; Elias and Heise, 1993). Single women and adolescents may not approach family planning services, for fear of being seen as sexually active or being refused service. Even medical research has been discriminatory, giving little attention to breast and cervical cancer; using only male subjects for research on heart disease; and, until recently, excluding female-specific symptoms such as cervical cancer or vaginal candidacies from the case definition of AIDS (Corea, 1992; Hamblin and Reid, 1991; Reid, 1992). Feminists and feminist studies have all along had grapple with the fact of the material bodies of women in their attempts to find the base for their theories of women's oppression, subordination and exploitation as well as strategies to overcome the same.

The World bank notes that public health financing in India is characterized by an emphasis on hospital rather than primary care; urban rather than rural population; medical offices rather than paramedics; services that have larger private rather than social returns; and family planning and child health excluding the wider aspects of female health. The constitution of India not only grants equality to women but also empowers the state to adopt measures of positive discrimination in favor of women. But the inequalities inherent in traditional structures have still a significant bearing on women in different spheres of life (Nagla, 2013).

Pregnant women are particularly vulnerable to vitamin and mineral deficiencies because of the increase in metabolic demands to meet foetal requirements for growth and development. It is estimated that 38.2% of pregnant women (aged 15–49 years) worldwide are anaemic (WHO, 2016).The causes of the high burden of maternal micronutrient deficiencies include poor access to and consumption of foods with adequate micronutrient content, cultural practices and values discouraging women from gaining weight, extensive physical labour and recurrent infections (Christian, 2010).Vitamin and mineral deficiencies in pregnancy are associated with adverse health outcomes in both the mother and her neonate. For example, iron deficiency accounts for 18 percent of maternal mortality (WHO, 2009) and is associated with premature delivery and low birth weight (Black *et al.*, 2008). Iodine deficiency during pregnancy increases the risk of miscarriage and foetal growth restriction (Zimmermann, 2008). Vitamin A deficiency affects approximately 19 million pregnant women worldwide and is associated with an increased risk of complications and death during pregnancy and in the postpartum period (WHO, 2009). Most women need additional iron to ensure sufficient iron stores to prevent iron deficiency during pregnancy (Bothwell, 2000). Direct iron supplementation in pregnant women is extensively used as a part of standard antenatal care to prevent and correct iron deficiency and anaemia during gestation (WHO, 2016). Anaemia is a major health problem among the Indian women. Anaemia is particularly widespread among women during pregnancy, when iron requirement increases nearly fivefold. According to the Rapid Survey of Children (RSOC) 2013-14, in India, it is observed that 85.2 percent women received at least one ANC check up. More than 60 percent women received first ANC in first trimester and 63.4 percent women received three or more ANCs. Yet only about 20 percent women in India received full ANC (Muzaffar, 2016).

In Indian society poor nutrition is caused not only by lack of food or poverty but there are also many socio-cultural factors which are responsible for this. Among many Indian families, the largest share of food is usually given to the bread earner, then next to boys, to the old or sick and lastly to girls and women in the household. Girls are generally neglected in matters of feeding and health care. More than half of the women do not get the recommended dietary intake of nutrients. Generally, the poor nutritional status of Indian girls and women is part of a vicious cycle that has particularly devastating consequences for pregnant and lactating mothers and their infants. Malnourished women are more likely to give birth to low birth weight babies, and if underweight baby is a female who survives, she is in turn likely to continue to be undernourished throughout her childhood, adolescence and adult life. This lack of nourishment has also detrimental effects on her reproductive and lactating capacities. Despite many nutritional programmes directed towards the needs of pregnant and lactating mothers, there is nutritional deficiencies in women starting from infancy to pregnancy and then again after crossing the childbearing ages.

Increasing population is the country's most urgent and pressing problem today, and root of all social and economic ills. The population control programmes is therefore seen as the panacea for all ills. However, the family planning programmes are overwhelmingly aimed at women. As women bear children, fertility reduction implies that women must give birth to fewer babies. It can be achieved by curtailing the reproductive capacities of women's bodies directly or by men taking care to prevent impregnation (Nagla, 2013).

Women's dignity and autonomy are ill-treated during the delivery of reproductive health services, because the doctrine of informed consent is not enforced or is misapplied. For example, the rate of caesarean sections is unnecessarily high in both developed and developing countries, in part because women are pressured to undergo the procedure without being given adequate information to make an informed choice between cesarean or vaginal delivery. The most obvious human right violated by avoidable death in pregnancy or childbirth is a woman's right to life itself. Article 6.1 of the Political Covenant provides that "every human being has the inherent right to life. This right shall be protected by law. No one shall be arbitrarily deprived of his life."

Article 9 (1), which provides that "everyone has the right to liberty and security of the person.... No one shall be deprived of his liberty except on such grounds and in accordance with such procedures as are established by law." A woman's right to liberty transcends her right to protect her life and health, and recognizes her right to reproductive choice as an element of her personal integrity and autonomy that is not dependent on health justifications. Under international human rights law, states cannot compel women to conceive children against their will, nor force men to impregnate women. A violation of liberty and security occurs when the state denies women access to means of fertility control, leaving them to risk unintended pregnancy. Article 7 of the Political Covenant provides that "no one shall be subjected to torture or to cruel, inhuman or degrading treatment or punishment." The applicability of this provision to medical interventions, and to denial of desired medical care, is evidenced in the sentence of article 7 that provides: "in particular no one shall be subjected without his free consent to medical or scientific experimentation" (Cook, 1993).

Women's reproductive functions have been used to control women themselves. States have advanced their chosen social, economic, and population agendas by implementing laws and employing practices that control women's reproduction. To gain autonomy, women must attain reproductive self-determination, their path to many of life's opportunities.

Birth control is an important instrument of emancipation for women, but there is a perceptible difference in consequences for women when birth control is imposed, or when the means to do so are unavailable, or means are hazardous to life. Fertility control can be liberating only when it consists in not just control of it but when it implies self-regulation done freely by women.

The practice of family planning is dominated by sterilization. The family planning technologies like IUDs, tubule ligation, laparoscopic tubectomies etc require professionals to install them and needs a follow-up also. But mostly the women do not get time for this and installing the intra-uterine devices causes excessive bleeding, cramps, backaches, dizziness, swelling etc. Sterilization process is used without taking into consideration the adverse effects it has on women. The brunt of sterilization is mostly bore by women when it comes to birth control. According to the World Bank 1996, female sterilization accounts for 90 percent of sterilization. This is highly unjust and a manifestation of gender inequality because men too are equally responsible for reproduction and can also go for sterilization. Women are much more likely to have used a modern method (58 percent) than a traditional method (19 percent). Female sterilization is by far the most commonly used modern method (37 percent) among currently married women. The three modern spacing methods (pill, IUD, and condom) have ever been used by 11, 6, and 14 percent of women, respectively. The contraceptive prevalence rate in India is 56 percent. Female sterilization accounts for two-thirds of total contraceptive use and 77 percent of modern method use. The prevalence of male sterilization is quite low—less than 5 percent in every state except Himachal Pradesh (6 percent) (IIPS, 2007).

The foundation stone of feminist theory is the notion of sexual politics that is women's bodies – both in and outside of intimate relationships are sites of patriarchal power – and are spaces where men are the most oppressive, and women are most oppressed. The control over women's bodies by intimate partner, family, community, society and the state manifests itself in sexual and reproductive rights. Furthermore, state policy, lack of access to effective and appropriate services, and patriarchal views of women and their reproductive role control women's decisions around contraception, pregnancy, abortion and determine if, when and how many children women should have. Linked to the issue of bodies and control, within feminist understandings and definitions the notion of power is also central (Washington and Tallis, 2012).

As noted, 'patriarchal relationships involve, to varying degrees and within different sites, inequalities of power, and without power women are likely to experience little control over sexual relations with men. It is within the context of unequal power relations that women are required to take preventative and protective actions aimed at minimizing their risk of contracting HIV' (Travers and Bennett, 1996).

Indeed, progress has been made and the impact is slowly being felt. However, unless the root causes of oppression and lack of autonomy are confronted and the whole range of oppression is tackled – including the more controversial issues – the sexual and reproductive freedoms of most women will continue to be compromised (Washington and Tallis, 2012). This compromise will never allow humanity (including both men and women) to enjoy the virtues of freedom, liberty and justice.

REFERENCES

Allen, J. (1983). Marxism and the man question. *In*: Allen, J. and Patton, P. (*eds.*) Beyond Marxism. Leichardt: Intervention Publishing.

Annandale, E. and Clark, J. (1996). What is gender? Feminist theory and the sociology of human reproduction. *Sociology of Health & Illness*, 18: 17-44.

Barrett, M. (1980). *Women's Oppression Today*. New York: New Left Books.

Begum, S., Dwivedi, S.N., Pandey, A. and Mittal, S. (2010). Association between domestic violence and unintended pregnancies in India: Findings from the National Family Health Survey-2 data. *Natl. Med. J. India*, 23: 198–200.

Black, M.C. (2011). Intimate partner violence and adverse health consequences: Implications for clinicians. *American Journal of Lifestyle Medicine*, 5: 428–439.

Black, R.E., Allen L.H., Bhutta Z.A., Caulfield L.E., De Onis, M., Ezzati, M. *et al.* (2008). Maternal and child under nutrition: Global and regional exposures and health consequences. *Lancet,* 371: 243–60.

Bothwell, T.H. (2000). Iron requirements in pregnancy and strategies to meet them. *Am. J. Clin. Nutr.,* 72: 257S–64S.

Cagatay, N., Grown, C. and Santiago, A. (1986). The Nairobi Women's Conference: Toward a global feminism? *Feminist Studies*, 12: 401–412.

Chhabra, S. (2008). Sexual violence among pregnant women in India. *J. Obstet. Gynaecol. Res.*, 34: 238–41.

Christian, P. (2010). Micronutrients, birth weight and survival. *Annu. Rev. Nutr.*, 30: 83–104.

Cook, R. (1993). International human rights and women's reproductive health. Studies in family planning, population council, pp. 73–86.

Corea, G. (1992). The invisible epidemic. New York: Harper Collins.

Dixon-Mueller, R. and Germain, A. (1993). Whose life is it, anyway? Assessing the relative risks of contraception and pregnancy. *In*: Dixon-Mueller, R. and Germain, A. (*eds.*) Four essays on birth control needs and risks. New York: International Women's Health Coalition.

Elias, C. and Heise, L. (1993). The development of microbicides: A new method of HIV prevention for women. Working paper no. 6. Programs division, population council.

Hamblin, J. and Reid, E. (1991). Women, the HIV epidemic and human rights: A tragic imperative. Paper presented at the International Workshop on AIDS: A Question of Rights and Humanity, at the International Court of Justice, The Hague.

IDS, (2006). Sexual and reproductive health and rights. *In*: Health Key Issues Guide. IDS: Brighton; IDS.

International Institute for Population Sciences (IIPS), (2007). National Family Household Survey (NFHS 3) 2005– 06, India, Volume I, Mumbai.

Jaggar, A. (1983). *Feminist Politics and Human Nature.* New Jersey: Roman and Allanheld.

Jejeebhoy, S.J. and Santhya, K.G. (2011). Sexual and reproductive health of young people in India: A review of policies, laws and programmes. New Delhi: Population council.

Josephine, D. (1996). *Feminist theory: The intellectual traditions of American feminism.* Continuum, New York.

Leeb, T.R., Lewis, T. and Zolotor, A.J. (2011). A review of physical and mental health consequences of child abuse and neglect and implications for practice. *American Journal of Lifestyle Medicine*, 5: 454–468.

MDG-ICR (2011). Millennium Development Goals- India Country Report, Central Statistical Organization, Ministry of Statistics and Programme Implementation, Government of India.

Muzaffar, N. (2016). Maternal health care in India: Some observations from RSOC, NFHS-3 and DLHS-3. *Int. J. Reprod. Contracept. Obstet. Gynecol.,* 1: 6–12.

Muzaffar, N. and Akram, M. (2015). Pregnancy and childbirth experiences: A review of the care agencies and the nature of care. *International Journal of Prevention and Treatment*, 3: 41–47.

Nagla, M. (2013). *Gender and Health.* Jaipur: Rawat Publications.

Pillai, V. and Gupta, R. (2011). Reproductive rights approach to reproductive health in developing countries. *Global Health Action,* 4: 8423.

Reid, E. (1992). Women, the HIV epidemic and human rights: A tragic imperative. Paper presented at the International Workshop on AIDS: A Question of Rights and Humanity, May, in The Hague.

Scholz, S. (2011). *Feminism; A Beginner's Guide*. USA: One World Publications.

Scott, S. and Morgan, D. (*eds.*) (1993). *Body Matters*. London: Falmer Press.

Tandon, N. (2008). *Feminism: A paradigm shift*. New Delhi: Atlantic Publishers and distributors.

Travers, M. and Bennett, L. (1996). AIDS, women and power. *In*: Sherr, L., Hankins, C. and Bennett, L. (*eds.*). *AIDS as a gender issue: Psychosocial perspectives*. (Social aspects of AIDS series). London: Taylor and Francis.

UNFPA, (1995). ICPD'94: Summary of the programme of action.

Washington, L. and Tallis, V. (2012). Sexual and reproductive health and rights. *A Journal on African Women's Experiences*, 2.

Wasserheit, J. and Holmes, K. (1992). Reproductive tract infections: Challenges for International Health Policy, Programs and Research. *In*: Germain, A. *et al.* (*eds.*), Reproductive tract infections: Global impact and priorities for women's reproductive health. New York: Plenum Press.

World Bank. (1996). *Improving Women's Health in India*. Washington, DC.

World Health Organization (2013). Global and regional estimates of violence against women: Prevalence and health effects of intimate partner violence and non-partner sexual violence. Geneva.

World Health Organization. (2009). Global health risk. Mortality and burden of disease attributable to selected major risks. Geneva.

World Health Organization. (2009). Global prevalence of vitamin A deficiency in populations at risk 1995–2005. WHO global database on vitamin A deficiency, Geneva.

World Health Organization. (2015). Health worker roles in providing safe abortion care and post-abortion contraception.

Zimmermann, M.B., Jooste, P.L. and Pandav, C.S. (2008). Iodine-deficiency disorders. *Lancet*, 372: 1251–62.

Chapter 2

Understanding Women's Health and Rights Issues

Madhu Nagla

INTRODUCTION

The concept of right to health as a human right has recently emerged as a result of ever growing consciousness about the dignity of human life, all over the world. Health care is considered as a socio-medical concept which implies that whatever is medically possible to promote the physical, mental and well-being of the patient must be done. Medical profession which is a noble profession has now becoming a business. Medical professionals often forget their responsibilities towards their patients and conduct their professional work without observing the code of ethics and thereby violate the rights of the patients. Growing incidences of malpractice and medical negligence keep the patient resulting into the poor health or sometime in medical complications. Since women who constitute nearly half of the population of any country and they have a additional responsibility of reproduction and motherhood, therefore, obviously they are more likely to be a recipient of health care.

Before any treatment or investigation, patients have the right to a clear, concise explanation in lay terms of the proposed procedure and of any available alternative procedure. Where applicable the explanation shall incorporate information on risks, side-effects or after-effects, problems relating to recuperation, likelihood of success, risk of death, and whether the proposed procedure is to be administered by or in the presence of students. A patient may refuse any treatment or investigation.

If a patient is in hospital or any other health care facility, the patient shall, unless incapacitated, be consulted about any decision to discharge or transfer the patient to another facility. Where it is appropriate to a patient's condition or treatment, the patient shall be given advice about self-care, drug administration, special precautions which may be necessary or desirable, and the existence of special association, facilities, aids or appliances which may be of assistance. A patient's consent shall be required before any procedure is carried out. No patient shall be treated or examined without his or her consent. If a patient is incapacitated and delay would be dangerous, a doctor is entitled to carry out any necessary treatment or operation. A patient's written consent shall be required for the inclusion of a patient in any research. The patient shall be adequately informed of the aims, methods, anticipated benefits and potential hazards of the study and the discomfort it may entail. The patient shall be informed that he or she is free to withdraw his or her consent to participation at any time. To ensure that the informed consent is not obtained under duress or from a patient in a dependent relationship to the health professional, the informed consent shall be obtained by a health professional who is not engaged in the investigation and who is completely independent of the official relationship between the patient and the health professional.

According to the human rights, which guarantees equality between sexes, many of the health disadvantages of women can be under scrutiny under equality. Gender disparities which affect many women, have lead to a host of health problems including unintended pregnancy, low birth weight, reproductive problems etc. Gender consideration often leads to denial of various human rights including the access to adequate information regarding sterilization in family planning, sex selective amniocentesistest, breast feeding and access to safe abortion. The present paper focuses on the understanding of women's health right issues in context of these above mentioned issues.

Human life is precious and every person has a fundamental right to live with dignity. It is the duty of a welfare state to protect and develop the life of every citizen and to promote his rights to health and medical care. Right to medical care is important because it relates to the very existence of human life. Medical care is as essential as the other basic needs of a person like food, water, shelter and clothing. Every nation has evolved its own system of laws to ensure the health rights of its citizens. These laws aim to establish a humane system of health care based on the principles of equity, justice and efficiency. By emphasizing the rights of the citizens for proper health care the welfare government tries to enhance the welfare of its people so that they can live healthy and predictive lives.

Right to health and health care is also a fundamental right under Article 21 of the Constitution of India. This has also been emphasized by the Supreme court of India in several obligation on he state to protect citizen's life from medical and other forms of negligence. Consumer Protection Act is applicable all over India but does not fall within the category of state-level health legislation.

CONTEXT

Reproductive health is matter of concern for women.There are several facets of it. Decision to conceive the child, use of different family planning methods, breast feeding and nuances of sex selective technology are some of the concerns which are exclusively related with women *vis-a-vis* her health.The present paper focuses on the emerging health right issues concern to women.

OBJECTIVES

- How do women adjust to possible health complications and procedures associated with family planning, sex-determination test, breast feeding and abortion.
- What makes them uncomfortable in relation to their health rights?

METHODOLOGY

Interviews formed an extremely interesting and rich source of information, and made the research process a thoroughly realistic. We have tried to present the feel of the field work experience by allowing the voices of some of those who were interviewed in the context of their autonomy and rights.

The following sections present the account of visits to a family Planning Clinic in the OPD of a medical college hospital and private health facilities during our study. The present paper is based on a larger study (Nagla, 2007) on the various facets of the gender inequality of health in which some ethnographic and health narratives are also one of the component. The data of the study was collected during April-June 2006. I was there during clinic hours, and the women attending the clinic were being seen throughout the interview. For me, it turned out to be as much as occasion to observe as to conduct an interview. The analysis of the present study is based on some case studies gathered during the field work done in relation to women with her health concerns in the city of Rohtak, Haryana. The empirical evidences are presented in the form of narratives gathered from the women during our field work. The paper seeks to discuss some of these questions in the context of evidence on the understanding of women and her rights in different areas of her health concern.

WOMEN STERILIZATION (FAMILY PLANNING METHOD)

Human right activists demand that the choice whether to choose contraceptives, or discontinue contraceptive use and choice of type of contraceptive should be individual woman's not that of the medical personnel providing the service. Providers of contraceptive technologies believe in the principle of free and informed choice, but in practice they often do not adhere to it, stating that they know what is good for the individual in question. Choices should be based on sufficient and unbiased information. The doctor should provide information about all methods (including barrier methods, and natural methods, access to safe abortion and sterilization), how to use them, their advantages and disadvantages in terms of both efficacy and adverse effects (health risks) and allow individual to choose the method once medical contraindications have been established. Unbalanced and incomplete information may be falsely reassuring and lead to inappropriate use and possible harm to women (Gupta, 2000).

The most common method of contraception used in India besides abortion is sterilization, and of this the major share is that of female sterilization. During the 1960s and early 1970s, vasectomy was promoted in India's family planning programme.Since then, at policy level, vasectomy has been almost totally replaced by tubectomy. India has started payment of incentives particularly after vasectomy since mid-sixties.This was considered as compensation for loss of ways for away from work of about five days. Paid leave after voluntary sterilization is given in India to government employees. There are some state governments and central government employees are given advance increments, loans with low interest rates etc. after voluntary sterilization of course with lower age and parity restrictions. Cash incentives to the motivators and or/to provider of services *e.g.,* surgeon, nurses and other para-medical staff after voluntary sterilization are also given. Laparoscopic sterilizations are often done in sub-optimal conditions, either in institutional or mobile settings. In rural areas, camps are organized in temporary locations such as school buildings or some other public facility on special occasions. In these camps a single surgeon performs 300-500 laparoscopies in 10 hours per day, which works out to one operation every two minutes. With the minimal care that is necessary for such an operation, only a maximum of 50 a day would be possible (Gupta, 2000). In Kumbakonam 1,225 women were operated in one day (Balasurbrahmanyan, 1986). In such as setting, it must be expected that the attitude of the health personnel would be callous. Obviously, follow-up care is not part of such mass programmes which provide the facility of sterilization and move on. Often these areas do not have hospitals or clinics where women who have problems can go for help.

Ramanathan *et al.* (1995) note that 48 sterilizations were performed by one surgical team in just over two hours is clear violation of the regulations. Counseling of women before the operation was inadequate, the surgeon never changed his gloves, the linen on the operating tables was never changed and the facilities in the building were grossly insufficient to support post-operation requirements.

A study of 9,066 laparoscopies conducted in camps over ten years reported surgical difficulties for 7.9 percent of the clients, complications for 5.3 percent, and failure rates of 0.6 percent per 100 women years' (Karkal, 1985:39). Prakash (1984) reports a death rate of 10-12 per 100,000 laparoscopic sterilizations, compared to an acceptable figure of 0.25 to 0.5. The Indian Association of Gynaecological Endoscopists issued a strong statement criticizing the way mass sterilization camps are conducted. Some even condemned the way of working of such 'professional laparoscopists' and their 'craze for speed' and the setting of daily targets which have resulted in both 'method failure' as well as medical complications for women (Prakash, 1984). The providers of the services, *i.e.,* doctors themselves were not aware of the standards, and the quality of the services provided by them was found be poor in all locations (Rajya Sabha, 2003). Mavalankar and Sharma (1999) in their study of sterilization in camps of Gujarat found that many potential clients are reluctant to undergo sterilization in spite of not wanting more children because of poor quality of care.

Unnithan Kumar (2003) finds that there is a widespread belief among Darana women and men as well as in the surrounding villages, that even when you go to public hospital to have a child, the doctors perform tubectomies (effectively terminating women's ability to conceive). Middle-class, high caste doctors force poor, low caste women to undergo sterilization with no thought for women's own choices, desires, or even their past reproductive histories.This is also evident in Ram's study (1998) of the relationship between maternity and modernity in Tamilnadu.

The situation in government hospitals and family welfare clinics is no better. Our study also observed the following situation in the field setting.

The women to whom we interviewed about the details of the entering into hospital upto the follow up procedures we infer from our data that more than seventy per cent women are illiterate therefore, they could not read the paper on which they signed before their sterilization. Neither they were informed or counseled for their sterilization in relation to the wider choices of different methods. The way sterilization camps were conducted, there is clear violation of the directions of the guidelines as well as violation of section 90 of the Indian Penal Code relating to informed consent. The women are only informed about that tubectomy is the best method and therefore, they are performing tubectomy on her for her goodness. Before, sterilization, it is mandatory for doctor to take the history of the patient and to see that whether the history of the person is compatible for sterilization or not. However, the history which is taken is restricted only to the menstrual and obstetric history, nothing more than that. The physical examination of pelvic is also done in a causal manner without bothering for change of gloves for each patient. Urine examination, haemoglobin examination is done in a routine manner. There is no cleanliness of toilets, and therefore, there are chances of infection which can be transmitted from one person to another. The operating surgeon did not conduct any final assessment of the women was done before performing sterilization. There are no cases of refusal of sterilization on the basis of relative contradiction, clinical assessment or laboratory examination in the health care facility.

In the context of sterilization, informed consent means that the user has been aware of the other choices of methods of contraception besides the possible health problems that might occur and grant her consent voluntarily without any inducement, force, deceit, bias or any other form of coercion. The informed consent of the individual acceptor is a must in case of voluntary sterilization. The consent may be considered as informed if the person consenting had the full information on:

(i) The nature of operation;

(ii) Its consequences, risks and the possibility that it may not succeed and;

(iii) Alternative to voluntary sterilization available.

Above information can also be given by the paramedical staff besides the doctors.

In view of the prevalent gender norms that rationalize the bargaining power of women, lack of informed choice and high infant as well as child mortality, female sterilization as a family planning measure in India raises questions about her rights.

Clients must be told that they have the option of deciding against the procedure at any time without sacrificing their right to other reproductive health services. The client must be told that a reversal of this surgery is possible, but the reversal involves a major surgery and its success cannot be guaranteed. Consent for sterilization operation should not be obtained under coercion or when the client is under physical or mental stress. Consent should not be obtained when a woman is sedated or when she experiences stress associated with some pregnancy related events / problems.

Clients must sign a printed application and consent form for sterilization. There are certain conditions that require doctors to be cautious, delay the surgery, refer the client to a specialty equipped centre, or counsel to opt for alternative contraception. There may be situations when it is better to counsel the female client's husband to go in for vasectomy. There are no absolute contraindications for tubectomy. Temporary contraindications include anaemia, severe hypertension, diabetes, local skin diseases etc. The best timing for performing tubectomy is after delivery also and it is called postpartum sterilization. Tubectomy can also be performed after periods when pregnancy is ruled out. This procedure is called interval tubectomy or tubectomy can be done after the woman undergoes MTP or spontaneous abortion. Female sterilization by minilap tubectomy can be performed by a trained MBBS doctor, whereas laparoscopic sterilization can only be performed either by a gynaecologist with DGO/MD/MS or a surgeon with a MS degree and trained in laparoscopy. Prior to performing sterilization operation, a careful clinical assessment of the clients should be made to ensure their fitness for surgery. Tubectomy is either done by laparotomy which entails opening of the abdomen by a small incision or by laparoscopy. Tubectomy by laparotomy is best done in the postpartum period when the operation is quite simple to perform as the uterus is large and felt per abdomen. This is a very simple and safe procedure. The operation is done at least 24 hours after delivery so that the woman has adequate rest and has sufficient time to make up her mind as this a permanent procedure. Her haemoglobin and urine are checked preoperatively. Consent of the women is enough for this operation. Husband's consent is not a must for this operation. The operating doctor confirms her physical fitness for this operation before proceeding for the surgery. Tubectomy can be performed under local anaesthesia, spinal anaesthesia or general anaesthesia. Preparation for surgery includes pre-operative assessment and instructions, a review of the surgical procedure and 24 post-operative care. Pre-operative assessment is essential to assess the client's physical fitness for surgery and also ensure that the consent for surgery is voluntary and well informed. This assessment can also provide an opportunity for overall health screening and treatment of RTI/STDS, if required Demographic information: on age, marital status, occupation, religion, education, number of living children, sex and age of the youngest child is required to be elicited.

Women are often provided inadequate time and information to consent to sterilization procedures, or are never told or discover later that they have been sterilized.

One of the women reported that:

"She had four children when she visited the family planning centre for some method of contraception. She did not want to have any children. She asked to the doctor to help her out for the conception. The doctor advised her to go for sterilization without suggesting any other method. She agreed for sterilization. After sterilization now she is having frequent problems of backache, menstrual cycle problem and weakness.

"I delivered a third child and doctor asked me to go immediately for sterilization. I along with my husband and my family members gave the consent for the same. After two days of sterilization, I had many complications. Doctors were unable to treat me properly. I still feel that I could have managed birth control without sterilization method".

"I completed my family and I am using Copper-T all through years. However after three years I went to family Planning for removing the Cooper-T as I was having some problems. I asked the doctors to suggest me some other methods as I turned 42 years. The doctor forcefully advised me for sterilization. I had sterilization, again I am having health problems."

Abortion is linked with sterilization in government facility. The blatant flouting the procedures for sterilizations, avoidance of informed consent, and follow up of sterilization cases is likely to have a serious long term consequences for the health of the women.

Women and Sex-Selection Test

Amniocentesis was first introduced in India in 1974 at the All India Institute of Medical Sciences (AIIMS) in New Delhi to detect foetal abnormalities. By 1975, it was known that the test was being used for conducting sex-selective abortion. However, sex-determination was banned first in 1988 in Maharashtra and then in other parts of the country. This ban, however, did not stop the lucrative business of sex-determination tests, it only made it more expensive. It was found that the violation of medical ethics by medical personnel in using technologies which were principally meant for detecting genetic abnormalities for detecting the sex of the foetus, and further misusing the liberal abortion laws of the country by performing sex-selective abortions (Gupta, 2000).

The amniocentesis procedure is usually performed between 14 to 20 weeks and sometimes as early as 11 weeks of pregnancy. In some cases, amniocentesis may be performed in the third trimester. The amniocentesis third trimester risks are lower and are not linked to premature labor. Amniocentesis is also carried out to determine uterine infections in case of ruptured membranes. It also helps to determine feral anaemia in babies with Rh disease. In such cases, it also helps the doctor to decide whether the foetus requires blood transfusions to save its life. During the third trimester, amniocentesis also helps assessing lung maturity. Amniocentesis is considered to be a safe procedure, but as it is an invasive diagnostic test, it has its share of risks. There are some amniocentesis risks that should be noted before carrying out the procedure. These risks include:

- ***Miscarriage*:** The rate of amniocentesis risks of miscarriage is about 1 in 300 to 1 in 500. The amniocentesis risks of miscarriage are high if carried out before 14 weeks of pregnancy. Miscarriages happen due to infection in the uterus, the water breaks or labor is induced prematurely. Amniocentesis risks for twins or multiple pregnancy is same as the slight risk of miscarriage in normal pregnancies.

- ***Cramps and Vaginal Bleeding***: Another risk of amniocentesis in some women is cramping and vaginal bleeding.
- ***Fetal Injury***: In extremely rare cases, the needle comes in contact with the baby. This may happen in case the baby moves an arm or leg and comes in contact with the needle. It is very rare to observe serious needle injuries in foetus while performing amniocentesis.
- ***Rh Sensitization:*** Again in rare cases, the foetal blood cells enter the mother's bloodstream triggering an immune response. This happens when the mother is Rh negative and the foetus has Rh positive blood group. The doctor may give the mother in such cases Rh immunoglobulin drugs to prevent production of antibodies against the foetal blood cells.
- ***Uterine Infections:*** Sometimes, amniocentesis may trigger a uterine infection that may lead to miscarriage. If the mother has hepatitis B or hepatitis C, it may increase the risk of transmission to baby in first or second trimesters. Amniocentesis also increases the risk of HIV from the mother being transmitted to the baby. Thus, one should avoid it in third trimester.

Some other side effects of amniocentesis include leakage of fluid and minor irritation at the puncture site. These were some amniocentesis risks. The following reporting by the woman will make us to understand that she is not informed about the health problems resulting out of the aminocentesis test:

"One of the women reported that she has gone for the amniocentesis test in the private health care and she found that it is male baby. She became and delivered a male child after a particular time. When the child grew older he developed lumps in his both hands. She consulted so many doctors, but could not get the satisfactory answer. At last, she went to AIIMS, Delhi for the same problem. After taking the detail history and diagnosis of his son, they could establish the fact that it is because of the fluid which was used at the time of performing

amniocentesis test. Similar types of problem are also encountered by the other children whose mothers went for the same type of test. Thus, in doctor's opinion and in her opinion it is side effect of the fluid which has been used for the test. Now, the child has grown and he has become young and of marriageable age, he is facing a lot of problem for finding a girl. The parents and prospective girls after knowing this problem are not ready to marry him. Thus, this younger boy is facing physical as well as social problems. He often asks to her mother, why you have done this wrong to me? However she cogently replies that it is the doctor who did not tell me the risk of the technology and doctor has made me the guinea pig for his end."

Women go to a clinic for the test and then to another hospital for abortion.Under the MTP Act, it is difficult to prove that woman is terminating the foetus merely on the ground of sex.Under the MTP woman have the right to terminate pregnancy due to a risk to their physical and mental health, which can be caused by poverty or contraceptive failure.

Another woman reported that:

"The woman recalled her amniocentesis test as a nurse giving local anaesthesia and a doctor inserting a needle through the abdomen. Ultrasound monitoring during the piercing of the amniotic sac was not followed. The doctor used a stethoscope to locate the position of foetus. They believed that the needle was inserted many times because the doctor was unable to get the fluid. During the test, the doctor had mentioned repeatedly that there were no side effects. When finished, the nurse gave them the fluid to take to a diagnostic centre for testing, which they did before going home. The woman did not know that they had faced risks of miscarriage or premature labour because amniocentesis was used without the use of ultrasound; accidental injury inflicted on the foetus by the syringe is generally responsible for such risks. She was also unaware that such procedure might have led to sepsis in the reproductive tract."

Conclusion

Women and Breast Feeding

Despite being known as a breast-feeding nation, India had to enact the Infant Milk Substitute Act in1992 to protect breast-feeding from the commercial onslaught of companies out to make a profit at the expense of the health of infants. The Act was later amended in 2003 and came to force on 1st January, 2004.

The main reason that more and more mothers are turning to infant formulas is because companies selling infant food make them psychological prisoners to the belief that their product is superior to mother's milk and thus more healthy for their new born, when just the contrary is true. Any such propaganda or advertisement, allurements to doctors or medical staff is a criminal offence and punishable under the Act.

The National Family Health Survey - 3, published in late 2006, said only 24.5 percent of new mothers initiated breastfeeding in the hour after birth, 46.4 percent breastfed exclusively the first six months and a slightly more encouraging 56.7 percent nursed beyond six months with the introduction of complementary food. But nearly half of under 5 children were underweight. The survey mentions these numbers in the same breath as a 57 in 1,000 live birth infant mortality rate compared to 44 in 1,000 live births of sub-Saharan Africa. An important developmental parameter, IMR continues to stay high despite the two-decade long campaign to bring it down.Breastfeeding promotion alone contributes to 11.6 percent reduction in IMR if coverage of promotion is 99 percent through one-to-one and group counseling, and can avert 21.9 million Disability Adjusted Life Years at 3 years. With such staggering statistics lined up, the country needs to give breastfeeding an impetus. The solution is simple: promote breastfeeding by committing money and resources (NFHS-3: 2006).

An International working group on infant feeding convened by the WHO (1991) recommended exclusive breast feeding up to the first four months. Exclusive breast feeding indicates feeding a baby with only breast milk and not with any supplementary foods (Ebrahim, 1978). The NFHS-I Survey in Kerala reported that forty nine per cent of mothers had squeezed the first breast milk (N =1423). This indicates that the governmental policy as partially helped and many still continue to avoid giving first milk to their babies.

Unenforced Law and Misinformation

If the benefits were this palpable, breastfeeding rates themselves are dismal. A study done by Breastfeeding Promotion Network of India (BPNI), headquartered in New Delhi, suggests the main stumbling block is the lack of support for mothers from the family, society, medical fraternity and also their work places. Mothers are often asked to throw away immune-property-rich colostrums or the first milk. Older women in the family, who dictate infant feeding practices for new mothers, cite inadequate breast milk supply and encourage mothers to switch to infant milk substitutes. Coupled with the aggressive promotion of these substitutes through surrogate advertisements, breastfeeding rates continue to be low. Surprisingly, it is not the law that is deficient, but its implementation and formation of support structure.

The Infant Milk Substitute, Feeding Bottles and Infant Food (Regulation of Production, Supply and Distribution) Act, 1992 does not bane the products under its scope, regulates marketing of breast milk substitutes, which the Act calls infant milk substitutes, to children under the age of two, clearly in consonance with the World Health Organisation recommendation of breastfeeding till 2 years.

"The IMS Act aims to curtail misinformation and misdirected education of pregnant women and mothers of infants about breastfeeding, and prohibits contact between industry and pregnant women or mothers of infants. Instead of just regulating the baby food industry, the Act also mandates creating awareness among pregnant women and lactating mothers about the benefits of breastfeeding. When read with other laws like The Maternity Benefit Act, the law could adequately serve to increase breastfeeding."

Apart from benefits to the mother and child, economic value of breastfeeding is quite high. According to 1998 BPNI estimate, the value of breast milk and breastfeeding to this country of 24.4 million annual births, based on the national breastfeeding patterns over a 2-year lactation period, was around three times the national education budget then.

Using available data on lactating mothers, frequency of nursing per day in both the exclusively breastfed group and those who had introduced complementary food, the researchers indicated Indian mothers produced an estimated total of 3944 million litres of breast milk. If this milk were to be replaced by infant milk substitutes it would cost $3 billion.

Little wonder then that the Infant Milk Substitutes manufacturers have been trying to subvert the IMS Act. Surrogate advertising and sponsored medical conferences were the norm till BPNI took on Food Products Major, Nestle, in 1994. Nestle products Cerelac and Lactogen were found to be violating provisions for advertising, labelling and sponsoring medical events. "The Act empowers four NGOs, including BPNI to prosecute erring companies, in addition to Health officers. But the government has done little in the way of budgetary allocation or legal support system.

In the face of strong lobby, the government has failed to meet the targets had set itself for the 10th five year plan ending 2007 *vis-a-vis* breastfeeding (50 percent initiating breastfeeding, 70 percent exclusive breastfeeding for 6 months and 75 percent complementary foods with breastfeeding till two years). And to the activists in BPNI, it is clearly the case of lack of information, of support, lack of skills among health workers in an institutional delivery and finally social taboos devaluing breastfeeding.

One of the woman in our study reported that she was not taught the way of breast feeding in the hospital:

"She delivered a child in the hospital. When she complained to the hospital staff for not enough milk" but the hospital staff did not make efforts to help for getting milk through breast. Thus, I and my child remained deprived of breastfeeding".

Another woman said that:

"Since she and her baby was exposed to pain killers at birth therefore, the feeding did not started immediately. To compensate the feeding of child she was encouraged for the formula milk. In the mean the child and mother both feel comfortable from bottle feeding. Thus the breast feeding is discouraged"

Another woman reported that:

"I had C-sections delivery and therefore, the breastfeeding did not started immediately. When she returned home, she was again exposed to more taboos and misinformation and therefore, the breast feeding did not take place,"

Breastfeeding offers health as well as emotional benefits to infants and mothers. The baby gets protected against allergies, bonding between mother and child contributes to reduction in postpartum depression, gives mother a rest from the reproductive cycle through lactational amenorrhoea, which has many benefits: no anemia, fatigue, protects against breast cancer, makes baby feel secure, and gives the baby the safest and the perfect food for full development.

Working Mothers and Breast Feeding

Agriculture taking a backseat and growing urbanization has meant most of the efforts of health workers get diluted. Daily wage earners, be it agricultural labourers or construction workers, traditionally they used to take their children to work place and breastfeed on demand. Increasing contractualisation of labour has meant employment practices that are not mother - and child-friendly. The woman said that:

> *"My nutritionally breast milk go waste because I have to return to work to supplement family income. My employer forbids me to take nursing breaks or bringing my infant to the work site. Thus, I abandoned breast feeding."*

This phenomenon is equally seen in urban organised sectors. Employers be it the state or private institutions often do not offer a maternity leave with benefits in excess of the minimum 6 weeks prescribed under the Maternity Benefits Act 1961. While the maternity leave available under this law varies from state to state with Haryana and Punjab providing for 6 months, others like Tamilnadu give 135 days or 3 months' leave. There is a long-standing demand that Act be amended to extend the minimum leave to 6 months and implement it uniformly in the country.

However, the lack of a policy framework to promote breast-feeding, the powerful supplementary foods lobby, the lack of support for mothers and health workers under-prepared in human lactation, have meant that the seven-day long push loses steam as the year rolls around.

The women on whom we focused our interview reported that as and when they complained of 'not enough milk', she is usually asked to buy formula milk or top feeding rather than making efforts for breast milk. Our Indian Medical Service in which the Infant Milk Substitutes, Feeding Bottles and Infant Foods (Regulation of Production, Supply and Distribution Act of 1992 mentions that

"Inappropriate feeding practices lead to infant malnutrition, morbidity and infant milk substitutes and related products like feeding bottles and teats do constitute a health hazard. Promotions of infant milk substitutes and related products have been more extensive and pervasive than the dissemination of information concerning the advantages of mother's milk and breastfeeding and contribute to decline in breastfeeding" (IMS Act, 1992).

Breastfeeding and its success depend on hormonal control particularly the flow of the mother's milk which depends on her state of mind. If there is any doubt planted in her mind about her ability to lactate, it is unlikely that she will succeed. Therefore, health workers or care providers have to play a vital role in building up the confidence of new mothers. However, such support is rarely forthcoming. If a woman complaints of "nor enough milk" she is usually asked to buy a formula feed rather than helped to gain confidence (Gupta, 2008).

Women and Access to Safe Abortion

Some 42 million unintended pregnancies are terminated each year an estimated 20 million of which are unsafe; two-thirds of all unsafe abortions occur among women aged between 15 and 30 years. Unsafe abortions kill an estimated 65000 to 70,000 women every year, representing 13 percent as all pregnancy-related deaths. In addition they are associated with considerable morbidity; for instance, more than 3 million suffer from the effects of reproductive infection, and almost 1.7 million will develop secondary infertility (WHO, 2007).

Abortion has been legal in India since 1972, when the Medical termination of Pregnancy Act was passed. Under the act, abortion is legal that it terminates endangers the life of the woman or causes grave injury to her physical or mental health or is likely to result in the birth ofa baby withphysical or mental abnormalities or is a result of rape or contraceptive failure. The act further stated that abortions could take place in government approved health facilities specifically approved for conducting abortions and by registered medical practitioner.

Data providing consistent estimates of induced abortion in India are scarce: whatever is available is through government reports and surveys. Available abortion statistics shows that five to six million abortions occur in unapproved facilities (Ganatara, 2000 and Arnold *et al.*, 2002). Illegal abortions are eight to eleven times as high as legal abortions (Chhabra, 1996; Jessani and Iyer, 1995; Chhabra and Nuna 1994).

In the Medical Termination of Pregnancy Act, it is the medical doctor who decided whether or not an abortion seeker fulfils the criteria spelled out in the Act. It is the doctor who decides as to how liberally or restrictively to interpret the Act in a given socio-political context. In addition to other factors, providers' attitude towards and understanding of women and their abortion needs influence the interpretation of the Act is an important variable influencing women's access to abortion services. Bandewar (2003) finds that the pattern of abortion practice indicates that perceptions and concerns for women's health in the context of their abortion needs do not go with their abortion care service pattern. This is because a large number of providers have mentioned that it was not advisable for women to use abortion as spacing method. One expects that they would provide contraceptive counselling to women seeking abortion care to avoid repeat abortions. Contraceptives were forced without leaving much space for making informed choices and denying opportunities to educate themselves *vis-à-vis* contraceptives.

The gap between perceptions and practices could be better explained with the help of forces at work which are pushing medical care service sector towards its commodification. Commercial interests of the medical community in abortion service provision in particular can further explain these gaps. Combating the irrational and unethical abortion care practices in isolation without understanding the dynamics of the larger health care system will be a difficult and perhaps even futile task. Further this is complemented by the convenient patriarchal attitudes towards women specific health care needs, such as, abortion care needs. One of the woman reports that:

"When I become pregnant for 3rd time I decided to go for abortion. I with a neighbour went to civil hospital. The lady doctor agreed for abortion but said that you must accept sterilization also. I become very much nervous. I did not want to go through operation and hence come back".

The women in our study had incorrect knowledge of the legality of abortion. They said that abortions among widows and unmarried girls are illegal. Some women had a more nuanced understanding of the abortion legislation in India, they explained that all abortions performed in private facilities or beyond 14 weeks' gestation are illegal. These women also believe that a husband's consent is required by law before the abortion can take place. One woman observed and said that doctors have a different opinion about the legality of the abortion:

"One of the doctor said that just because abortion is legalized, does not mean that doctors should be so liberal in doing this."

The Mumbai High Court judgment disallowing the abortion of a 26-week-old foetus has sparked off a nationwide debate on abortion and a woman's right of choice. But for a majority of Indian women, 'medical termination of pregnancy' (MTP, the medical term for abortions) remains largely unsafe (Hindustan Times, 2008).

Unsafe abortions are those performed illegally, by untrained practitioners with faulty equipment, leading to injuries, infections and even death. India has the highest number of unsafe abortions in the world. According to government estimates, 8.9 percent of maternal deaths in India every year — around 15,000 — are caused by unsafe abortions. The irony is apparent when doctors say MTP, if done right, is among the safest medical procedures. Of the 6.4 million abortions performed in India in 2002 and 2003, 56 percent or 3.6 million were unsafe, says the Abortion Assessment Project I, 2004. The study — one of the largest in recent times — was managed by the Mumbai-based Centre for Equity into Health and Allied Themes and Health watch Trust. It included qualitative and quantitative studies across various states by non-governmental organisations (NGOs), researchers and healthcare professionals (Duggal and Ramachandran, 2004).

It also pointed out problems of reach and access with public investment in abortion facilities being woefully inadequate. Only 25 percent of abortion facilities in the organised sector are government-owned; the rest are private clinics. These are so expensive that they completely exclude the poor sections.

"There's inadequate, inequitable distribution of facilities for safe abortions. Contraceptive usage is low in India, hence the great demand for safe abortion services," said Dr. Jaydeep Tank, chairperson of the MTP Committee at the Federation of Obstetric and Gynecological Societies of India (FOGSI). Besides, only six per cent of India's 23,000 primary health centres (PHCs) provide abortion services."Besides risk to life, unsafe abortions have serious long-term repercussions like life-long disabilities and reproductive tract infections," said Sushanta Banerjee, senior advisor at Ipas, an NGO (Hindustan Times, 2008)

For a country with a 'liberal' law on abortion, Banerjee said awareness about it is extremely low even three decades after it was enacted. "In Jharkhand, for instance, we found that 82 percent of women didn't even know abortion was legal," he said. In a related study by the Population Council in Rajasthan in 2002, the figure was 84 percent and in Maharashtra at least 37 percent of those who had had abortions thought they were illegal. This misconception leads many women to unqualified professionals. Other barriers to safe abortion are "social stigma and myths attached to MTP", said Tank. "Awareness about abortion through drugs like Mifepristone and Misoprostol is also low, despite they being legal and easily available." (Reference:).

Social barriers like spousal consent and judgmental doctors are also deterrents, though the law requires no such consent. Under the government's Reproductive and Child Health Project, safe abortions are a key concern and some progress is being made — maternal mortality due to abortion was 11 percent in 2001. "We need to generate awareness at the community level about contraception and safe abortion, in both rural areas and urban slums," said Thomas Chandy, CEO, Save the Children in India. Ipas also advocates training of mid-level service providers like nurses and non-allopathic doctors in remote areas where access to trained doctors is a problem (Reference:)

Only two in five of the estimated 6.4 million abortions that take place annually in India are safe. The number of *women* aborting an unwanted child has dipped globally. But the rate of unsafe terminations continues to be almost as bad. Around 41.6 million women underwent abortions in 2003 compared to 45.5 million in 1995 — a drop to 29 per 1,000 women from 35 (The Times of India: 14th October, 2009).

Abortion remains highly restricted, and unsafe abortion is common and continues to damage women's health. The evidence is strong that empowering women with the means to decide for themselves when to become pregnant and how many children to have significantly lowers unintended pregnancy rates and thereby reduces the need for abortion.

One woman went to the family planning centre for the abortion and she shared her experience with us:

> *"I went for the MTP to the government facility they agreed for the MTP but without going for contraceptive in the form of Cooper-T. I cannot leave the hospital. Secondly, since I was in my early twenties therefore, they asked me to bring accompanied person, either husband or someone else."*

One of the women reported that:

> *"I went to the family planning clinic for the MTP. But the doctor was not ready to do MTP as he was telling other health personnel that these women they do not come for contraceptive advice and even if they come it is very difficult to convince them about family planning. Most women come here to get rid*

of pregnancies through MTP. They never plan pregnancies. These types of accusation are made against us. Thus I feel that the MTP is done with negative attitude to realize me that I have committed a crime and therefore, I am guilty of the same."

Access to Post Abortion Care

The mortality rates and severity of short or long term complications of unsafe abortions may be strongly influenced by the quality of care received after the abortion. Acute complications such as uterine perforation or the perforation or injury of other internal organs may be fatal if emergency care is not urgently provided. Infection will progress locally and systematically as long as the proper medical and surgical therapy is not given. The later and he less efficient the care received, the more severe the consequences are likely to be and the greater the risk of death. Therefore, it is recommended that the assessment of the woman's condition and the provision of post abortion should be available on a 24 hours basis and provided with the urgency demanded by the severity of the condition (Look, 2011).

Medical Termination of pregnancy is a legal provision provided to women. Liberalization of abortion has led to the fact that women are all aware that they can get an MTP done literally on demand any time

In one of the study Das, Rai and Singh (2004) found that medical termination of pregnancy was done also with laparoscopic legations, in contravention to medical standards. A bicycle pump with a nasal tube attached to its end was used to pump air into the abdomen, and in some cases, the bulb of a blood pressure instrument was used to pump air. Carbon- di-oxide was not used at all.

In India, abortion is regulated on grounds of the health of the mother. It has since been widely interpreted in practice to mean that the health of the mother would suffer from too many pregnancies. Abortion is widely used as a contraceptive measure by women. Further, the sex-selective abortion on non-medical grounds brought out the difficulty with the slogan "a woman's right to choose'. It threw up + -0853 new dilemma- can the right of women to decide regarding abortion be extended to women's use of prenatal diagnosis and abortion of a female foetus? Most Indian feminist, while supporting women's right to abortion, condemned the practice of sex-selective abortion and succeeded in having it banned in 1994 (Gupta, 2000: 602).

The field data confirms that respondents were rarely aware of the legality of abortion, most were more familiar with the government legislation curtailing right to abortion.

CONCLUSIONS

The paper falls in three main parts. The first part reflects on the understanding of women and her health rights, the second in the context of different parameters of women's health where she is directly relating herself to health *i.e.,* women and family planning; women and breast-feeding; women and abortion; women and sex-selection test. Finally the paper concludes by problematising the autonomy and right of the women in the above context.

REFERENCES

Arnold, F. *et al.*(2002): 'Sex-Selective Abortions in India'. *Population and Development Review*, 28(4): 759–85.

Balagopal, Gayathri (2009). "Access to Health care Among Poor Elderly Women in India: How far do Policies Respond to Women's Realities?" Gender *and Development,*17(3): 481–491.

Bandear, Sunita (2003): "Abortion Services and Providers' Perceptions: Gender Dimensions". *Economic and Political Weekly*, XXXVIII(21): 2081.

Banerjee, Sushanta K. and Tank, Jaydeep (2009). "Expanding the provider base: Improving access, saving lives. "*Prevention of Unsafe Abortion in Asia Oceania Region, New Delhi: Impression Communications*, pp. 93–103.

Ganatra, B.R. (2000). 'Abortion research in India: What we know and What we need to know', *In*: Ramasubban, Radhika and Jejeebhoy, Shireen J. (*eds.*), *Women's Reproductive Health in India*, New Delhi: Rawat Publications.

Jessani, A. and Iyer, A. (1995). 'Abortions: Who is Responsible for Her Rights?' *In*: Karkal, Malini (*ed.*), *Our Lives our health*, Coordination Unit, New Delhi, The World Conference on Women, Beijing.

Bhatt, Rohit V. (1991). "Camp Laparoscopic Sterilization Depth's in Gujarat State, India, 1978-1980". *Asia-Oceanic Journal of Obstetric and Gynaecology,* 17(4): 297-301.

Bhatt, Rohit V. *et al.* (1978), "Female Sterilization in Small Camp Setting in Rural India", *Studies in family Planning*, Vol. 9, No. 2/3, Feb-March.

Balasurbrahmanyan, V. (1986), *Contraception: As if Women Mattered: A Critique of Family Planning,* Centre for Education and Documentation, Bombay.

Barua, Alka and Apte, Hemant (2007). "Quality of Abortion Care: Perspectives of Clients and Providers in Jharkhand". *Economic and Political Weekly*, XLII(48).

Beser, E.V. and Aydemir, Boxkaya, H. (1994). "Body Mass Index and natural Age at menopause". *Gynecologic and Obstetric Investigation*, 37: 40–42.

Brambilla, D.J. and McKinlay, S.M. (1989): 'A Prospective Study of factors Affecting Age at Menopause'. *Journal of Clinical Epidemiology*, 42: 1031–39.

Bromberger, I.T., Mathews, K.A. and Kuller, L.H. (1997). 'Prospective Study of the Determinants of Age at Menopause'. *American Journal of Epidemiology*, 145: 124–33.

Chhabra, R. and Nuna, S.C. (1994). *Abortion in India: An Overview,* Ford Foundation, New Delhi.

Chhabra, R. (1996). 'Abortion in India: An Overview'. *Demography India,* 25(1): 83–92.

Das, A., Rai, R. and Singh, D. (2004). "Medical Negligence and Rights violation". *Economic and Political Weekly*, pp. 3876–3879.

Duggal, Ravi and Ramachandran, Vimla (2004). "The Abortion Assessment Project-India: Key Findings and Recommendations". *Reproductive Health Matters*, 12(24): Supplement.

Ebrahim, G.J. (1978). *Breastfeeding- The biological Option,* Macmillan Tropical Community Health manuals, London: Macmillan Press.

Ellen, B.G., Bromberger, J., Crawford, S., Samuels, S., Greenndale, G.A., Harlow, S.D. and Skurnick, J. (2001). 'Factors Associated with Age at natural Menopause in a Multi-ethnic Sample of Middle women'. *American Journal of Epidemiology*, 153(9): 856–74.

Elul, Batya *et al.* (2004). *Unwanted Pregnancy and Induced Abortion in Rajasthan, India: A Qualitative Exploration*, Population Council of India.

Gupta, Arun (2008). "Manipulation by Assistance: Undermining Breastfeeding". *Economic and Political Weekly*, XLIII(36): 6–12.

Gupta, Jyotsna Agnihotri (2000). *New Reproductive Technologies, Women's health and Autonomy*, New Delhi: Sage Publications.

Hindustan Times (2008). *Most Unsafe Abortions in India*, 8th August.

Hindustan Times (2008), August 9.

Jacob, K.S. (2009): 'Caste and Inequalities in Health', *The Hindu*, 22 August.

Karkal, Malini (1985). *Family planning in India: A critical appraisal.* Meeting of the National Committee for Natural Family Planning, Washington, DC.

Look, Paul E.A. Van (2011). *Sexual and Reproductive Health: A Public Health perspective,* The Netherlands: Elsevier.

Luoto, R., Kaprio, J.and Uutela, A. (1994). 'Age at natural Menopause and socio-demographic Status in Finland'. *American Journal of Epidemiology*, 139: 64–76.

Mavalankar, D. and Sharma, Bharti (1999). "The Quality of are in Sterilization Camp: Evidence from Gujarat". *In*: Koenig, M.A. and Khan, M.E. (*eds.*), *Improving Quality of care in India's Family Welfare Programme,* New York: Population Council.

Mane, Purnima (2008). "Population, Gender Inequality and Health- India in a Global Context'. *Demography India,* 37(2): 176.

Nagla, M. (2007). "Feeding the family in India: An approach to household food consumption". *International Journal of Consumer Studies*, 31(3): 295–302.

Kohli, Namita (2008). "Most Unsafe Abortions in India", *Hindustan Times.*

National Sample Survey Organization (1998). *Maternal and Child Health Care in India* 52nd *Round.*

National Family Health Survey (NFHS-3) *India* 2005-06 (2009), Mumbai: IIPS.

Pandey, Arvind (2008). "Population, Gender and Health". *Demography India,* 37(2): 167–169.

Patel, Vibhuti (1992). Review of the effects of the Structural Adjustment programme on Women' Unpublished paper presented to the Development Studies Institute, London School of Economics, 27 November.

Papanek, V. (1984). *Design for the Real World, Human Ecology and Social Change*, London: Thames and Hudson.

Pradhan, M.R. (2009). "Female Sterilization and Ethical Issues: The Indian Experience". *Social Change*, 39: 3.

Prakash, P. (1984). "Use of Laparoscopy for Sterilizations". *Economic and Political Weekly*, 17: 453–454.

Rajya Sabha (2003). *Unstarred Question No. 752*, answered on 28.07.2003.

Ramanathan, M. Dilip, R. and Padmadas, S.S. (1995). "Quality of Care in laparoscopic Sterilization Camps: Observations from Kerala, India". *Reproductive Health Matters*, 6: 84–93.

Ram,K. (1998). "Maternity and the Story of Enlightenment in the Colonies: Tamilnadu women, South India", *In*: Ram, K. and Jolly, M.(*eds.*), *Maternities and Modernities in Colonial and Post-Colonial Experiences in Asia and the Pacific*, Cambridge: Cambridge University Press, pp. 114–43.

Rosenzweig, Mark R. and Paul Schultz, T. (1982). Market Opportunities, Genetic Endowments, and Intrafamily Resource Distribution: Child Survival in Rural India. *The American Economic Review,* 72(4): 803–15.

Shah, Rashmi S. (1998). 'Menopause ad HRT: Growing Public Health Challenges', *ICMR Bulletin*, p. 28.

Standford, J.L., Harge, P. and Brinton, L.A. (1987). 'Factors Influencing the Age at natural menopause'. *Journal of Chronic Diseases*, 40: 995–1002.

Syamala, S. and Sivakami, M. (2005). "Menopause: An Emerging Issue in India". *Economic and Political Weekly*, XL(47): 19–25.

The Times of India (2009), 14th October.

Unnithan-Kumar, Maya (2003). "Spirits of the Womb: Migration, Reproductive Choice and Healing in Rajasthan". *Contribution to Indian Sociology*, 37(1–3): 184.

World Health Organization (1991). *Indicators for assessing breast-feeding practices*, Report on an Informal Meeting, WHO, 11-12 June, WHO Geneva.

World Health Organization (2007). *Unsafe Abortion: Global and Regional Estimates of Incidence of Unsafe Abortion and Associated Mortality in* 2000, Geneva, Switzerland: WHO.

WHO (1991b). *Indicators for assessing breast-feeding practices*, Report on an Informal Meeting, WHO, 11-12 June, WHO Geneva.

Wyon, John Benjamin and Gordon, John Everett (1971). *The Khanna Study: Population Problems in the Rural Punjab,* USA: Harvard University press.

World Bank (2002). *World Development Indicators 2002*, Washington D C: World Bank.

Chapter 3

Dynamics of Gender Variation and Formation of Gender Identity

Poornima Jain and Tarun Joshi

INTRODUCTION

Identity is the one of the most important aspect of human life and it is assigned during the entire lifetime in one form or another. One such identity is of *gender,* which literally have different meanings for different people. In the feminist circles it is presumably associated with *women studies, women upliftment* and thus unifocal to a great extent. While in general it is being understood as synchronous to sex and labelled in a binary set of male and female or masculine and feminine. However, gender is nothing of it, but it is a social construct where individuals align themselves with different sets of roles and are identified accordingly. Now, since it is sociological in origin and society always possesses anomalies and exceptions, gender types can also fall under a vast umbrella of possibilities and combinations which are beyond the socially approved stereotypes.

Gender like all identities, is socially constructed. Social constructionism is one of the key theories sociologists use to put gender into historical and cultural focus. Social constructionism is a social theory about how meaning is created through social interaction- through the things we do and say with other people. This theory shows that gender is not a fixed or innate fact, but instead it varies across time and place. Gender norms are learned from birth through childhood socialization. We learn what is expected of our gender from what our parents teach us, as well as what we pick up at school, through religious and cultural teachings, in the media, and various other social institutions.

Gender is broadly classified into two categories namely *gender stereotypes* and *gender non-conformers*. Gender stereotypes include the traditional men and women which are in accordance with socially accepted gender roles and duties aligned to their sex which are male and female respectively; while gender non-conformers comprise of the categories which defy the socially constructed roles and duties in alignment of their sex. The most popular gender non-conformers are LGBTs where L(lesbian) and G(gay) are representing homosexuals, who are attracted towards the individuals of same sex; B represent bisexuals, who are the individuals which are attracted towards the individuals of either sex. And the most interesting T which represents transgenders, who see their physical bodies as mismatched to their gender identity and dress and act like the opposite gender.

Each of the gender categories possesses their set of problems which are sometimes interconnected and sometimes unique in their nature. In the stereotypical sets of gender, women face a variety of problems as they find themselves oppressed and exploited in a patriarchal world, especially in the third world countries where their voice is unheard in the presence of traditional mindsets which undermine the potential of women and limit them to a narrow dimension which will always be under the domination of a man. On the other hand men suffer a situation where they are deemed as emotionless and become the soft target of accusations in the pressures of women movements and they have no ideological backing to back them is such a situation. It is generally expected from a man to take care of the family and even if the family is broken due to divorce they are expected to provide for the maintenance of their spouse and children. In the guise of positive feminism, radical feminist movements hold men responsible for every problem associated with women. If there are flexible women roles in neo-sociology then why there is stereotyping of men with a particular identity is a matter of debate.

The problems of gender non-conformers are the greatest as they are the gender minority and face humiliation and discrimination on every ground on the basis of their gender identity. They are held responsible for breaking sociologically accepted norms of gender roles and duties and are deemed as misfits and discouraged for opting roles which are inconsistent with their biological sex. Homosexual pairing in India along with many other countries is illegal and is a punishable offence under section 377 of Indian Penal Code. The rights of LGBTs are largely absent and even the United Nations who have identified the need for special human rights for women and children, is turned blind in the case of human rights for non-conformers (LGBTs).

GENDER ROLES (BINARY STEREOTYPES)

As children move through childhood and into adolescence, they are exposed to many factors which influence their attitudes and behavior regarding gender roles. These attitudes and behaviors are generally learned first in the home and are then reinforced by the child's peers, school experience and television viewing. However, the strongest influence on gender role development seems to occur within the family setting, with parents passing on, both overtly and covertly, their own beliefs about gender (Witt, 1997).

It is difficult for a child to grow to adulthood without experiencing some form of gender bias or stereotyping, whether it be the expectation that the boys are better than girls at math's or the idea that only females can nurture children. As children grow and develop, the gender stereotype they are exposed to at home be reinforced by other elements in their environment and are thus perpetuated throughout childhood and into adolescence (Witt, 1997). One hypotheses also proposes that the gender differences in health behavior are due primarily to 2 complementary aspects of gender roles namely, males greater risk taking then females and females greater health concerns. Males are socialized to take risk, whereas females are socialized to be more cautious and more concerned with protecting health (Waldron, 1997). Males have greater propensity for antisocial (*i.e.,*externalizing) behavior. Although the genders did not differ in moral judgment stage, females evidenced greater moral self-relevance, and less anti-social behavior (Morrison *et al.*, 2001).

The expectations about what women and men should be guide and shape how women and men actually are. The process begins in infancy and continues throughout our lives. Although these beliefs are informative, providing a road map for our interactions with others (Kite, 2001).

The body of human male and female is slightly different in physiology and morphology because of the specialized function of reproduction and procreation thus the difference to a great extent is biological and more stable in nature but what function and roles both the sexes perform in society may differ greatly in time and space and are considered as dynamic in nature. The set of rules which dictate what should be considered masculine and feminine are more flexible. One such example is of an anthropological concept of couvade which is a custom in which the husband has to take over the symptoms of post natal illness and disability while the wife goes about the ordinary business of life (Riviere, 1974) after the birth of a child. The stereotypical role of child care and nurturing is associated with the female but here male is performing this role, however, in a customary sense.

Males in different societies choose different grounds on which to rank each other. Our society reflecting its own particular preoccupations stratifies men according to physical strength and athletic ability in the early years, but later in life focuses on success with women and ability to make money. It is sometime thought that competition for women is the ultimate source of men's competition with each other. In this view if women did not exist, men would not have anything to compete for with each other (Murphy, 2004). However, these beliefs are always shaped on majoritarian beliefs and there as there are also women who play sports and even at international levels and they do know how to earn money and success.

Traditional relationships with women have provided men a safe place in which they can recuperate from the stresses they have absorbed in their daily struggle with other men. If women begin to compete with men and have power in their own right, men are threatened by the loss of refuge (Murphy, 2004), as they believe it is an intrusion into their territory and is against the dominant characteristic of masculinity. There has been a considerable increase in the proportion of women managers in recent years, from 21% in 1976 to 46 % in 1999, and a call for feminine leadership to capitalize on this increase (Powell *et al.*, 2002) attributing to the shift of gender roles in modern times.

Again society tries hard to maintain the assigned roles and stereotypes associated with men and women, thus it puts allegations like, the entry of women in offices and job markets has led to neglect of the primary role of maintaining family and nurturing children. Although it has become more accepted that if the mother is employed it does not necessarily have a negative effect on family life and the development of the child; moreover, the double earner family model is indispensable for the financial security of the family (Repassy, 1991).

GENDER NON CONFORMERS (LGBTS)

The battle of sexes between the well-recognized categories seems to be legitimate and looked upon as natural and healthy while this is not the case with the minorities whose gender and sexual orientation is rather complicated. However, in views of the specialists like Sigmund Freud and Alfred Kinsey the tale does have a different narration. According to Freud sexual life does not begin at puberty, but starts with clear manifestations soon after birth. Sexual life comprising the function of obtaining pleasure from zones of the body –a function which is subsequently brought into the service of that of reproduction, but the two functions often fail to coincide completely (Freud, 1940). According to him, all human beings are polymorphously perverse. Human can derive sexual pleasure from almost anything and when it comes to sexual attraction, everyone is inherently bisexual, possessing the capacity to develop attraction to men or to women (Lehmiller, 2013). Similarly, Alfred Kinsey had searched for the traits and levels of homosexuality and heterosexuality in individuals through a typical scale. The classic Kinsey scale ranges from 0 (defined as an exclusive pattern of heterosexual attraction and behavior) to 6 (defined as an exclusive pattern of homosexual attraction and behavior) with 3 representing equal levels of both (Lehmiller, 2013).

Ratings	***Sexuality levels***
0	Exclusively heterosexual
1.	Mostly heterosexual incidentally homosexual
2.	Mostly heterosexual with significant homosexual experience
3.	Equally heterosexual and homosexual
4.	Mostly homosexual with significant heterosexual experience
5.	Mostly homosexual incidentally heterosexual
6.	Exclusively homosexual

Source: Wiley Blackwell: The Psychology of Human Sexuality (Lehmiller, 2013).

Kinsey thus, characterized sexuality as a very flexible thing, although he failed to explain or measure asexuality which is the absence of any sort of attractive feeling towards either sex. These approaches of Freud and Kinsey portrayed gender and sexuality in a very paradoxical manner where there can be numerous combinations of them in contract with the binary system of differentiation.

The *gender non-conformers* are widely misunderstood and confused with each other. But there is a marked difference in all the categories with a few incidences of overlapping as well. Hence, LGBT comprises of lesbian-women and gay-men who conform to the binary model of gender but oppose the same in terms of their sexuality as they both seems to be attracted by the members of their own sex and are popularly called as homosexuals. The 'B' stands for bisexual who feels attracted towards members of both the binary sexes but conform to a stereotypical gender as a male or female.

Homosexuals are present in both the stereotyped genders but there is a slight difference between the orientation pattern as data from three studies assessing a total of 3,645 participants show that for most women, high sex drive is associated with increased sexual attraction to both men and women. For men, however high sex drive is associated with increased sexual attraction to any one sex or the other, depending on the individual sexual orientation. The results suggest that the correlates of sex drive and the organization of sexual and sexual orientation are different for women and men (Lippa, 2006).

However, the most interesting category resides in the letter 'T' which stands for transgender. The term transgender was coined in the late 1980s, by men who did not find the label transvestite adequate enough to describe their desire to live as women (Carroll *et al.*, 2002). The transgenders are gender non-conforming and believed to be born in wrong body *i.e.*, women in a male body and *vice versa*. There are two categories of transgenders; the one who does not change their sex through sex-reversal surgeries because many traditionally gender-identified persons did not necessarily want to reconfigure their bodies surgically and hormonally and did not share the desire to pass or to fit into normative gender categories of male and female (Carroll *et al.*, 2002); and the other who make this change to fit their gender identity with their body, the latter category is referred to as transsexuals. The very popular form of transgenders which is often glamourized is the lady-boy of

Thailand, they have long been a part of Thailand's cultural landscape and the term use for transgender in Thailand is Kathoey (Totman, 2011). However, this change may result in serious consequences as changing one's natural anatomy may pose difficulties in a variety of ways, like: testosterone is the crucial hormone in female-to-male (FtM) transsexuals for the development of secondary sexual characteristics of the desired gender. A major safety concern is whether testosterones have a stimulatory effect on the breast that can increase the risk of developing breast cancer (Shao *et al.*, 2011).

The societal beliefs of a dominant sex and gender also shape the attitudes towards nonconformity. Parents welcome what they perceive as gender non-conformity among their young daughters, while their responses in relation to sons are more complex. Many parents across racial and class background accept or encourage some tendencies they consider atypical for boys, but this acceptance is balanced by efforts to approximate hegemonic ideals of masculinity (Kane, 2006).

Towards the deviant community the society is harsh and hostile and it also distances itself from them, because there is a general belief that it is only through societal marginalization and hostility towards non-conformers that the accepted stereotype will be reinforced effectively, and allowing them to break the stereotype will only lead to social imbalance as their beliefs may turn contagious. The fear of society towards homosexuals in called as homophobia and towards transgenders as transphobia. While homophobia is increasingly compared to racism and sexism, discrimination against lesbian women and gay men is much more widely accepted then other forms of discrimination. Heterosexually identified individuals are effectively discouraged from raising lesbian and gay issues because their own sexuality might be put in question (Sanders, 1996).

In a study in US for both sexes, transphobia and homophobia were highly correlated with each other and with right wing authoritarianism, religious fundamentalism (Nagoshi *et al.*, 2008). Although, talking about the religious fundamentalism, while gay men and lesbians have been consistently involved in the institutional forms of Judeo-Christianity throughout history, those institutions have themselves failed to accept or support openly gay individuals or couples, either professionally, liturgically/ pastorally, or doctrinally. It has instead encouraged homophobia in society thereby fostering antigay oppression which dehumanizes gay individuals, undermines gay coupling, and exacerbates familial tensions between gay and non-gay relatives (Clarke *et al.*, 1989). A contemporary social movement understanding violence against gay men and lesbians as "homophobic" suggests a solid basis for coalitionist action. But important aspects of the imposition of gender conformity are a common thread in the experience of female, male and transsexual victims and the motives of perpetrators (Tomsen and Mason, 2001).

Societal pressure may be immense, but since most homosexuals get their first experience of prejudice within the family, it becomes difficult for homosexuals either to put trust in a supportive community or to withhold trust from an outside enemy (Norton, 1975).

Similarly, the existence of transgender and gender-nonconforming people has been documented throughout history and across many cultures. In the twentieth century, transgender expression become medicalized and sex-reassignment become available, initially enforcing a binary understanding of sex/gender, evading the social stigma attached to gender non-conformity (Bockting, 2014). Research on transgendered individuals has tended to come from medical, psychiatric, or deviance perspectives, with little attention to the social context in which these individuals exist or their efforts to resist normative expectations of sex and gender (Gagné and Tewksbury, 1988). Gender is a ubiquitous social construct that wields power over every individual in our society. The traditional dichotomous gender paradigm is oppressive, especially for transgendered people whose sense of themselves as gendered people is incongruent with the gender they were assigned at birth (Burdge, 2007).

Homosexual men and women and even transgenders are socially disintegrated and thus, as a result of this disintegration may suffer from depression and other psychotic conditions and thus revert to the consumption of sedatives and drugs. They have been described as at high risk for alcohol and drug abuse, due to psychological variables such as stress levels or the cultural importance of bar settings. In a study there was a substantially higher proportions of the homosexuals sample used alcohol, marijuana, or cocaine than was in the case in the general population (McKirnan and Peterson, 1989).

International evidence demonstrates that there are elevated rates of suicide and alcohol abuse amongst lesbian, gay, bisexual and transgender (LGBT) youth. Also, data from interviews and focus groups with young LGBT participants suggest a strong link between homophobia and self-destructive behaviors (McDermott, 2008).

The conflict is not only between what is stereotyped and what is deviant but there exist an inherent sense of identity within the subgroups of the deviant community which leads to prejudice. Heterosexism against bisexuals and transgenders exist not only in the straight community, but in the gay and lesbian community as well. As the LGBT community developed, power relations arose which resulted in the four different groups (L/G/B/T), assigning them different social locations, prejudice in gay and lesbian communities against bisexuals and transgenders is heterosexism because it is among other things, an accommodationist attempt to disavow these more radical forms of sexuality (Weiss, 2004). There is even intra-category conflict as it was found in a North American study, where, a sample of female to male (FtM) transsexuals were sexually attracted to men, aiming their identity and sexuality in context of a culture of transgender empowerment (Bockting *et al.*, 2009).

To live in a society and to differ from the majority is itself an invitation for prejudices and challenges. Thus, the LGBT community is highly vulnerable and is always susceptible to a multitude of challenges and problems as the deviant members of society. Likewise, there is an allegation on homosexuals for them not fitting well for parenting. The quality of the parental relationship has been implicated increasingly over the past two decades as a factor contributing to the social and emotional development of the child (Block *et al.*, 1981). However, opponents of lesbian and gay parental rights claims that children with lesbian-gay parents are at higher risk for a variety of negative outcomes. Yet most research in psychology concludes that there are no differences in developmental outcomes between children raised by lesbian-gay parents and those raised by heterosexual parents (Stacey and Biblarz, 2001).

The growing number of families formed by homosexual, transvestite (cross dresser) and transsexual fathers/mothers has not only become a social, but also socio-anthropological fact, requiring traditional convictions to be rethought. The diversity of family configuration present in other societies permits us to affirm that kinship and affiliation are always social in nature, not being merely derived procreation (Zambrano, 2007).

INDIAN PERSPECTIVE

Homosexuality in Indian society is considered inappropriate and shrouded in secrecy. Identity finds its roots in self-perceptions in relation to specific social setting and the subjective adoption of a role or roles by an individual. Certainly negative notions about homosexuality create a dilemma for homosexually oriented men to choose gender and sexual roles and appropriate identities (Pandya, 2011).

The most significant problem of the sexual/gender minorities is of a legal permit to portray who they are. A large number of countries worldwide have legalized homosexual rights. South

Africa was the first country to constitutionally safeguard the rights of homosexuals in 1994. But ever since India was a British colony Section 377 of the Indian Penal Code (IPC) of 1860 defines homosexuality as a crime punishable by imprisonment. The outdated law violates the fundamental rights of homosexuals in India. Despite the fact that literature drawn from Hindu, Buddhist, Muslim and modern fiction testify to the presence of same-sex love in various forms, homosexuality is still considered a taboo in India, by both the society and the government (Agoramoorthy and Minna, 2007).

Homosexuals are more prone to HIV/AIDS as it is much easier to get HIV infection from anal sex as presence of (micro-traumatic) lesions in the oral, rectal or urethral mucosa that permits direct blood-bloodstream or secretions-bloodstream contact (Caceres and Griensven, 1994). Indian coordinator for UNAIDS stated that treating homosexuals as criminals increases stigma and therefore hinders the fight against HIV/AIDS. The existence of homosexuality law is a stumbling block to prevent gay men from coming forward to test for HIV/AIDS (Agoramoorthy and Minna, 2007).

In Indian society, having sexual relationship with people of the same sex is considered abnormal. Homosexual behavior are seen in society as immoral, dirty, and unnatural. As a result, these behaviors are secretly practiced without adequate knowledge about safe sexual practices; hence, men who have sex with men (MSM) tend to be more vulnerable to sexually transmitted infections (STIs) and a host of psychiatric morbidities (Pandya and Pandya, 2013).

In a study of homosexual men in Gujarat it was found that eleven respondents mentioned that they were confused with their own self, sex feelings, attraction and interests in same-sex sexual activities. One respondent with bisexual orientation said, "I feel bad for my feelings for other men, and sexual activities I do. I do not know why god has made me such". Other respondent who identified himself as *koti* stated, "People laugh on my effeminate behavior. I try to become like other men but I just can't, sometimes I can't control my feelings and desires to cross-dress. I want to stop cross-dressing, sex with other men but I can't stop." Such experiences often lead to the development of dual self-identities. Duality in turn creates an identity confusion and role conflict which is usually expressed through non-acceptance of one's sexuality, secret homosexual activities, risky sexual behaviors, multiple sexual relationships, self-destructive behavior, substance abuse, unstable relationships, and internalization of homophobia (Pandya, 2011).

All unmarried men in the study concurred that they want to marry, and desire to father a child. Fathering a child is demonstration of proven manhood and the fulfillment of one of the social requirements of married men. Married men shared reasons for their marriages. Primary reasons were parental pressure and their own conviction with the notion of heterosexual marriage. They had fear if they had not married, it would defame their parents' status; and siblings would not be able to marry. This itself show invisible layer of internal stigma associated with own homosexual orientation and self-discrimination as the biggest personal barrier in development of healthy sexual identity (Pandya, 2011).

A cross-sectional study among 200 men having sex with men in Surat city explores their initial MSM experiences. Findings in a study reveal that MSM are sexually active with slightly more bisexual than homosexual. The discussion revealed that slightly over half (53%) MSM were bisexual followed by 47% who engaged solely in homosexual relationships in line with varying patterns of homosexual and bisexual. Though many of the respondents had reported of heterosexual attraction, the majority perceived themselves as feminine and felt attraction towards males. Many of the MSM had realized their sexual inclinations after marriage and some were forced into heterosexual marriages by their parents and therefore their bisexual inclinations. The majority (57%) had reported of their first homosexual encounter while playing with friends, resembling the findings of Deb *et al.,*in 2009, which reported that, a male friend was the first sexual partner in majority of the cases (50.9%) among the MSM. An important finding is that many were forced or raped into their first MSM experience by cousin, friend or elders and caretakers (Mukesh and Bansal, 2010).

Talking about another interesting category of *gender non-conformers* is the Indian form of transgender called as Hijra. The Hijra (eunuch/transvestite) is an institutionalized third gender in India. They are neither male nor female, but contain elements of both (Nanda, 1986). Indian society has been tolerant of diverse sexual identities and sexual behaviors as is evident from its mythologies and ancient scripts like the Kama sutra. The transgendered Hijra community has evolved to form a unique within Indian society, existing alongside the ubiquitous heterosexual family. Some of the aspects of their lives such as their social structure and attaining of Nirvan (emasculation, not to be confused with nirvana) (Kalra, 2012), may intrigue the ones researching psychology.

Stories of sexual variation in ancient Hindu texts give hijras a measure of mythological and historical legitimization; this Hindu textual affirmation inevitably influences their religious practices. The most important goddess for the hijras is the Mother Goddess, specifically in the form of Bahuchara Mata. It is in her name that hijras perform their ritual function by giving blessings of fertility or prosperity to a newborn child or married couple, and in her temple in Gujarat they act as servants of the Mother goddess (Loh, 2011).

In India, transgenders earn their daily bread by begging, performing religious ceremonies and most painfully through sexual work. It is unfortunate that society is least bothered about the psyche of their fellow human beings. When society gets the information that a person is transgender, they face social ostracism within and outside family. So most of them will not be able to complete their studies and there is no employment opportunity for them. These all add to their vulnerability. State mechanisms of police who are considered to be the protectors of rights are unfortunately becoming predatory of their rights. (Soman, 2013).

THEORETICAL APPROACHES

There are various theories of gender socialization and how children learn gender identity, when they become aware that the two sexes (male and female) behave differently. Some of the theoretical approaches are as follows:

SOCIOLOGICAL THEORIES

Functionalist Approach for Gender

As we know that functionalist approach holds society with the interdependent parts which constitute the whole. So, gender in this approach, gets place in very functional way which is formed in the beginning of history. Ancient times, there was very useful and efficient division of labor between men and women, in hunter and gatherer societies have men as hunter and outsider, women as mother, nurse and housekeeping (Lindsey, 2011). According to functionalists, this division of labor derives from biological differences between men and women, also Murdock held this issue as, sexual division of labor exists in every culture and it is not a result of biological "programming" but a logical basis for organizing in society (Giddens, 2009).

Parsons, one of the leaders of functionalist thinker, claims that acting according to proper roles for man and woman in the family also help for socialization of children. He mentioned from the roles as instrumental role - providing shelters, food etc- for father and expressive role –providing care and security for children, emotional support- for mother (Parsons and Bales, 1956).

Conflict Theory in Gender

According to Engels, capitalism makes male dominance more powerful, and he has explained this claim in three states. Firstly, capitalism provides power for men by giving them chance in order to have high income and private property. Secondly, women became the consumer part of society, because they do not produce, but get money from their husband and spend for satisfy their need or enjoy. Thirdly, capitalism divides men and women in working way. It puts men to factory and women to house, however, it does not pay for women's workings in the house, but pays for men for his working in factory, so it puts importance to male's job by paying money (Macionis, 2010).

Symbolic Interaction Theory in Gender

Symbolic Interaction Theory claims that concepts such as – race, ethnicity or gender – are not naturally and objectively existed, but they occurred through society. Society named "females" or "males" are endowed with distinct character features defined as feminine or masculine. Gender does not exist by itself, but with the interaction among people in society. So, they claim that, society is "doing" gender, and they show as an example Erving Goffman's "Dramaturgy" study (Lindsey, 2011).

According to Goffman's explanation, we have some roles inside of us and when their time comes, we use them in front of the stage. Thus, gender is one of our roles and we present them as male and female in society.

PSYCHOLOGICAL THEORIES

1. Psychodynamic Theory

Psychodynamic theory is the oldest perspective on sexuality in the field and is credited to Sigmund Freud. He believed that our gender identity develops as a result of strong but unconscious sexual urges we have as a child. Between the ages of three and five a child will go through what he regards as the *phallic stage* in which he/she will develop strong sexual urges towards the parent of the opposite sex and therefore great jealously towards the parent of the same sex. A normally developing child will resolve this conflict by identifying with the parent of the same sex and copying his/her behavior.

The oedipus complex: This is the name given to the unconscious dilemma a boy experiences when he is very young. During the *phallic stage* he develops an attraction towards his mother and a fear of his father, who he believes may castrate him. In other words he is torn in two directions. In order to prevent the castration he rejects his mother and identifies with his father. He does this by aping his behavior and copying his masculine characteristics.

The electra complex: This is the name given to the unconscious dilemma a girl experiences when she is between three and five years old. During the phallic stage she develops an attraction towards her father and a fear that she will lose her mother's love. In order to keep her mother's love she rejects her father and identifies with her mother. She does this by aping her behavior and copying her feminine characteristics. In this way female behavior is transferred from one generation to another.

Gender disturbances: Freud believed that children who were brought up in households where one parent is absent are likely to have a much weaker sense of gender identity. He went even furthor by claiming that a boy brought up without a father is likely to develop into a homosexual. Recent research by *Rekers and Moray (1990)* also suggested that boys who grow up without a father-figure are more likely to have gender disturbances

Freud's theories have been very influential but very few psychologists accept everything he has to say. His theories are based on the unconscious and for that reason are difficult to put to the test. Freud himself had very little evidence to support his case.

There is also the argument that recent decades have seen an increase in lone-parent families but not an equivalent increase in the homosexual population. This fact works against Freud's theory. The theory also tends to assume that homosexuality is abnormal and that gender disturbances are a bad thing.

2. Social Learning Theory

In 1941 *Miller and Dollard* proposed the theory of social learning. In 1963, *Bandura and Walters* broadened the social learning theory with the principles of observational learning and vicarious reinforcement.

Unlike Freud's psychoanalytic approach, which focus on internal conflicts in socialization, social learning theory focuses on observable behavior. For social learning theorists like *Albert Bandura*, socialization is based on rewards (reinforcing appropriate behavior) and punishments (extinguishing inappropriate behavior). As with other behaviors gender roles are learned directly through observation and imitation. In gender socialization, different expectations lead to different expectations lead to differential reinforcement from parents, peers, and teachers for doing either boy or the girl thing.

Gender identity is developed when children associate the label of boy or girl with the rewards that come with the appropriate behavior and then act out gender roles according to that perception. According to social learning theory, boy and girls are not parallel in the acquisition of gender role knowledge during the primary socialization years. Because fathers are not as available as mothers during early childhood, boys have limited opportunity to model the same gender parent. Thus in early childhood boys struggle to put together definition of masculinity based on incomplete information. They are often told what they should not do than what they should do, "don't be sissies" and the classic "big boys don't cry" are examples. Girls on the other hand have an easier time because of the continuous contact with the mother. The lack of exposure to males at an early age leads boys to view masculinity in a stereotypical manner. Males express more insecurity about their gender identity, and cross gender behavior in boys ("sissies") is viewed more negatively than when it occurs in girls ("tomboys").

This theory falls down on the nurture side of the nature/ nurture argument and doesn't take biological differences into account. Nevertheless it is a well-researched theory and has a lot of evidence to support it. *What the theory doesn't explain* is why children tend to be more observant of the behavior of the same-sex parent, or why many children brought up in one-parent families don't develop *gender disturbances.*

The theory does have certain limitations like children are not the passive recipients of rewards and punishments that social learning theorists envision. Because children routinely choose gender-inconsistent behavior, the reinforcement and modeling process are far more complex. Most importantly social learning theory minimizes the importance of social change, a significant factor in gender socialization. Also modeling is not always so stereotyped as they present, since the case of single parents, blending families, and divorce lead to the creation of a wide range of models.

3. Cognitive Development Theory

The major proponents of *cognitive development theory* were *Jean Piaget* and *Lawrence Kohlberg*. According to cognitive developmental theory, gender identity is postulated as the basic organizer and regulator of children's gender learning. Children develop the stereotypic conceptions of gender from what they see and hear around them. Once they achieve gender constancy — the belief that their own gender is fixed and irreversible — they positively value their gender identity and seek to behave only in ways that are congruent with that conception

Cognitive development explanations for gender socialization contrast sharply with social learning theory. *Jean Piaget* (1896-

1980) took interest in how children gradually develop intelligence; thinking and reasoning laid the foundation for cognitive development theory. His work is consistent with symbolic interaction theory regarding his ideas that cognitive abilities are developed in stages through ongoing social interaction. Behavior depends on how a person perceives a social situation at each cognitive stage. Cognitive theory stresses a child's active role in structuring and interpreting the world.

Like social learning cognitive development theory cannot account for all gender role socialization. The cognitive development model also has been criticized because a key assertion is that children will actively choose gender typed behavior only after they understood gender constancy (realization that gender is fixed and does not change with time), gender constancy appears by age 6, but gender type preferences in play and toy selections are already in place by age 2 or 3. For the model to fit neatly with the stages outlined in the cognitive development, gender identity must come before an understanding of gender constancy and research till date has been unable to confirm this sequence.

4. Social Cognitive Theory

Social cognitive theory was propounded by *Albert Bandura*. This theory taps into the strong points of all previous theories to understand the degree to which the children actively choose their gender roles and how much imitation and reinforcement are needed for gender roles to be learned. This theory has been used to explain the connection between gender and the selection of sports role models. As predicted by the social learning theory that girl and boys nominate role models of their own gender. However, girls often pick males rather than females. Social cognitive theory explains these choices according to the image of sports as a male domain and the level of influence wielded by men in the domain. When combined with the symbolic interaction perspective, this theory provides a good foundation for interdisciplinary approaches to gender role socialization.

Of all the theory of gender socialization, social cognitive theory appears to offer the best integrative model to explain contradictory research results on gender related to the influence of a child choice of role models.

However this theory is yet to provide answers to two important questions about primary socialization. First when does "active self-socialization" occur before or after the selection of role models? Second, which is more in the process that child active choices or the availability of the role model itself? Can a child act out beliefs about gender if there is no role model?

DISCUSSION AND CONCLUSIONS

The complex interplay of light and shadow will always be present between society and its individuals. Although, a society has a complete right to decide what is good for it but it should not be at the expense of marginalizing and de-socializing a part of its members. The accommodation of differential types of gender and sexual orientation within the framework of society is a big challenge as social reform has its own pace and for it to reach every single mind it will take a little more time. But with the rise of individualization of society the trend of respecting one's own choice even if it is completely non-synchronized with the majority, the peaceful and equal environment for the gender non-conformers can be sighted in near future although it requires a serious effort on part of human right activists along with governmental and non-governmental organizations.

The role of entertainment industry is immense for propagating the gender variant envelope. The famous television series The L word which followed the lives of several lesbian, bisexual, and transgendered women living in Los Angeles, California; and the series entitled Queer as Folk follows the life of five gay men living in Pittsburgh, Pennsylvania. And also the popularity of Neil Patrick Harris an American homosexual actor who played a very opposite role of a womanizer in the famous series called How I

Met Your Mother. These attempts pushed the envelope of non-conformity and gave an opportunity to the non-conformers to feel comfortable of what they are, when almost everyone in society became their critique.

Focusing on the challenges, pressures and prejudices experienced by individuals to maintain binary enactments of gender where they are not free to express what is their real self and always presumed to be what society desires them to be. Since, the gender non-conformity is not a new concept and is experienced throughout the human history; it would be just unfair to dictate how one should behave in matters which are purely personal. The only way in which we can achieve equal rights for each one of us is positive campaigning and providing proper education about the different gender/sexual orientation and roles without scandalizing them as being something obscure. The government and other authoritarian agencies should look upon these diverse sets of individuals through emic approach and should not try to impose their beliefs as gender orientation can only be identified as a personal choice.

REFERENCES

Agoramoorthy, G. and Minna, J.H. (2007). India's homosexual discrimination and health consequences. *Revista de saúdepública*, 41(4): 657–660.

Block, J.H., Block, J. and Morrison, A. (1981). Parental agreement-disagreement on child-rearing orientations and gender-related personality correlates in children. Child Development, pp. 965–974.

Bockting, W. (2014). The impact of stigma on transgender identity development and mental health. *In*: Gender Dysphoria and Disorders of Sex Development, Springer US, pp. 319–330.

Bockting, W., Benner, A. and Coleman, E. (2009). Gay and bisexual identity development among female-to-male transsexuals in North America: Emergence of a transgender sexuality. *Archives of Sexual Behavior*, 38(5): 688–701.

Burdge, B.J. (2007). Bending gender, ending gender: Theoretical foundations for social work practice with the transgender community. *Social Work*, 52(3): 243–250.

Caceres, C.F. and Van Griensven, G.J. (1994). Male homosexual transmission of HIV-1. *Aids*, 8(8): 1051–1062.

Carroll, L., Gilroy, P.J. and Ryan, J. (2002). Counseling transgendered, transsexual and gender-variant clients. *Journal of Counseling and Development* (JCD), 80(2): 131.

Clarke, J.M., Brown, J.C. and Hochstein, L.M. (1989). Institutional religion and gay/lesbian oppression. *Marriage and Family Review*, 14(3–4): 265–284.

Freud, S. (1940). The development of the sexual function. *Standard Edition*, 23: 152–156.

Gagné, P. and Tewksbury, R. (1998). Conformity pressures and gender resistance among transgendered individuals. Social problems, pp. 81–101.

Giddens, A. (2009). *Sociology*. 6. Edition dü. Cambridge: Polity Press.

Kalra, G. (2012). Hijras: The unique transgender culture of India. *International Journal of Culture and Mental Health,* 5(2): 121–126.

Kane, E.W. (2006). "No way my boys are going to be like that!" Parents responses to children's gender nonconformity. *Gender and Society*, 20(2): 149–176.

Kite, M.E. (2001). Changing times, changing gender roles: Who do we want women and men to be?

Lehmiller, J.J. (2013). The psychology of human sexuality. John Wiley and Sons.

Lindsey, L.L. (2011). *Gender Roles: A Sociological Perspective*. 5. Edition dü. New York: Pearson.

Lippa, R.A. (2006). Is high sex drive associated with increased sexual attraction to both sexes? It depends on whether you are male or female. *Psychological Science*, 17(1): 46–52.

Loh, J. (2011). 'Borrowing' Religious Identifications: A Study of Religious Practices among the Hijras of India.

Macionis, J.J. (2010). *Sociology*. 13. Edition dü. London: Pearson.

McDermott, E., Roen, K. and Scourfield, J. (2008). Avoiding shame: Young LGBT people, homophobia and self destructive behaviours. *Culture, Health and Sexuality*, 10(8): 815–829.

McKirnan, D.J. and Peterson, P.L. (1989). Alcohol and drug use among homosexual men and women: Epidemiology and population characteristics. *Addictive Behaviors*, 14(5): 545–553.

Morrison, E.M., Barriga, A.Q., Liau, A.K. and Gibbs, J.C. (2001). Moral cognition: Explaining the gender difference in antisocial behavior. *Merrill-Palmer Quarterly*, 47(4): 532–562.

Mukesh, K. and Bansal, R.K. (2010). Initial Homosexual Experiences of Msm in Surat City. *National Journal*, 1(1): 17.

Murphy, P.F. (*ed.*) (2004). Feminism and masculinities. OUP Oxford.

Nagoshi, J.L., Adams, K.A., Terrell, H.K., Hill, E.D., Brzuzy, S. and Nagoshi, C.T. (2008). Gender differences in correlates of homophobia and transphobia. *Sex Roles*, 59(7–8): 521–531.

Nanda, S. (1986). The Hijras of India: Cultural and individual dimensions of an institutionalized third gender role. *Journal of Homosexuality*, 11(3–4): 35–54.

Norton, R. (1975). Prejudice against homosexuals. *Patterns of Prejudice*, 9(4): 7–12.

Pandya, A. (2011). Psycho-socio-cultural issues of men who have sex with men in Gujarat, India. *International Journal of Psychology and Behavioral Sciences*, 1(1): 18–23.

Pandya, A. and Pandya, S. (2013). Socio-cultural Context and Sexual Health Risks of Men who have Sex with Men (MSM) and their Female Partners in Gujarat, India. *International Journal of Scientific and Research Publications*, 629.

Parsons, T. and Bales, R. (1956). Family Socialization and Interaction Process. London: Routledge.

Powell, G.N., Butterfield, D.A. and Parent, J.D. (2002). Gender and managerial stereotypes: Have the times changed? *Journal of Management*, 28(2): 177–193.

Repassy, H. (1991). Changing gender roles in Hungarian agriculture. *Journal of Rural Studies*, 7(1): 23–29.

Riviere, P.G. (1974). The couvade: A problem reborn. *Man*, 9(3): 423–435.

Sanders, D. (1996). Getting lesbian and gay issues on the international human rights agenda. *Human Rights Quarterly*, 18(1): 67–106.

Shao, T., Grossbard, M.L. and Klein, P. (2011). Breast cancer in female-to-male transsexuals: Two cases with a review of physiology and management.*Clinical Breast Cancer*, 11(6): 417–419.

Soman, A.P. (2013). Penal laws and rights of transgender: International perspective with special reference to Section 377 of the Indian Penal Code, 1860. *Scientific Committee of Reviewers*, 276.

Stacey, J. and Biblarz, T.J. (2001). (How) does the sexual orientation of parents matter? *American Sociological Review*, pp. 159–183.

Tomsen, S. and Mason, G. (2001). Engendering homophobia: Violence, sexuality and gender conformity. *Journal of Sociology*, 37(3): 257–273.

Totman, R. (2011). The third sex: Kathoey: Thailand's ladyboys. Souvenir Press.

Waldron, I. (1997). Changing gender roles and gender differences in health behavior.

Weiss, J.T. (2004). GL vs. BT: The archaeology of biphobia and transphobia within the US gay and lesbian community. *Journal of Bisexuality*, 3(3–4): 25–55.

Witt, S.D. (1997). Parental influence on children's socialization to gender roles. *Adolescence*, 32(126): 253.

Zambrano, E. (2007). "Unthinkable" parenthoods: Homosexual, transvestite and transsexual mothers and fathers. *Horizontes Antropológicos*, 3(se): 0–0.

Chapter 4

Baptizing U.S. Women into the Spirit of Freedom and Equality: A Closer Look at Gender and Transformation of Power in Elizabeth Cady Stanton's Popular Talk *Our Girls*

Julie M. Geredien

INTRODUCTION

Elizabeth Cady Stanton was a U.S. suffragist whose activism originated in the abolitionist movement. In 1840, without her parents' consent, she married Henry Brewster Stanton, who spoke out strongly for immediate abolition. When the couple traveled on their honeymoon to the World's Anti-Slavery convention in London, Stanton, along with all the other American female delegates, was denied a seat at the convention. It was in this context that she met a Hicksite Quaker named Lucretia Mott, who introduced her to the woman's rights movement and provoked her to begin thinking critically about participation in reform. Stanton had strong intellectual capacities and soon found herself in a major leadership role advancing woman's suffrage.

In her ensuing life's work seeking justice and equality for women, Stanton revealed a broad and deep concern for human development and dignity, and she is now remembered as much more than an advocate for women's voting rights. To understand her seriousness and vision, it is important to appreciate that the real beginnings of her feminist thinking are rooted intimately in her context as a girl growing up in Seneca County, New York. There she was in close proximity to the Haudenosaunee Nation[1], and she and members of her family had meaningful encounters with the Iroquois people throughout her life.[2] The women of the Iroquois League were for Stanton real-life examples of people living free from the political, economic, religious and socio-cultural oppression that plagued U.S. women.

Stanton saw how Iroquoian women were assured of human equality in all domains of life. The Great Law of Peace, which was the spiritual and ethical foundation of Iroquois society, promised that "Much as all men stood as 'towering trees' of the same height, 'Women Chiefs' would also be of the same height to one another and to the men". (Hewitt, 1926: 3).

The emotional, moral and spiritual problems that Stanton perceived as afflicting the lives of most U.S. women simply did not exist in the social ecology supporting the female citizens of the

---

[1] Another name for the Haudenosaunee Nation was the League of Peace and Power. During colonial years the French called them the "Iroquois League," and only later were they referred to as the "Iroquois Confederacy." The French knew them as the "Five Nations" (before 1722), and later as the "Six Nations," comprising the Mohawk, Onondaga, Oneida, Cayuga, Seneca, and Tuscarora peoples. For more on Iroquois history, Deganawidah and the Great Law of Peace that united the nations of the Iroquois League, please see my chapter in *Practical Spirituality and Human Development*, called "Practical Spirituality and the Transformation of Power: How the Great Law of Peace and Iroquoian Culture Awakened Social and Spiritual Vision in Early American Suffragettes".

[2] Writing in the Seneca Falls Historical Society Papers reveals that: Both her [Stanton's] cousin, Peter Skenandoah Smith, and her nearest Seneca Falls neighbor, Oren Tyler, were adopted into Iroquois clans. As she told the Marcellus Observer in an interview, she would, throughout her childhood, have other encounters with the Iroquois people. (Wagner, 2001: 42).

Confederacy. The right of Iroquoian women to speech, to divorce, to spiritual leadership, and to dignity through participation in governance, agricultural labor and life-long learning became an inspiration to Stanton and a validation of the realistic attainability of the U.S. suffragists' seemingly radical goals and demands. "If U.S. women were to aspire to the levels of self-sovereignty and equal participation within Iroquois society, they would need to take on active and universal responsibility."

In this essay I focus on Stanton's speech, *Our Girls*. *Our Girls* and its companion piece, *Our Boys,* were her most popular talks in the lyceum lecture circuit[3] during the 1870s, also known as the Reconstruction era in the United States. In *Our Girls*, Stanton challenged not only gender roles in society, but many underlying assumptions within mainstream 19th century U.S. culture, concerning the meanings of democracy and public health, for example. In her effort to rid sexism and all forms of prejudice and domination from the foundations of the society, she raised serious

[3] Lyceum is a Latin representation of the ancient Greek word Ëýêåéïí ("Lykeion"), which refers to a gymnasium in classical Athens dedicated to Apollo Lyceus. The ancient lyceum is remembered as the location of the traveling school of Aristotle. The Lyceum Movement in the United States was a movement of educational reform beginning around 1830 and extending into the years after the Civil War. Though based on the idea of Mechanics Institutes established in England as a practical way to train apprentices in the rapidly evolving technologies of the industrial revolution, the Lyceums in New England served a more encompassing civic function. They were "progressive democratic institutions" that provided connection to a broader culture in a time when there was no television, film, radio or internet. The Lyceums admitted all people and kept dues very affordable. Whole communities would gather together, not only to attend classes on literature, philosophy, art appreciation, and the current science of the day, but also to discuss ideas and to build agreement on how to address local concerns. The movement played a vital role in establishing many local public libraries, schools and colleges. See word press site on the history of the lyceum movement: https://nolalyceum.wordpress.com/about/history-of-the-lyceum-movement/

questions about human dignity, human development and justice. Although her presentations did not directly address the legal and constitutional issues in the way that her suffrage speeches like *Declaration of Rights and Sentiments* did, Stanton turned her audience's attention to a much more interior and weighty ground of social transformation: the education and socialization of young boys and girls.

In the first part of the essay, I review the major themes and underlying concerns in this talk. These include the law of restoration and meaning of integral health; the role of human agency in projects of self-cultivation and society-making (dignity as both empowerment and constraint); the need to redefine beauty and to look toward the dawn of a new civilization. I discuss how the content of *Our Girls* challenged conventional notions about human development, sociality, democracy and marriage, and explain the paradigm shifts involved in how Stanton understood each of these. Then I consider how the historical context of the speech, and Stanton's work as a suffragist, beginning with the Seneca Falls Convention, can be understood in relation to a larger spiritual zeitgeist permeating that time period. My aim here is to reveal a unity in the nature of transformation itself and in the rise of new levels of human moral and spiritual consciousness needed for the realization of the true meaning of gender equality.

In the latter part of the essay, I review how themes and concerns in *Our Girls* reflect not only the zeitgeist of that day, but also a re-emergence of much older philosophical concepts and spiritual insights, related more generally to Judaic understandings of the third and tenth Sefiroth and Greek ideas like *pleroma*, signifying "fullness" and "completion" and specifically, to the Roman goddess of wisdom, Minerva, who Stanton mentioned at the close of the speech. I maintain that these older philosophical concepts and spiritual insights can help us to understand the archetypal forces Stanton called upon in the speech and also, the larger human spiritual heritage she was calling upon when she referred to the ideal of "perfected womanhood." Stanton gave the speech a baptismal power intended to open humanity to enlightened participation in the holy ground of "everything". Her references throughout the talk, to "full symmetrical development" and the ideal feminine, point to the spiritual and ethical foundation of democracy that Stanton knew to be necessary for justice.

Finally, I reflect on how U.S. women in the 21st century, having overcome many of the socio-centric and legal barriers to participation that thwarted 19th century women, are now often given the message, through culture and technology, that it is possible for them to "have it all" and so to reach material and conventional social standards of fullness or self-completion. I conclude that though girls and women are empowered today with many positive and negative rights, they nevertheless remain in many ways impoverished and disunited. The realization of genuine gender equality and the fulfillment of human potentialities can only be attained when both men and women recognize the oneness of humankind and realize the meaning of dignity not only as empowerment, but also as constraint. This includes a world-encompassing vision of justice, "radical democracy"[4] (republican

---

[4] I use "radical democracy" at times in this chapter to refer to Stanton's vision of a renewed democracy, although this term was actually put forth decades later by John Dewey. I believe Stanton would have appreciated Dewey's recognition of the need for deep structural transformation in all existing institutions, and his insistence that democracy was itself the cure for the ills of democracy. Dewey wrote in *Later Works*: The end of democracy is a radical end. For it is an end that has not been adequately realized in any country at any time. It is radical because it requires great change in existing social institutions, economic, legal and cultural. A democratic liberalism that does not recognize these things in thought and action is not awake to its own meaning and to what that meaning demands. (Dewey, *LW* 11: 298-9; Bernstein, 2010: 77) . Recognition of the need for deep structural change that "has not yet been adequately realized" before, is central to Baha'i understandings of individual and social transformation that are put forth also for the first time throughout this time period in the 19th and 20th

(*Contd...*)

ideal of democracy) and ethical governance, in which appreciation for the unifying realities of reciprocity and mutuality within all life assures that diverse values, points of view and principles regulate one another symmetrically in different deliberative contexts[5], bringing about equality, integration and harmony and uprooting domination and tyranny from human relations.

OUR GIRLS

The text of *Our Girls* was a part of oral tradition and changed over the years and across audiences. In 1869 when Stanton began, the speech was called *The Coming Girl.* Later, in 1872, the title changed to *The Girl of the Future.* It wasn't until 1875 that the title by which it is remembered today, *Our Girls,* came into being. (Gordon, 1997: 484).

Many people associate the talk with a critique of the fashion and beauty standards of the 19th century, which were set by male ideals of feminine beauty. Stanton is known to have argued that conformity to these false standards had deleterious health effects on women and hindered all aspects of their development. But while this is a generally accurate representation of some of the speech's content, it misses the speech's stream of insight about natural law, and Stanton's vision of a new dawning civilization. These make aspects of her popular talk more than mere commentary on fashion

---

(Contd...)

century. Shoghi Effendi, The Guardian of the Baha'i Faith, wrote in "The Goal of a New World Order" *The World Order of Baha'u'llah,* concerning how the Principle of the Oneness of Mankind would re-organize institutional, cultural, and inner life: It implies an organic change in the structure of present day society, a change such as the world has not yet experienced...

[5] See George Harris' book *Agent-Centered Morality: An Aristotelian Alternative to Kantian Internalism*, for relevant related discussions on practical reason, symmetrical and asymmetrical regulation of norms, and the need for an empirical "integration test".

and social critique: at points it became a call for the renewal of democracy and an aesthetic of justice that negates all forms of oppression and promotes "full symmetrical" human development.

To understand the nature of this call, it is helpful to remember her much earlier address, the *Declaration of Rights and Sentiments*, given at the historic Seneca Falls Convention in 1848. There, Stanton, speaking publicly for the first time in her life, expressed a moral and political appreciation of the unity of humankind that revealed her underlying respect for the laws of reciprocity and mutuality that govern relationships.[6] The universality of these moral and spiritual laws can be appreciated when, for example, we note the similarity between Stanton's words and those of Lakota White Buffalo Calf Woman:

> When one sits in the Hoop of the People, one must be responsible, because all of Creation is related, the hurt of one is the hurt of all. And the honor of one is the honor of all. (Lakota White Buffalo Calf Woman)

> God, in His wisdom, has so linked the whole human family together that any violence done at one end of the chain is felt throughout its length, and here, too, is the law of restoration, as in woman all have fallen, so in her elevation shall the race be recreated. (Stanton)

Stanton understood that all individuals share responsibility for human well-being. Because of its inherent inter-relatedness, humankind participates together in the burdens of human vulnerability, and in its achievements, even if this is not immediately apparent due to the limitations of sensory perception

[6] These "laws" of inter-dependence can also be understood as the Buddha's central teaching of Dharma, or mutual causality. Understanding of transformation, deep ecological relationship and the reciprocity of causal factors is approached in the present day through general systems theory. Joanna Macy, a scholar of Buddhism and an environmental activist has written extensively on this, calling it the "dharma of natural systems."

in one's individual life. In *Our Girls*, Stanton built on this foundational comprehension of the unity of humankind, by advocating for dignity in balanced terms, both as empowerment and constraint: that is, she asserted the need to recognize the individualism of intrinsic human rights (empowerment) and the collectivism of a metaphysical or religious unified ground of being that protects shared vision (constraint).

In the above statement from *Declaration of Rights and Sentiments,* concerning the law of restoration, the metaphysical or religious ground that supports Stanton's appreciation of dignity as constraint was established. Dignity as constraint reaches beyond individuals and toward a shared vision of dignity based on consciousness of the internal, co-arising, or mutual dimensions of actual life experiences. It extends beyond concern for human dignity to concern for the status and welfare of all life. Dignity as constraint is therefore prescriptive. Its purpose is to protect humankind from what is perceived of as a threat to its survival and to provide it with an authoritative sense of right direction for its future. (Jacobsen, 2012: 187).

Dignity as empowerment on the other hand, depends on "the Kantian ground of capacity for moral agency, the ground based on human vulnerability, and the relational ground, all of which grant dignity to individuals." (187) For Stanton, empowering girls involved engaging their agency and desire to participate as citizens in the transformation of self and society. However, she knew that dignity as empowerment must rest on the relational ground of dignity as constraint in order to create true progress. By calling attention to the significance of the integral nature of health, woman's empowerment could indeed rest on this foundation. Applying logic of unity one could begin to perceive comprehensively the multiple inter-woven dimensions of health and also where its inter-related strands were being violated. As one discerned how social custom and human constructed law hindered realization of health and prevented rightful paths of development, one could develop a full human moral response to this injustice and become an empowered agent of rightful change. In *Our Girls*, she declared outright that:

> I do not believe that it is in harmony with God's laws that any woman should move up and down the earth with her ribs lapped. And the fact the mass of American women are diseased, old before they are thirty years, proves that some great law is violated. ... Health is the normal condition for all women, weakness, disease, pain and sorrow are the results in all cases of violated law.

By introducing this view of health as the normal condition, which ought to be recognized as an essential criterion for just development, Stanton was also urging the moral realization that violations in health signal to citizens the need for encompassing collective and individual learning, and for the specific assertion of negative and positive rights. In her book *Dignity and Health*, Nora Jacobsen provides readers with an articulation of these:

> A (negative) right against unwilled interventions by others that are damaging to the circumstances or conditions that are essential if one is to flourish as a human being; and ... a (positive) right to support and assistance in securing' such circumstances and conditions (Beyleveld, D.; R. Brownsword, 2001: 18 and Jacobsen, 1995: 187).

Stanton saw that as the standard of flourishing was applied to discern instances of violated law, integral health would become a normative ethical orientation." It would help to motivate a sense of rights and to uncover "world-guiding" and "prescriptive" precepts for humankind. (Manne, 2015) In *Our Girls*, Stanton directed her listeners' attention to a range of problems related to human development and health, so as to move listeners beyond mere acknowledgement of the issues, and toward empowered participation in change and deeper comprehension of law itself.

I will now consider how Stanton perceived health as an integral reality that encompasses all aspects of our nature. This view of health positions women as agents of integrity and is therefore directly related to how Stanton understood the social processes through which flawed and fragmented expressions of legal code could become reformed and rightly aligned expressions of justice.

While the aforementioned corseting of women seems to refer more directly to how social norms were effecting women's physical health, and so violating law and mandating citizen action, other sections of the speech more clearly also address mental and spiritual health, viewing them as related to physical health and as bodily imperatives in their own right. For example, Stanton highlighted the dangers of leaving woman without the proper social infrastructures to fulfill her creative and intellectual potentials. She observed that

> The more fire and genius a girl has with no outlets for her powers, the more complete is her misery when all these forces are turned back upon herself.

Where others saw woman's degradation and failings, Stanton perceived crises in human development, violations in natural law, and moral and spiritual potentialities that had not had proper social structures or "outlets" in which to be developed:

> The pent up fires that might have glowed with living words of eloquence in courts of justice, in the pulpit, or on the stage, are to-day consuming their victims in lunatic asylums, in domestic discontent and disgust, in peevish wailings about trifles, or in the vain pursuit of pleasure and fashion, longing for that peace that is found only in action.

Becoming a transformative repository for the shame and loss of the society, Stanton expressed with remorse the vast number of girls who "live and die unloving and unloved" yet, who, in a just society, "might have stood high in the shining walks of life a blessing to others and themselves." Here, the dissonance created by the images of the actual life lived by the "unloving and unloved" gifted girl in an oppressive society evoke a sense of pity. Robbed of her integrity, this girl is deprived of her well-being and ability to participate constructively in self-development and society-making. She continues to suffer in large part due to cultural norms that impede necessary interpersonal attunement and social integration in the present-moment time of day-to-day life; and also, due to social obstacles that block necessary emotional and cognitive growth in the long-term unfolding of developmental time.

Throughout the talk, Stanton expressed concern like this, evoking at other times, a sense of dismay and even outrage at the nature of the injustice. For instance, she noted that while some girls, as described above, are tragically overwhelmed by the internal force of creative and moral energies, others are simply disgracefully prevented from accessing these capacities. She saw the imposition of false male ideals of feminine beauty and behavior as the culprit. Adherence to 19th century women's fashion trends was an example of how false ideals of beauty and behavior contaminated girls' minds and harmed their bodies. She gave a factual account of the women's dress in that day that was calculated to provoke consternation and alarm in listeners:

> the tight waist prevents a free circulation of the blood and action of the heart and lungs, contracts the ribs and paralyzes a belt of the nerves and muscles at least six inches in width round that part of the body.

Bound in such restrictive clothing and given only sedentary indoor activities, a girl often becomes

> ... moody, listless, weary, strolls when she should run, cries when she should laugh and this at the very age when she should manifest new power, vigor and enthusiasm.

In Stanton's observations of integral health she especially pointed to how the physical and social are closely bound to myriad inter-related processes of maturation. For instance, she concluded that stifling clothing and lifestyle is directly related to the stifling of the human mind and denial of the soul:

> When we remember that deep breathing has much to do with deep thinking we see the relation between scholarship and clothes. ... even to the mermaid is vouchsafed more breathing power than to the woman of the 19th century.

When Stanton pointed out to people how a girl's clothing influenced her ability to breathe, and how this in turn directly related to her ability to think deeply for herself, she was demonstrating her comprehension of correspondence and interaction between biological and spiritual law; she was also confirming, through practical wisdom, that sociological (as well as ecological) conditions can directly impact physiology and can in turn, strongly affect moral and cognitive development. Her understanding of the need for integration across the developmental systems implicated in individual and social life, informed her vision of how integrity in social law could be attained.

Indeed, her understanding on this subject can be said to resonate with some of the social significances of what has been generally called the "Medicine Wheel." The Medicine Wheel is a broad synthesis of the Western concept of wheel and generalized insights from indigenous cultures about healing.[7] It represents how the "holy" and the "healthy" share common ground in religion and medicine, and also, as Andrew Weil, M.D. explains in his book *Health and Healing*, is a meaningful symbol of "the circle as a

---

[7] The term "Medicine Wheel" is not a Native American expression. Instead, it is of European and American origin. What the symbol has been called in Native America depends on the language of each particular Nation. This is protected among some Native American Nations and therefore will not be discussed here. For some this has often been lost and "Medicine Wheel" is the common used phrase. (Oxedine, Jamie K. *NATIVE AMERICAN MEDICINE WHEEL Comparison in Life*.) Available at http://www.powwows.com/2014/04/08/native-americanmedicine-wheel-comparison-in-life/.

universal symbol of wholeness and perfection." (Weil, 1983: 43) Respect for the holy (spiritual law) and the healthy (biological law) are meant to be woven together, each regulating the other in a range of deliberative contexts, bringing about a holistic, balanced way of living.

In terms of social development and how integrity in social law can be attained, Medicine Wheel wisdom unites dignity as empowerment and constraint: its' symbolic imagery directs focus away from the limits of region and human-constructed culture, and towards the possibility of a more unified path to progress. An individual is empowered by this wisdom toward positive and negative human rights to health, but also constrained by understanding of one's self as living in the context of a much larger whole and in relation to an ideal of integrity and integration. By engaging such insights herself, Stanton presented a way in which the individual can become an interactive moral participant in social transformation, rather than merely a political player aiming for limited legal change, or a conformist, seeking personal advancement by adhering to social norms injurious to the progress and well-being of humankind.

For example, if allowed to elaborate further, I believe Stanton would advance the understanding that the gifted girl with a strong aesthetic capacity for engagement and creative participation must not only be free to access outlets to nurture her abilities as a thespian, judge or spiritual educator. The underlying purpose of theater, court or spiritual learning, and its role in the making of civilized society and democracy must also be energized by the contributions of the girl of "fire and genius" as she gains access to the social avenues through which to learn, serve and creatively innovate. As she is able to develop integrity the quality of her reasoning and way of life becomes a source of renewal and vitalization, not only for herself, but for the world. In this way, self-healing and self-regulating social systems, free from oppression, organically come into being as paths to self-development are opened for all. Such systems, by their nature, can certainly not be imposed.

The key point here is this: for Stanton, changes in law, and movement toward social transformation, had to be regarded hand in hand with concerns for actual human development in specific real-world life contexts. Changes had to be based "not on common speculative notions, but on common practical notions" that are integrated, and that directly support integral health and sustain improved long-term survival. (Maritain, 1951: 77) This meant that, law, as Stanton envisioned it, had to be realized through a particular kind of sociality, one essentially non-coercive and conducive to the attainment of universal or common agreement. In accord with the general wisdom of the Medicine Wheel, Stanton acknowledged that people must come to agree practically upon a common orientation for governing actions, and then, like the gifted girl described above, must work on an on-going basis, to bring those guiding biological concerns for health and fulfillment, and spiritual concerns for ethics and aesthetics, into the world as creative insights and responsive actions. (Vatter, 2013: 245).

Talks like *Our Girls* prove that Stanton's appreciation of the ground of inter-relatedness and mutual influence, that enlivens dignity as constraint, was not merely philosophical or ideological. This ground was not realized through any authoritarian interpretation of the Bible, or any set of imposed or assumed cultural beliefs about either spirituality or well-being. Rather, it was realized freely and internally, in direct relation to the underlying internal togetherness of scripture, to life's inter-dependent web of relationships and to real life needs for creative growth and restoration. To approach these deeper unifying realities requires major paradigm shifts in how we view human development and human sociality, which I will now explore further.

First, I will focus on the paradigm shift in human development that Stanton boldly put forth. An underlying message in *Our Girls* is that just law, embodying the laws of health, relates one to a sacred or providential order of things. This order protects the way a person achieves "fullness of being, either in its growth or behavior." (Vatter, 2013: 247) In *Our Girls*, it becomes clear how Stanton viewed laws of health as reflecting "God's law": if observed and obeyed, laws of health can reveal "an ideal formula of development of a given being". (247) However, ideal development should not be understood in conventional terms, as either static or abstract. Stanton instead emphasized that "perfect" development reflects a mature relation to the realities of a dynamic world. It embodies flexible, adaptive, coherent, energetic and stable[8] processes of learning and growing that are attuned both to individual variability and to the social ecologies that provide for all a necessary ground of security and belonging, or commonwealth.

In a contingent life-world, humans must relate to the realities of change and development, not through a set theoretical consensus to a meta-ideal or assumption of a meta-perspective, but through "a trans-subjective space of truth"[9] in which sacred or providential order can be inwardly felt and known. This space is respectably attained both deliberatively and contentiously when truly radical democratic structures for inclusion and perspective-taking are enlivened by citizens of both genders, and all generations, in local

---

[8] These five adjectives form the acronym FACES, which was created by interpersonal neurobiologist Daniel Siegel. See his book *The Mindful Brain* to learn more about FACES flow and domains of neural integration that are the biological substrates of optimal development and mental health.

[9] There are practices for reaching this "trans-subjective space of truth", for example, the community making process facilitated by the Foundation for Community Encouragement, which involves individual and group ontological transformation as people journey through a stage of "emptiness" and are able to move beyond patterns of bias perception and habitual limited ways of relating. Also the Baha'i process of consultation empowers people to come to practical agreements and conclusions, not by permitting or forcing some to stifle deeper feelings and responses, but rather, by calling upon "truth force" (what Gandhi called *satyagraha*). Abdu'l Baha affirmed that in consultation, "The shining spark of truth cometh forth only after the clash of differing opinions."

commons, as found in the structure of clans and nations in the federalized Haudenosaunee Nation or Iroquois League. (Bernstein, 2010: 122) Just law supporting fullness of being and rightful development is therefore beyond human political constructions of "positive" law. (Vatter, 2013: 247, 249).

This leads to necessary discussion of the second paradigm shift, concerning human sociality. When one states that just law is not positive law, one is affirming that just law is not uncovered through I-We sociality, but through I-Thou sociality, to use the terms offered by pragmatist philosopher Robert Brandom. In I-We sociality the community is privileged over the individual as "the arbiter of what is true and objective." (Bernstein, 2010: 121) Individual human consciousness is subsumed by the collective. The community forgets that it is a perspective and takes itself as an absolute, falling into the trap of conventionalism. This means that I-We sociality cannot give rise to the "trans-subjective space of truth" in which distinct individuals come to recognize and agree upon just expressions of law in a given context. People engaged in I-We sociality are fearful of individuality and cling to custom and convention, despite its deleterious effects on holistic well-being.

For Stanton, living in the U.S. in the19th century, the common fixed assumptions of what is "right" or acceptable in human development, were not only wrong in content, but also wrong in the form through which a citizen was structurally imagined as democratic, equal and participatory. While founding U.S. documents spoke generally and absolutely about liberty, equality and independence, the specific meaning and application of these terms, though made to appear universal, were actually only based on one dominant groups' positivist I-We social assumptions.[10]

[10] In her book, *Yurugu, An African-centered Critique of European Cultural Thought and Behavior*, author Marimba Ani (Dona Richards) provides important terms for understanding the underlying nature of culture. The

(*Contd...*)

Right form and content for government and citizenship, supportive of noble civic aspirations, and of both the biological and spiritual aspects of human sociality, can only become known when one establishes much more open-minded and inquisitive social practices for discerning what is real and true; that is, practices which acknowledge the need for original position and for distinct perspectival forms, through which one can call attention to subjective dimensions within one's thinking and views, benefit from the epistemic value of one's personal reactions and feelings, and locate with one's fellow citizens common ground of practical reasoning with one's fellow citizens.[11] In this authentic, egalitarian I-Thou sociality, that contrasts with the I-We, every perspective has a rich intrinsic value, and a woman's embodied perspective is recognized as inherently equal in value to a man's, despite major differences in kinds of individual and social life

(Contd...)

conceptual framework for analyzing culture, which includes the concepts of *Asili* (the logos, germ/seed of a culture within which its various aspects cohere), *Utamawazo* (cognition that is culturally structured by the *Asili*) and *Utamaroho* (the vital force or energy source of a culture, set in motion by the *Asili*) is very helpful not only for uncovering the oppressive dynamics of I-We sociality that Stanton was addressing in her day, but also for analyzing the different means by which she worked to transform self and society; these included regenerating culture and the meaning of democracy (focus on *Asili*), re-structuring cultural cognitions pertaining to women's capacities and human development (focus on *Utamawazo*), and setting in motion new kinds of vital forces, through symbolic acts like calling for the "baptism" of women into the "spirit of freedom and equality" (focus on *Utamaroho*).

[11] In my book, *Toward a Cosmopolitan World Social Body: A Treatise on Harmony* (to be published 2018 by Cambridge Scholars Publishing) I provide a structural analysis of the ancient concept of harmony, and put forth that this structure can serve as a neutral egalitarian original position that supports living social creative ethical practices; in addition the tri-partite nature of Soul and City can help to mobilize I-Thou sociality by providing a structure for different perspectival forms.

experience.[12] "Within the context of I-Thou sociality, the dharma of natural systems is understood in terms of "laws" like the law of inter-dependency, that are already instantiated within all life. Our task is to live in conscious harmony with this evolutionary force and to establish within our institutional structures universal guiding principles that reflect its wisdom."

Because the individual is brought directly into an experience of her individuality, the experience of unconscious (passive) and conscious (coerced) submission in I-We sociality is not tolerated in I-Thou sociality. With intentional focus placed on integral health, "one becomes more sensitively attuned to the mutual aid, cooperation and reciprocity that characterize the world of being, so that internal and external forms of oppression, related to gender,age,ability, creativity, race, ethnicity or nation-state identity, become disturbingly obvious". These violations provoke an experience of the moral power[13]inherent in the individual's sense of an unfulfilled right.

---

[12] In fact, when differences are understood from the point of view of form and I-Thou sociality, one realizes that while people in I-We sociality may believe there is a real ground of greater commonalities in content to be found in a given selected group of people in I-We assumed patterns of relationship, in actuality, because of the mystery of each individual's relation to the Unknown (Mystery, or a Transcendent and Inaccessible God) differences "among people of different demographics, and even time period, which would seem so vast and insurmountable, are rendered as equalin form, if not content, to differences among a self-selected group of say, all white Western males ages 35-55 in the State of New York in 1848. The gifts of pluralism that await humankind, and that Stanton envisioned in the new civilization, can only be receivedwhen a far greater vision of integrative social practice is noetically and creatively awakened, so that the multiplicity of difference available in I- Thou sociality can become a transformative ground of truth-seeking for any kind of group-those with members with seeming great similarities, and those constituted of people with sharply contrasting generic profiles, statistically speaking."

[13] Known as *orenda* by the Iroquois

They also awaken the creative power within the individual's agency as one's vision turns toward a guiding ideal of justice.[14] In the struggle against perceived injustice and error that ensues, one's deepest desire for justice and true freedom becomes known and the authentic Subject within each citizen is permitted to rise. (Touraine, 1995) It is through the struggle for equality that one comes to attest to the truth of a deeper sacred order, a "law of all laws," as Trotsky termed the class struggle that forbids a person or group from blocking a dignified outlet for fulfillment of any individual's real developmental needs.[15]

Stanton clearly valued how this movement from I-We to I-Thou sociality centered each girl in a sense of her own agency and noble purpose. She continually sought to affirm each girl as an authentic Subject, capable of her own point of view, and of engaging courageously with life struggle. She placed each girl in I-Thou relation to her own creative being and set her sights toward pursuit of the highest good:

> It is a great truth to impress on the mind of every girl that she is an independent creative will power, made primarily for her own happiness, making self-development and self-support and the highest good of the race the end of her being.

One can see here how Stanton restored to U.S. girls the inmost substance of human strength, by reminding them of their innate capacity for integrity. When girls were freed from attachment to superficial values and narrow social aims they could realize their inner power and live much more complete lives, dedicated to the vast vision of the well-being of all humankind.

---

[14] Agency here relates to human capacity for both moral and aesthetic engagement, both agent-neutral (impartial) and agent-centered (partial or impartial influencing one's felt sense of partiality) modes of participation. See George Harris, *Agent-Centered Morality,* for more on these understandings of human agency, moral and aesthetic norms.

[15] For more related to this reference of Trotsky, see Bernstein 2010 p 296 and Dewey, "Significance of the Trotsky Inquiry" (1937) *LW* II: 331.

While she affirmed their capacity for vigor and steadfastness, she also sought to protect it from the threatening forces in the society that could deny or harm it. She did this by challenging the false belief that women were "naturally weak" and susceptible to "disability", a view popularly endorsed by those in the medical profession, which excused a woman from responsibly engaging the inherent moral power of her independent creative will, as described in the passage above. Unchallenged belief in natural weakness would inevitably damage a woman's deeper integrity: it made her subject to fatalism and superstitious modes of thinking, the products of I-We structured sociality, and left her disengaged from the real concerns of human life. Stanton noted that:

> ...so long as physicians continue to teach this theory [of "the natural weaknesses and disabilities of woman"], women instead of having a feeling of guilt, when their children or themselves are always out of health, they will continue to throw all their sins on a mysterious providence.

In this passage, Stanton was addressing the more serious ideological and psychological dangers of I-We sociality. Physicians who endorsed the natural weakness of women were affirming their own sacrosanct social order of acquiescence that, in addition to impacting social conceptions of gender and accepted norms for active participation in society, were also more broadly useful for the preservation and expansion of their own profession; the theory of woman's natural weakness and disability mentally entrenched the notion that a separate category of needy or "feminized" people actually existed, rather than conceding that all humans must share equally in the ground of human poverty. Establishing this category and preserving it overtime was an unconscious survival strategy useful for creating a populace that would perpetually lack perception of the role of their own agency in creating individual and public health, and so, would continuously produce the category of "patients", and by default, maintain the doctor's social position and authority. Such a populace would not be prepared to question the foundational premises of Western medicine as it advanced to encompass new domains like "behaviorism" and eventually, new medical fields, like psychiatry, which at this period in history, conventionally called on practices like "straight-jacketing" that were even more violent to women than corseting. The integral health of all was profoundly jeopardized by the loss of woman's integrity when she accepted a doctor's blanket assumptions about her natural weakness and inferior ability.

Stanton clearly perceived this social danger in the I-We power structure that supported physicians' authority: she saw how such use of authority not only affected women's self-perception, but also influenced assumptions about reality generally. In many ways she appears to have viewed it as more threatening to human development than the authority of politicians. She understood how the 19th century physicians' denial of the "great immutable laws of life" prevented not only women and their children from progressing, but also the whole of science itself. Stanton affirmed that scientific inquiry and investigation would greatly assist human advancement. But a science free from imposed bias had to be recovered through a rigorous and genuine "scientific education" made available to both genders.[16]

> With the scientific education of our youth of both sexes, and a strict observance of the great immutable laws of life, another generation might show as marked a change in the human family as we already observe in the lower animals, which science has done so much to improve during the last century.

---

[16] An example of how gender equality in science influenced human advancement is in the field of primatology. Male primatologists commonly focused on patterns of aggression and social hierarchy in primate behavior, often leading to closed conclusions about human nature and the necessary role of dominance and status in human interactions. However, women are said to have "revolutionized" the field when they were allowed to participate themselves in research. Their often close personal relations with the animals helped them to uncover deeper patterns of behavior and examples of primate altruism and caring that are helpful for human understandings of intimacy, survival and peace. See http://www.iflscience.com/editors-blog/how-three-women-known-trimates-revolutionized-field-primatology/ for details.

Throughout the talk, the aesthetic, spiritual and scientific ideals of progress that she called upon, inspired I-Thou sociality, while negating the superficial and popularized ideals of mere social advancement that she felt kept U.S. women trapped in forms of mimetic desire and acquisition, caring more about pleasing men and false notions of self-worth, than about living by the noblest principles of a true participatory democracy:[17]

As today's reader of *Our Girls* considers how Stanton defended and protected girls' identity as agents capable of participating fully in all domains of education and of serving the highest good of humankind, I believe it will become evident that the paradigm shifts she advanced, in conceptions of human development and sociality, direct attention to a new moral frontier, in which women themselves bring about a larger awakening of political integrity:

> Again when American women begin to care more for principle, than pleasing, more to be, than to seem, and understand their true dignity as citizens of a republic, they will not ape foreign customs, manners and fashions all out of joint with our theory of government. ...

In statements like this and the one below, Stanton united concern for ideal paths of development and for emergent I-Thou sociality to provoke a new sense of civic responsibility:

---

[17] Theophus Smith writes about how mimetic desire and acquisition, emerging from biological survival drives, are at the root of all social violence. Homeopathic violent cures for violence in society make use of the natural tendency to feel mimetic desire so as to generate reflexively beliefs about the need for exclusionary logic, conformity and a sense of superiority through participation in social norms of acquisition. See *Conjuring Culture: Biblical Formations of Black America.* Stanton obviously perceived that needs for belonging and a fear of social exclusion kept women ensnared in paradigms of "pleasing"; women needed to understand that they did indeed have full capacity to engage their own inner faculties, and therefore, to direct their own lives and to participate nobly in society by reasoning for themselves.

> I urge you one and all to study the laws of health and obey them, that you may bravely do your part in the future in maintaining the strength, virtue, honor, and dignity of this government.

I believe these passages point to a third paradigm shift that is offered in *Our Girls*, related to democracy and woman's role in the transformation of government. This shift begins with Stanton's insistence that girls not neglect the gift of intellect, but rather care responsibly for its creative and spiritual dimensions.

> God has given you minds, dear girls, as well as it is your duty to develop your immortal powers.

In addition to this lofty duty and overall directive, Stanton instructed young women more specifically to contribute to social change practically, at a root level, through respectable work, and to attain secure levels of wealth independently. On the subject of a girl's employment and financial independence, she stated that:

> ...she is to be a creator of wealth herself...To train your daughter to a good trade or profession is far better than to leave her an unhappy dependent or a fortune without the necessary knowledge to take care of it. Every thinking man must see how entirely a woman's virtue and dignity are involved in her pecuniary independence.

By engaging in an ethical trade or profession, Stanton saw that young women could "strike a blow at licentiousness and excess" in all domains of life. The impact of this would be "felt throughout the land." Girls had to be encouraged to enter profitable employments, "not only for their own personal happiness" but also "for the safety of public morals." Here again is the shift away from personal and conventional expectations of social development and participation, and toward much grander calls for self-cultivation and authentic civic engagement.

Stanton also coached girls to recognize how their virtue and dignity would help them to approach the republican democratic ideal of the citizen. As they became responsible agents, and used their minds, they would be able to participate not only in society-making, but also in visionary civilization-building. She pronounced that:

> I would have girls regard themselves not as adjectives but nouns, not mere appendages made to qualify somebody else, but independent, responsible workers in carrying forward the grand eternal plans in the redemption of mankind.

At the center of this paradigm shift in how we respect the ontology of womanhood and woman's practical role in the transformation of governance, was Stanton's assertion that real beauty did not involve subjective concerns for one's physical aesthetics, but rather was attained through intellectual engagement and civic participation. She insisted that the aesthetic dimension rested upon the quality of one's inner life and on the

> culture of the intellect, the tastes, sentiments, and affections of the soul, on an earnest unselfish life purpose to leave the world better than you find it.

A woman's physical appearance is transformed by noble virtues and brings

> a halo of glory about the head, in a personal atmosphere of goodness, and greatness that none can mistake.

Stanton instructed that beauty and leadership were brought together through moral power, which can only abide in the true Subject. The authentic leader, capable of I-Thou individuality and sociality, is one who exemplifies the qualities of "kindness, nobility, generosity and magnanimity." Stanton particularly prevailed on women to animate within their selves a public service ethos that was about more than uniting state and civil society. Traditional public service and public sector ethos is usually characterized by the following:

> first, and most important, it is about the setting aside of personal interests... working altruistically for the public good. Secondly... it is about working with others, collegially and anonymously, to promote that public good. Thirdly, it is about integrity in dealing with the many and diverse problems which need solving if the public good is to be promoted (O'Toole, 1993: 3; Temple, 2000: 112).

However, the public service ethos that Stanton counseled for women also entailed a fourth dimension that expanded and refined one's notion of the "public good": this involved dedication to ideal vision and participation in spiritual realities related to the meaning of democracy itself. This kind of vision and participation could re-make democracy. When Stanton urged girls to develop themselves spiritually, as in her guidance—

> You must cultivate those immortal powers that gradually unfold and grasp the invisible as from day to day the visible ceases to absorb the soul.

—she did so with the understanding that it was spiritual development that would best prepare them to become transformers of political structure and to attain the "halo of glory" and the spiritual beauty that comes with this kind of noble action. When girls could "grasp the invisible" and evolve beyond perceptions of only "visible" life realities that subsumed them, they could then also instate a new visionary democracy, not yet present anywhere in the world, leaving behind their everyday sensory dependence on conventions, norms and outdated laws that stifled and absorbed them. Standards of caring for full human maturation and civic participation would guide individual and social change and create transformation through radical acts of beauty.

Stanton believed that with adequate focus placed on individual agency and new kinds of education, democracy could become "the cure for the ills of democracy." In *Our Girls*, she promoted this transformative idea, which Dewey would later speak of as a revitalizing return to the idea of democracy itself,

> Of clarifying and deepening our apprehension of it, and of employing our sense of its meaning to criticize and remake its political manifestations (Dewey, *Later Works* 2: 325; Bernstein, 2010: 80)

Stanton perceived that like any valid tradition, democracy could be "made and re-made", that it involved certain habits of reasoning, attitudes and loves, and that its "terms" and "parameters" could be continuously "scrutinized and revised." (Stout, 2005: 5; Abeysekara, 2008:101) Because the ground of all being is a unified ground, inclusion of women into democracy could thoroughly revive democracy, and through the laws of restoration that Stanton referred to in *Declaration of Rights and Sentiments*, it could also elevate all humankind. I consider this to be the most far-reaching point about gender and transformation of power that Stanton offers. It represents a turn away from conventional, socio-centric views of change that are linear and occur only in minute increments and implies a major alteration in modern notions of causal relations.

Stanton insisted that it was because of her love of country and belief in its free institutions that she desired

> to see this government maintained and perpetuated as it only can be by baptizing its women into the spirit of freedom and equality.

If women were thus empowered and constrained by authentic dignity, Stanton saw that they would become more than public servants upholding the status quo in American democracy; they would actually become vessels for "the redemption of mankind." (see earlier quote "I would have girls regard themselves not as adjectives but nouns…")

Stanton strengthened her articulation of a vital public service ethos by positioning it as necessary for "saving" both individuals and humankind; and she instilled in listeners' some measure of fear about the ability of their nation-state to endure adversity if women should be prevented from fully embodying this "spirit of freedom and equality". She predicted that if U.S. males did not use the advantage of their political power to help the women of their nation in this rightful path of participation, speedily inaugurating "some grand reform in this direction," then the imbalances and deficiencies that would manifest in the U.S. as a nation-state would leave the people at risk of "sturdier foreign races" taking their advantage over those in the U.S.

In this regard, the zeal of her seeming nationalism, which inspires pride in the political heritage or tradition of democracy, and in the egalitarian character of its people, can be likened to aspects of Gandhi's practical spiritual approach to motivating individual and social transformation, apparent in writings like *Hind Swaraj or Indian Home Rule*,[18] which has strong nationalist overtones, helping to inculcate within its readers a new-found sense of honor and active agency.

[18] In Gandhi's 1909 book, *Hind Swaraj or Indian Home Rule*, Gandhi reminded the Indian people of their heritage and ethos. He wrote as the Editor: A nation with a constitution like this is fitter to teach others than to learn from others. This nation had courts, lawyers and doctors, but they were all within bounds. ... the common people lived independently and followed their agricultural occupation. They enjoyed true Home Rule. The word "Swaraj", translated into English as 'Home Rule" needs to be understood as it relates to dignity as empowerment and human agency. Swa translates to "self" and raj to "rule," so swaraj, like the Iroquois understanding of the Good Mind, is a form of self-rule or "home rule," with people awakened and active as citizens, connected to their local place, as in the true meaning of "commonwealth." Gandhi's nationalism, like Stanton's, was not based on exclusionary emotions, but rather on a desire to call out and to nurture what is of highest value in his fellow Indians. As evidence of this, consider this quotation from Chapter 15, "Italy and India," which describes the nature of his patriotism: By patriotism I mean the welfare of the whole people, and if I could secure it at the hands of the English, I should bow down my head to them. If any Englishman dedicated his life to securing the freedom of India, resisting tyranny and serving the land, I should welcome that Englishman as an Indian. This too is similar to Stanton's concern for what will bring practical relief and transformation to all people.

An example of Stanton's use of this kind of motivating pride in the political heritage or tradition of American democracy can be found in her description of her experience in Europe seeing U.S. Americans "moving about among the Kings, Queens and nobles of the old world." Stanton expressed her delight in "the unconscious way in which Americans ignore all distinctions," exemplifying a kind of self-possession. In contrast, the middle classes in Europe "manifest in the presence of the nobility the most pitiful unrest and obsequiousness,"[19] causing Stanton to remind her audience that

> We never fully appreciate the beneficent results of our republican theory, that all men are created equal until we see our people in contrast with the cringing masses in the old world.

But like Gandhi, Stanton was actually generating nation-state pride by reclaiming the notion of democracy as tradition, which people had failed to "fully appreciate"; she certainly was not affirming the common rendering of democratic norms found in every day secular U.S civic life. Stanton also had a fairly keen understanding of the political heritage of this tradition in the U.S. The "republican theory" that she referred to was actually inherited, not as much from the Greeks as from the Iroquois, who the founding fathers borrowed from in large part when they created national symbols and a federal nation-state structure. Stanton recognized Iroquois law and governing structures as an ideal and virtuous form of republican democracy that, unlike the U.S. borrowed and partial renderings of it, actually protected principles of gender

[19] Archived text of the speech at University of Maryland explains that Stanton shared with listeners an anecdote about how Harriet Elizabeth Georgiana Leveson-Gower, the Duchess of Sutherland (1806-1868), asked to meet the American abolitionists after the World's Anti-Slavery Convention of 1840. In her memoir, *Eighty Years and More*, ECS described how nervous her visit made the English middle class and how easily Lucretia Mott greeted the duchess.

equality and total citizen participation in government. Iroquois girls living under the Iroquoian Great Law of Peace were able to embody the Great Values and the practices of the Good Mind, and to be assured of their rights to responsible participation within the various domains of life.

Stanton's understanding of "democracy as tradition" in the U.S. was vitalized by her respect for this political heritage and for the dignity manifested in the lives of neighboring Iroquois women. This appreciation is a major underlying aspect of the paradigm shift that she hoped to create in how people in the U.S. view their own legally-constructed democracy. She envisioned the "coming girl" in the U.S. living under just and equitable laws grounded in the kind of reverence for the whole of life that was present among the Iroquois; and she saw this U.S. girl as likewise empowered to become "healthy, wealthy, and wise," to hold with dignity "an equal place with her brother in the world of work, in the colleges, in the state, the church and the home." She called the new girl "an independent, self-supporting being, not as today a helpless victim of fashion, superstition, and absurd conventionalisms."

In addition, Stanton's "girl of the future" was to be nourished through her spiritual ancestral roots, through remembrance of humanity's history. Connecting aspiration and vision ahead with respect for the past was a bridge of perception that safeguarded recognition of the unity of life and facilitated in the realization of dignity as constraint. Stanton spoke of how restoration of respect for a matrilineal line of spiritual leaders would revive "that glorious period when old maids will be honored and revered." In her efforts preparing girls for their future, Stanton urged them to look to women leaders both from her day and from an inspiring and exemplary past, including a

> long line of [female] geniuses, saints and philanthropists who have devoted themselves to art, religion and reform.

She listed women active in many spheres of life — Caroline Summerville, Maria Mitchell, Harriet Martineau, Angelica

Kauffmann, Harriet Hosmer, Rosa Bonheur, Elizabeth Barrett Browning, George Sand, Charlotte Bronte and Harriet Beecher Stowe—and made her naming of them a potent spiritual act of conjuration[20], affirming that:

> All these and many more have risen up in spite of the stone on their heads and walked forward as easily as did Samson into the gates of the city.

In this reference to Judges 16:3, Samson is gifted by God with great strength and by his example, encourages others to join him. Here the works of the female exemplars Stanton named are not diminished because of their identity as women; instead, like Samson, the women triumph over the notion their status is flawed or sinful, and participate with him in a spiritual transformation of power. The girl of the future would likewise be able to know victory.

Finally, it is possible to perceive how the paradigm shifts I have so far outlined, in our understandings of human development, sociality, democracy and participation, are all involved in Stanton's views on love and the institution of marriage. Considering all domains of girls' needs and lives, Stanton did not neglect this topic; she pointed to a future in which reformed practices in education and marriage would unite physical and spiritual development in

---

[20] Conjuration is a means of re-envisioning and transforming reality in black spirituality and culture. In African American tradition the Bible is used to invoke Divine powers in order to change conditions of inequality and injustice. The practice originated in the United States during slavery. People like Moses, events like the Exodus, and archetypes like the Suffering Servant are called upon to transform culture and society. In the passage quoted, Stanton is in some sense calling upon the African American practice of conjuring, by symbolically associating the women she names with a biblical reference to triumph. The gate image is relevant to the archetypal forces of transformation called upon in Stanton's reference to "baptism" at another point in the speech. See Judges 16:3 for reference to Samson and Theophus Smith's book *Conjuring Culture: Biblical Formations of Black America* for more on conjuration.

girls and would make possible for all realizations of dignity both as empowerment and constraint. She believed that these reforms in cultural expectations and institutions bring about an elevated and just harmony in human relations between men and women and would lead to the betterment of the world:

> Again no girl should marry until she is at least twenty-five years of age as she does not reach physical maturity before that time. Thus many years could be devoted to reading, thought and study, to a preparation for that higher companionship of the spirit and intellect with pure, cultivated, scholarly men.

Ultimately, Stanton saw that the outcome of this education and the full emergence of the coming girl into womanhood would be not just a modified democracy but "the dawning of a new civilization." She foresaw how the guided development of women would correspond with the creation of new social structures and higher "outlets" that would allow the force of women's natural capacity for pure love and altruism to flourish fully and to flow with refinement into the society. She promised that

> In the higher civilization now dawning upon us, the love element of pure, refined women, guided and controlled by conscience, science, and religion will find higher purer outlets for its forces.

I will now summarize the four major paradigm shifts discussed:

- Ideal human development is not rigid, fixed or abstract; rather, it is dynamic, contingent on context and directly related to the comprehensive standard of integral health; it reflects recognition of the sacrality of life and of there being a providential or sacred order through which rightful development is attained.
- Authentic sociality is not based on limited group identity, conventions and norms of conformity; rather, it is agent-

centered and relates individuals to the larger totality of life and the mystery of what is beyond the individual.

- Democracy is not a fixed tradition, inherited only from the Greeks, and perpetuated through imitation and habit; rather, it is revitalized through spiritual perception and public service ethos and can be re-made through remembrance of culture, history and acts of beauty.
- Marriage is not a contract for perpetuating status quo social order, and love relationships are not meant to maintain limiting gender roles and inequalities; rather, marriage and love are means through which people, as equals enter into higher companionship and encourage the force of the "love element" to enter the world.

Below is an additional review, using some of the terms I have introduced to the reader, of Stanton's radical vision of gender and the transformation of power that ends not just in certain rights, like the vote, attained for women, but in the dawning of a whole new civilization:

1. Girls shift from I-We to I-Thou sociality and recognize their rights and sense of agency, their natural moral and creative power.
2. Girls work particularly to overcome sanctioned and imposed biases in their thinking and errors in their self-perception (such as they are "weak" or "disabled"). They engage in science education and recognize violations in laws of health pertaining to physical, intellectual, emotional, social, moral and spiritual development; they link their sense of rights to their responsibility to fulfill their development and to become active citizens capable of transforming social structure.
3. Girls recognize democracy as a tradition that can be "made and re-made"; they connect to a matrilineal line, realize and focus on spiritual development and critical discernment of social reality; they become baptized into the spirit of freedom

and equality and capable of realizing dignity both as empowerment and constraint.

4. As girls become young women, they extend education and enter into "higher companionship" with men. Focus on gender equality, advanced learning, and a fully enlivened public service ethos makes them a vital force in laws of restoration and the "dawning of a new civilization".

As one reflects upon the above summaries, it is important to remember that *Our Girls*, unlike other famous speeches by Stanton, was not a declaration or a political address. It was a piece of popular oratory, was performed on the Lyceum circuit during the sensitive time of the Reconstruction Era, and was used to provoke not only new social awareness about how 19th century conventions harmed girls, but also inspirational realizations about human potential and the re-making of democracy. In this talk, Stanton looked beyond more superficial or external socio-centric methods of legal change, and toward soul-centered ways of healing people's perceptions and influencing their hearts, minds, desires, aims and dreams so that they would become able to re-configure the power structures internal to human relationships and sociality.

Though Stanton was a profound thinker, and influenced by the research, reflection and scholarship of women like Matilda Joslyn Gage, who later authored *Woman, Culture and State*, *Our Girls* obviously is not a piece of academic philosophy either. However, with its emphasis on addressing real-world practical issues like health and education, it does reveal how gender issues and the work of woman suffragists like Stanton influenced public discourse and established philosophical and spiritual roots of pragmatism that American philosophers like Charles Peirce, William James and John Dewey would later grow their work from while in more sheltered academic settings, in the late 19th and early 20th century.

When reviewing Stanton's efforts and seeking to understand their context, I offer that it is also helpful to remember something of the zeitgeist, that is the defining spirit, of that time in history, as manifested in the ideas, beliefs and actions that emerge in the world during that period. The fact is, that at the very same time that Stanton initiated her work as a suffragist, by taking a leading role in the Seneca Falls Convention, in the United States, similarly bold assertions of women's dignity, spiritual equality and right to participate in governance were made by Fatimah Baraghani, also known as Qurratu l-¿Ayn (*Solace / Consolation of the Eyes*), at the Conference of Badasht, held in an area of Persia, now known as Iran. Fatimah's exceptionally forthright and gallant actions eventually caused her to become, in 1852, the "first woman suffrage martyr." [21] There, on the continent of Asia, this Iranian "feminist" took transformative action to establish a break from old, oppressive laws and the unjust dress codes of Islamic women that prevented them from being able to participate in governance.

Although the particulars of the matter in regard to clothing are very different—with Iranian Islamic women oppressed by laws pertaining to the veil, and U.S. mostly Christian women endangered by Victorian standards of femininity— the severity of the injustices that afflicted women on both continents during this time period, and the recognition, by both these suffragists, of the violation of "God's law", are quite similar. Since this history is not widely known, I will below briefly outline and describe the events in Iran and the most striking parallels between the Conference of Badasht and Seneca Falls, which as mentioned, marked the tumultuous but ardent beginning of suffrage in the U.S.

The Conference of Badasht, in Iran, was made possible and planned in part by Mírzá Husayn-'Alí Núrí (Bahá'u'lláh), in order to address the issues of the Bábi Faith's relation to Islam and the status of the Báb, who was imprisoned at the time. Fatimah, who was revered by many as the spiritual return of Fatima Zahra, the

[21] This is how Shoghi Effendi referred to her in *God Passes By* (1944). See page 75. For more on this topic, please also see "Tahirih and Women's Suffrage" by/on behalf of Universal House of Justice published in Bahá'í Studies Bulletin, 4:2 1990-01 first written or published 1988.

daughter of the prophet Muhammad, unveiled herself in a large assembly of about eighty men, and spoke out on how Bábi law replaces Islamic Sharia law. In doing so, she forged new understanding about the equality of the spiritual and social station of men and women in relation to God and society. (Maneck 1994).

The conference took place in Persia in a "Paradise garden," and when Fatimah quoted from the Quran, "verily, amid gardens and rivers shall the pious dwell in the seat of truth, in the presence of the potent King," the significance of the dissonance between Islamic theology and practice was clarified. To make the Islamic paradise requires that people be able "dwell in the seat of truth" and to participate in I-Thou sociality. At the time, veiled women could not visit the Persian Paradise garden for public discourse. The rules of Sharia that barred women from the dress and behaviors that would allow them to participate were obviously only human constructs and did not reflect the Word of God itself, as provided for humanity in scripture.

Fatimah established the break from Islam Sharia by proclaiming herself to be the *Word* spoken on the day of judgment by the Qa'im, since the representation of her person at Badasht upholds a divine standard of justice. (Momen and Lawson, 2004) Through this practical action she forged a path through which women could establish their unshakeable moral and spiritual rights as equal to men. She also served in an authentically creative way to initiate the emergence of the Bábi Faith itself, as distinct from, though continuous with, Islam. She provided a way for people to comprehend the distinct Bábi realization of law, separate from Islamic Sharia, and in doing so she also participated in the larger pioneering process of bringing forth the Bahá'í Faith. Despite harsh reactions from many assembled in the garden and divisive tensions between Fatimah and a prominent male Bábi leader, Quddús, Mírzá Husayn-'Alí Núrí (Bahá'u'lláh) himself revealed his respectful solidarity with Fatimah's actions at the Conference and there named her Tahirih (The Pure One). This name was later confirmed by the Báb and it is the name by which she is loved and revered by many Bahá'ís today.

It is possible to perceive a great spiritual zeitgeist encompassing the planet during this time in the 19th century; it was in this period that the Bahá'í Faith emerged. The equality of men and women, as well as the unity of the races, were recognized and affirmed by Bahá'u'lláh, the founder of the Bahá'í Faith, and by its subsequent appointed leaders, to signal the advent of divine justice[22] and to be principles of universal peace that would serve as the egalitarian foundation of a New World Order in which the welfare and security of all humankind would be protected. Bahá'u'lláh articulated in innumerable Tablets the requirements and wondrous nature of the dawning civilization that Stanton also was heralding through her advocacy for women and for the oppressed everywhere. Bahá'ís recognize notable parallels between the Conference at Badasht and the Seneca Falls Convention. The salient similarities are listed below:

1. *Both the conference and the convention transpired in July 1848.* The Seneca convention was held over just two days in mid-July, but the Badasht conference ran for over three weeks, from late June to mid-July 1848, and overlaps in time with the convention.
2. *A strong declaration of "independence" was made at both meetings.* *The Declaration of Rights and Sentiments* was modeled on the template of the *Declaration of Independence* and Tahirih's removal of the veil was a profound gesture declaring the independence of the Bábi Faith from Islam, and was followed by a speech she gave herself.
3. *Both gatherings involved a strong woman in a public arena that has before been closed to women.* Seneca Falls featured Stanton and Badasht featured Tahirih.
4. *Both gatherings had a portion of attendees who responded negatively to the statements made.* At Seneca Falls, many

[22] See Shoghi Effendi's *The Advent of Divine Justice*, a letter written by him to the Bahá'ís of North America, dated 25 December 1938.

people were strongly disapproving immediately or shortly after the convention closed, when Stanton's proposal was ridiculed. Badasht had men present so dismayed by Tahirih's unveiling that they left, and one man is reported to have slit his throat in response.

5. *Both gatherings also involved a strong man involved in the tension present at the gathering, but who, by the end, supported the leading women and reconciled differences with them through healing, understanding and communication.* Frederick Douglas was this man in the United States convention, and Quddús, a recognized leading follower of the Báb, in the Iran conference.[23]

Why highlight these synchronicities? Why attempt to contemplate zeitgeist or historical details that point to the reality of a larger, global movement for gender equality? I believe such inquiry and observation helps one to understand something about the nature of transformation itself. The practical spirituality of women like Stanton and Tahirih makes possible the transformation of power as it re-structures and re-scales one's sense of temporal and spatial reality and renews conceptual realizations of human unity.[24] The spatial distance separating movements for reform are overcome in the recognition of a greater human solidarity. For example: while Stanton in North America dedicated herself to co-writing a *Woman's Bible* and declared woman's independence from corrupted interpretations of Christian theology and Victorian morality that oppress women within both the institutions of the Church and the State, Tahirih, her contemporary on the neighboring continent of Asia, declared woman's independence

[23] For more on this, see Bradford Miller's article, "Seneca Falls First Woman's Rights Convention of 1848: The Sacred Rites of the Nation" found at https://bahai-studies.ca/wp-content/uploads/2014/05/8.3-Miller.pdf

[24] Herbert Reid and Betsy Taylor describe the "re-scaling" of spatial and temporal being that is involved in the recovering of the commons and the realization of global solidarity. See their book, *Recovering the Commons: Democracy, Place, and Global Justice.*

from corrupted interpretations of Islamic theology that likewise oppressed woman's ability to participate in making the paradigmatic society. The temporal distance separating socio-spiritual movements are similarly overcome in the recognition of a common evolving spiritual heritage and need for a greater unified peaceful civilization.

The Ideal of "Perfect Womanhood" and Concepts of Fullness in Our Girls

Throughout *Our Girls*, Stanton underscored the need for girls to pursue full development and to respect the universal dimensions of the human spiritual experience within their physical embodiment of the female gender. Whereas women were conditioned by the world from a young age to understand their identity reflexively in terms of "the duties of wives and mothers and housekeepers" Stanton insisted that "all these incidental relations should ever be subordinate to the greater fact of womanhood." She argued that:

> You may never be wives, or mothers, or housekeepers, but you will be women, therefore labor for the grander and more universal fact of your existence.

Furthermore, the theological notion that woman, in this more archetypal, universal and grand sense was created solely for the enjoyment of man, becomes absurd if the fulfillment of a man's mundane needs and worldly social desires are considered a reflection of God's intentions when the male-female human dynamic was called into being. Stanton quoted Frances Power Cobbe, "a distinguished Englishwoman", on this point:

> Believing that the same woman, a million of ages hence, will be a glorious spirit before the throne of God, filled with unutterable love and light and joy, we cannot satisfactorily trace the beginning of that eternal and seraphic existence to Mr. Smith's want of a wife for a score of years here upon earth,

or to the necessity Mr. Jones was under to find somebody to cook his food and repair his clothes.

It is the moral search for greater purpose and a meaningful life, and the spiritual quest for truth that give a life dignity and peace through right action. Both genders know equally these human longings. The only path of human development worth pursuing is that which steers a girl on this grand search and places her in a coherent, flexible and stable relation to an absolute form of the good: an ideal of the perfected woman, a being, as Cobbe described, "filled with unutterable love and light and joy." Stanton here shared Greek philosophical wisdom with her listeners, challenging them to realize their full noetic capacities:

> "There is a knowledge of the truth," says Plato," that gives rest to the soul and thus saves life." But the mere capacity for this knowledge unsatisfied, gives the soul not rest but restlessness. Your life work dear girls is not simply to eat, drink, dress, be merry, be married and be mothers, but to mould yourselves into a perfect womanhood.

The task of moulding oneself into "perfect womanhood" required that girls seek the conditions that "best secure a full symmetrical development"; and at another point in the speech, she elaborated on this concept of aesthetic development, turning the listener's attention toward the artistic pursuit of truth and goodness in one's own life, that invited one to participate creatively in daily radical acts of transformative beauty. This unifying of truth, beauty and goodness, extends beyond limited personal acts in one's individual life; it can be understood as an evolving and broadening movement of willingness to dialogue across subjective, objective and inter-subjective domains of inquiry, finding resonance and new insights in the intersections of arts (including formal contemplative and spiritual practices), science and humanities, respectively.[25]

[25] Roger Prentice, has created an education program based on this model called SUN Walk. He correlates the subjective, objective, inter-subjective/

(Contd...)

"Symmetrical development" comes only from this fertile and creative ground of human exploration and discovery, and is represented in the divine potentiality and holistic totality of "true womanhood."

In religious and spiritual traditions, the feminine as an active integrative reality is associated with moral and mystical aspects of the human relationship-oriented quest and consciousness-making. When barriers for ethical development are removed, holy human desires for union and perfection can be felt and can guide right action. In these traditions, the realities of the Divine Feminine do not pertain exclusively to females, but are equally relevant for both genders[26]. When "true womanhood" is associated with "full symmetrical development" and the creative and generative weaving together of beauty, truth and goodness, one realizes that *both* sexes live in relation to the ideal feminine. This relation is inherently aesthetic and artistic.[27]

(*Contd...*)

arts, sciences, humanities with modes of trans-disciplinary, situational learning through creativity, criticality, and caring, respectively. All of this is within context of Community. See https://sunwalkmodelofholistic education. wordpress.com/author/sunwalked/ for more on this Baha'i-inspired approach to holistic education.

[26] For more on this understanding of the feminine and functions of the Sophianic Feminine, see Austin, R.W.J. (1999) "The Sophianic Feminine in the Work of Ibn 'Arabi and Rumi. In The Heritage of Sufism." The Legacy of Medieval Persia Sufism (1150-1500). Vol. 2 (Edited by Leonard Lewisohn). Oxford: One World, pp. 233–246.

[27] In *The Woman's Bible*, Stanton clarified the inclusive feminine meaning of the word Elohim, which is feminine and plural, though translated as a masculine singular. Eloh or ALH is feminine singular and IM is plural, but usually terminates a masculine plural, hence the erroneous translation as a masculine singular. The true meaning of Elohim as a feminine plural is retained in Genesis 4, 26 "And Elohim said: Let US make man." Stanton explained that it signifies "female potency united to a masculine idea." This understanding of the source of social ethical creativity and the spiritual import of gender equality is one of Stanton's most powerful underlying cognitions that she develops and expresses over her decades of service and justice work.

Stanton saw however, that womanhood itself had become a degraded reality. While one might hear the expression "be a man" in order to inspire a person of either gender to gain rightful courage for action, the notion of commanding someone to "be a woman", *i.e.,*"be integrative, artistically inclusive and committed to the loftiest ideals of human development and nurturance", would have an ambiguous import, because in general, so little social dignity was conferred to woman and the ideals of "true womanhood" had been lost in a misogynist U.S. society. To restore this ideal, Stanton advised listeners to

> Regard yourselves precisely as the artist does his painting or statue, ever stretching forward to some grand ideal. Remember that your daily, hourly lives, every impulse, passion, feeling of your soul, every good action, high resolve and lofty conception of the good and true, are delicate touches here and there gradually rounding out and perfecting in yourselves a true womanhood.

Stanton grasped that aesthetic or "full symmetrical" human development was in fact, the art of creative living itself. Furthermore, one's relation to the ideal feminine, and its generative power, had both creative and destructive potentials, depending on the outlets available for its realization. She described "a beautiful girl just eighteen, full of genius, force and fire," who read Shakespeare "with rare power" and who appreciated "the nicest shades of his thought." Her "longings", "hopes" and "aspirations" centered around the stage. Stanton noted how friends tried "to change the current of her thoughts, her heart's desire, the purpose of her life." They had

> the power to say her nay, to control her action, thwart her will, pervert her nature, darken all life…

However, far from a life of conformity and submission, a life lived in authentic relation to ideal of perfected womanhood is one of internally integrative spirituality: an independent life of vision and dedication, that resonates with Hamlet's essential creed, "to thine own self be true." It cares passionately for unifying beauty, truth and goodness both in self and world. Stanton therefore demanded to know how these so-called friends could

> fill the mighty void that one strong passion unsatisfied makes in the human soul [and] ...what the guardians of this girl propose for the sacrifice they ask? Can they substitute another strong purpose, will or wish as they desire? Are human souls like garden beds where passions can be transplanted as easily as flowers?

While conventional or "popular" femininity is generally associated with sociality, and is subject to the trickeries of mimetic desire, in *Our Girls*, Stanton advocated for an embrace of the sacred or sophianic feminine that could restore vibrant and courageous respect for true individuality.[28] This is the move from I-We to I-Thou sociality, that can renew democracy, and that was reviewed in the previous section. *Our Girls* can be understood as a call to re-organize sociality around this inherently democratic human reality of each individual's freedom and independence and around the deeper mysteries of representation, imitation and intimacy when all humans so orient their individual soul to this vision and ideal.

Here, it should become apparent that Stanton is in some sense, serving in a high priestly social role, sanctifying whole new ways of relating to ourselves and each other in the world. Remember the statement of hers quoted in the previous section of this essay, that:

> It is because I love my country and believe in its free institutions that I desire to see this government maintained and perpetuated as it only can be by baptizing its women into the spirit of freedom and equality.

[28] That is, sacred and civic respect for the distinct particularities and variabilities of each individual life.

Stanton seeks for women an ontological, experience of freedom and equality that will inwardly restore the "spirit" or truth of their meaning. This kind of direct elucidation would "clarify" and "deepen" their apprehension of democracy, as the American philosopher John Dewey would say. The possibility of attaining this inner depth and criticality of perception is the reason why she wants them to be baptized into these realities, and not just merely taught about their significance. By seeking a baptism for women into the spirit of freedom and equality, Stanton is indirectly but strongly affirming a particular kind of democracy and recognition of human constituent power, one grounded in realization of moral power and creative agency, described as "radical democracy" decades later by Dewey, and also called upon when the French philosopher Jacques Maritain sought to create a visionary philosophical and spiritual foundation for a Universal Declaration of Human Rights. It is important also to remember that, in that day, the very notion that a woman would have the ordained power and authority to baptize would have been considered heretical by many. Being a woman herself, and asserting such a necessity for women, was in itself a radical democratic act of naming a hitherto unexpressed and oppressed developmental need that was urgently connected to the fulfillment of self and society.

Here, it may be helpful to broaden our understanding of baptism in order to appreciate the many reasons why, when referring to government and free institutions, Stanton would choose a religious word with implications that are seemingly not related to the State. Baptism is the first Christian sacrament, and like the other six sacraments now associated primarily with the Roman Catholic Church but also still with other Christian traditions, is a sacred ceremony that endues the receiving individual with specific qualities of grace or Divine energy. The Christian Sacraments can be understood as "symbolic tasks for growth into spiritual maturity and for healing..." each representing "powers we are meant to bestow on others as well as to receive from others." (Myss, 1996:

71) By insisting that U.S. women need to be baptized "into the spirit of freedom and equality" Stanton was recognizing a spiritual foundation of democracy that dwells within all peoples, not a mere technical, legal or human-constructed foundation that can only be constituted by the select few (white males within a certain age range and conventional ability level).

Carolyn Myss is a 21st century medical intuitive, who like Stanton, perceives deep connection between, on the one hand, the social and cultural habits surrounding physical health, and on the other, one's consciousness of emotional well-being, mental health and spiritual integrity. In her book, *Anatomy of the Spirit*, Myss provides clues to understanding the symbolic power of Baptism, which Stanton called upon in *Our Girls*. Myss offers that baptismal power resonates with the symbolic power of the first chakra, Root chakra or Muladhara, and also with the tenth sefirah, Shekhinah. She explains that the Christian, Indic and Judaic traditions all similarly hold that "releasing one's spirit into the physical world through fear or negativity is a faithless act of choosing personal will over the will of the heavens." (77)

Significantly, like Myss, Stanton's thinking and feeling was strongly organized around concern for integral health; and like Myss, Stanton also realized the unity of authentic religious teachings, especially the underlying ground of consensus among them, regarding, for example, the feminine aspects or attributes of God's presence within the Creation. I believe this is further proof that genuine concern for integral health is inextricably related to the most serious questions pertaining to our humanity and necessarily relates biological and spiritual dimensions of human experience to one another. Stanton was particularly interested in deepening Biblical understanding through the understandings of unity articulated in the Kabbalah, which she recognized as teaching consistently that "man and woman are from the creation co-equal and co-existing, perfectly equal, one with the other." (1993:108) In *The Woman's Bible*, Stanton herself described the Bible as an "occult book" and stated that

> Read in light of occult teachings, it becomes something more than the old battle ground of controversy for warring religions... Occultism alone furnishes the key to this ancient treasury of wisdom. (106)

Myss, who is able to diagnose accurately the ills afflicting people she has never even met in person, calls upon this "treasury of wisdom" to educate people about her spiritual comprehensions of human anatomy. For example, she explains that the archetypal forces of the Tribal chakra (Muladhara), the sacrament of Baptism, and the sefirah of Shekhinah all similarly transmit into human energy and biological systems the sacred truth of the unity of life. She explains their common significance as follows:

> We are interconnected with all of life and to one another...By connecting to the energy of any of these three archetypal forces we can connect to this truth.

Understood in terms of collective human evolutionary social development: tightly bound tribal group identity through one's own biological family, that grounds human connection to the physical sensory world, provides for one's survival when born, and organizes obedience to community or nation-state governing structures as one grows, regardless of those structures' ethical basis in principles of justice, must expand and mature. It must open itself to a more inclusive and flowing tribal identity, inclusive of all humankind as equal members of one common family. Men cannot hinder this realization by insisting that only they are recipients of the democratic, participatory "spirit of freedom and equality". The three related archetypal forces (Baptism, Muladhara and Shekhinah) are involved in humanity's on-going work across the planet, to manifest a genuine ethical and spiritual foundation for governance and shared life together, based on universal consensus at this root level of our being about the unity of life. All therefore must be baptized into the spirit of freedom and equality: it is not a spirit intended only for the few or chosen.

Interestingly, the Shekhinah, the correlate of the sacrament of Baptism in Kabbalist tradition, is the only sefirah understood as representative of the feminine, besides the sefirah of Binah, sometimes referred to as the "upper feminine" or upper Shekhinah (aligned with sacrament of Ordination and Ajna, the chakra of mental powers).[29] The Shekhinah is concerned on a spiritual and cognitive level of integration with realization of the symbolic power of the tribe of Israel. This tightly bound and "chosen" tribe, is to be understood as an embodiment pointing to, evolving towards, the mystical community of Israel, known as the higher Knesset Israel, including all humankind in shared realization of indwelling divine presence. Myss writes:

> In a more symbolic and universal perspective, the Divine consciousness creates and protects all tribes of the human race. Shekhinah is also the doorway into the Divine: "One who enters must enter through this gate" (Zohar, 1:7b) (1996: 81).

This helps us to appreciate how, when Stanton called upon the archetypal force in the sacrament of Baptism, she was engaging her mental powers and her personal integration of the powers of Ordination, (linking the upper and lower sefirah, Shekhinah and Binah) to herald in a new social order in which the divine presence is recognized as inhabiting, settling, dwelling in every life, in every tribe of the human race. No individual or "chosen" group abides "above" or absolutely superior to another. She was able through

[29] In *The Woman's Bible*, Stanton has a whole chapter devoted to discussion of the Kabbalah, and in particular, understandings of the feminine force of Binah and the significance of perfect gender equality in the relations between Chokmah and Binah. She explained the three uppermost sephira "complete" and "make evident" the supernal Trinity, "also called AMA, Mother, the great productive Mother, who is eternally conjoined with the Father for the maintenance of the universe in order." (1895, 1993:108) She also described this source of creativity and equality as the "Ancient of Days" conforming himself "simultaneously into the Father and the Mother" and thus begetting the Son. (106)

this action to unite dignity as empowerment and dignity as constraint. By asserting an oppressed human developmental need and breaking with conventional boundaries that prevent secular and sacred from uniting in the civil society, and that keep women from serving in the sacred social functions deemed exclusively for men, Stanton released energies of empowerment associated with baptism; and by recognizing the universality of the "spirit of freedom and equality" within herself, as well as the deeper governing life laws of inter-relatedness, reciprocity and mutual influence that are the basis of this universality, she welcomed in realizations of dignity as constraint that are likewise associated with baptism.

It may also be worth noting how the Zohar reference to the Shekhinah, as the gate through which one enters into the Divine, recalls her reference to the success of the female exemplars, which she likened to Samson's victory walking forward "into the gates of the city", *i.e.,* into spiritual perception of the unity of all life and in accord with its laws of inter-relatedness and reciprocity. From this perspective, women have a spiritual political power when they are baptized into the "spirit of freedom and equality" and gather together in real life-world contexts; this is because, unlike their context within constructions of political power that rely on cultural norms of exclusion and forms of institutionalized structural violence, in their act of gathering together the Shekhinah can be said to rest upon them.

This renewed spiritual understanding of the power of tribe and law is reflected not only in Judaic writings, but also Christian and Islamic; for instance, in the Gospel of Matthew, 18:20 where it is said that "Where two or three are gathered together in my name there am I in their midst." (DeRoo, 2009: 27) Here it is evident that Christ, as an exemplar leader for humankind, rather than hoarding power and creating the divide of political "haves" and "have nots" in the human social world, instead shares the glory of God (understood as Shekhinah), His divine power, with all those who receive baptismal energies, recognize reciprocity and equality and seek freedom together through illumined consciousness and justice. The "fullness" that comes to rest upon peoples, of any number, when they are gathered together in this way, is associated in Christian thought with the Greek word *pleroma*, meaning the totality or fullness of the Godhead that dwells in Christ, and is believed to have entered into Christian thinking through the work of Philo of Alexandria, a Hellenist Jewish philosopher, who is said to have harmonized Jewish scripture with Greek philosophy. Of course in Eastern religion there are even more ancient associations with "fullness" and divine presence, that pre-date the Christian, Judaic and Greek; consider for example, the goddess Lakshmi who is known to take away poverty and misfortune and to bring wealth, power and sovereignty. Her sacred name is *Shri*, which since Vedic times has been the cosmic sound of auspiciousness and abundance. When the word *Shri* is spoken before addressing an individual, the person's holiness in relation to the whole of life is felt and openly acknowledged. It is akin to the sacrament of Ordination in this way, and its associations with wisdom and knowledge also align it to Binah, the "upper" spiritual and intellectual counterpart to Shekhinah. When *Shri* is used in naming that individual's sanctified spiritual presence is understood to exemplify the qualities of real human leadership and the person is understood to possess true political authority[30]. I believe the fullness of development that Stanton advocated for in *Our Girls* can be better comprehended when it is related to this spiritual heritage of meaning about the nature of human and divine realizations of completion.

One final point may be worth noting concerning the nature of the archetypal force invoked by Stanton when she expresses desire particularly to baptize women. The divine presence of Shekhinah is also understood through the metaphor of "daughter": in a poor but powerful condition of dependency, she is the recipient of all the virtuosic forces of God's presence in the world; ultimately this

[30] See https://qz.com/545655/the-ancient-story-of-goddess-lakshmi-bestower-of-power-wealth-and-sovereignty/ for an introduction to these concepts.

daughter is the ground of being through which "everything" becomes a habitation for God. Stanton's vision of a new civilization was in essence one of a Tabernacle of Unity[31], in which no one is deprived of the presence of the "spirit of freedom and equality".

[31] I believe Bahá'í understandings of the concepts of tabernacle and unity provide relevant insight into themes raised in *Our Girls*, pertaining to freedom, equality, and genuine mental sanctuary. Below are brief elaborations on these Bahá'í concepts, found in the *Tabernacle of Unity*, (a small book of Bahá'u'lláh's tablets written to Zoroastrian individuals, while he was in the prison city of 'Akká, including two letters answering questions put forward by Parsi Zoroastrian scholar and civil rights activist, Manikchi Sahib) and the *Tablet of Unity*, (one of Bahá'u'lláh's tablets believed to have been addressed to Sayy id Asadu'llah of Rasht also while Baha'u'llah was imprisoned in 'Akká). The meaning of *tabernacle* concerns the dawning of humans' civilizing instinct, because it is related structurally to the significance of all primitive shelters, caves, tents, and places of safe haven and protection, where one can attain sanctuary. It is in the shelter or the "tabernacle", removed from immersion in the exigencies and hazards of exposed living and non-reflective movement, that one can access more integrative and reflective cognitive powers and insights pertaining to mutual causality, peace and unity. In this sense, the Sabbath or the 7th day of God's rest after making Creation is also associated with the word tabernacle. So too could be the first three sefirah, which are particularly virtuosic forces through which a truly enlightened and inclusive epistemology can emerge in relation to our evolutionary needs to protect practical reasoning about collective development. In the *Tabernacle of Unity*, one sees how tabernacle refers to this pure and sanctified quality of mind, or to Intellect as the "universal divine Mind" capable of providing true guidance and shelter for humanity. In addition, the *Tabernacle of Unity* can serve to remind one of the physical Tabernacle of the Covenant, such as made by the Levites, under instruction by God. This literal tabernacle, known to God's "chosen people", can now be known to all on a spiritual and cognitive level that encompasses the whole of humankind. This is because God's dwelling place in this Day is meant to be everywhere on Earth, with all humans recognized equally as sons and daughters of God and members of one family. The meaning of *unity* is discussed in the *Tablet of Unity*. Bahá'í scholar Moojan Momen outlines the six kinds of unity that Bahá'u'lláh discusses in this Tablet. These involve unity in Religion, Words, Ritual Acts, Rank or Station, Wealth and Souls. These six kinds of unity embody the spirit of equality discussed in this paper and promulgated by Stanton herself. To view this article, and provisional translation of the text, visit https://bahai-library.com/bahaullah_lawh_ittihad_momen

Her proposed inclusion of women, "daughters of God", within previously male-dominated institutions signals a profound questioning of old assumptions about authority as well as a deep structural re-ordering of perceptions of reality and human sociality, based on comprehension of an underlying co-dependent, mutually arising ground of unity, that is inclusive of all life. If the United States accepted its poverty, in regard to its currently lacking standards of participation and vision of spiritual progress, it would then, like the daughter of God associated with the Shekhinah, be able to receive the influx of the released capacities brought about through the inherent creativity and virtue of gender equality and harmony. The United States would now be able to pursue her own "full symmetrical development" and to realize her ideal potentials, becoming a beacon of hope and guidance for the peoples of the world, many of whom, in Stanton's view, were still far behind Americans generally in recognizing the natural equality of all people and in refusing to respect notions of caste or inherited aristocratic status and power.

At the end of the speech, Stanton made a valiant reference to Minerva, the Roman goddess of wisdom and strategic warfare, most likely hoping to stir the U.S. listeners' mythic imagination and inward sense of their own capacity for moral vigilance and higher forms of mental discernment.[32] Minerva was a great

[32] The birth of Minerva from her Father's head, like the birth of Athena, can be understood as symbolically associated with the third sefirah of Binah. Binah is the upper Feminine counterpart of Shekhinah, the feminine force that resides at "ground level". Binah represents limit, structure and the potential for a good relation between Wisdom (which allows Divine reasoning) and Knowledge (which is how our thought processes construct secure understandings). The virtues associated with Binah are related to epistemology and clear mental powers that let us engage symbolic sight, for example. That is why Myss links this sefirah to the sixth chakra of Mind or Ajna that involves our reasoning abilities and "our psychological skill at evaluating our beliefs and attitudes." As a goddess, Minerva helps people to connect to this archetypal quality. One can also see how the recognition of her authority in arts, medicine, commerce and even strategic warfare, reflects a sacred or ordained energy, and so correlates also with the sacrament of Ordination as Myss suggests herself.

daughter, conceived by Metis, after she was swallowed by Jupiter. Inside the confines of Jupiter's body, Metis armed her daughter and dressed her in armor. When Jupiter could no longer tolerate the internal pressure and headache, Vulcan split open his head and Minerva burst out, in a volcanic-like motion. Romans later associated Minerva with Athena, the Greek virgin goddess of music, poetry, medicine, commerce, weaving and the crafts, and there is a similar story of Athena being birthed from Zeus' head.

Stanton offered a non-violent depiction of the myth, calling it "beautiful" and describing Minerva in more Athena-like terms, as "springing" from her Father's brain; however, she most likely called upon this story and used Minerva as her prophetic symbol of the "coming girl" in order to play with the more forceful undertones of emergent feminine transformation of power that lie within the associated Roman mythology. It is worth remembering that a prophecy was received by Jupiter when he impregnated Metis: that his own child would overthrow him, or cause his downfall.It was for this reason that Jupiter attempted to suppress the creative power of the feminine altogether, literally consuming Metis and keeping her down. The name Metis signified a proportional "mix" or integration of wisdom (spiritual power) and practical cunning (biological evolutionary survival power), and came later through the French to represent people of "mixed" ethnic ancestry. Though literally associated now with indigenous tribes in Canada of mixed ancestry, the underlying meaning of Metis can be symbolically associated to Jacob's line, who are inheritors of promises not yet fulfilled and who are scattered, and "mixed" across the earth.

The goddess Minerva, like Athena, is an archetypal force that represents the Divine Feminine but is not confined to gender expectations or conventional standards of femininity in its embodiment; indeed the story or surah of the return of Joseph

(Yusuf), Jacob's son sold into slavery[33], and the profound creative and ethical realization of human reconciliation and unity that he represents, can be understood in the prophetic language of monotheistic world religion like Islam to embody the underlying wisdom and logos within Stanton's closing reference to the Roman goddess. As the Minerva myth reveals, the feminine force is invincible, and the life lived in accordance with "God's laws", despite all kinds of oppression, is able to fulfill its promise; Minerva seems only to have developed more advanced civilizing abilities and immune system adaptations to adversity due to her unusual in utero life and her mother's subjugation. Stanton closed the speech by stating:

> That beautiful myth of the goddess Minerva springing from the brain of her Father, fully armed and equipped for the battle of life, has a deeper significance than the world dreams of today.

The Promise of Gender Equality and Women in U.S. Society Today

Today, the United States is a seemingly even more diverse and complex place than it was when Stanton offered *Our Girls* to American audiences during the time of Reconstruction. What would she say about issues pertaining to gender and democracy today if she were to assess her country? Most significantly, I believe she would hold that neither the public service ethos, which had most likely sparked hope and aspiration in many of the young girls who heard her speak, nor the integrative realities of the ideal feminine in action, which were alive within Stanton and the most ardent woman suffragists of her day, have been able to become embodied in institutional practices and cultural norms. The challenges of

---

[33] See Genesis 37–45 and in the Quran 12.4–102; also article *The Bahá'í Tradition: The Return of Joseph and the Peaceable Imagination* by Todd Lawson, found at https://bahai-library.com/pdf/l/lawson_joseph_peaceable_imagination.pdf

post-Civil War life, including political and territorial divides and problems of racism, fear of challenging religious authorities, as well as the challenges of attaining the far more socio-centric and limited aim of the positive right of the vote itself, caused not only deep divide in the woman's suffrage movement, but also very real digressions in the public's attention, and all this distracted many women from the weightier and far more comprehensive moral and spiritual concerns and tasks that Stanton raised and put forth.

I believe Stanton would agree that dignity as empowerment has manifested in the U.S. with the emergence of many "negative" rights, protecting women against "unwilled interventions by others that are damaging" as well as many "positive" rights supporting and assisting women "in securing such circumstances and conditions." (Beyleveld, D. and R. Brownsword, 2001: 18) For example, women are now much more empowered to defend their reproductive rights, divorce rights, and right to equal pay, and a fair minimum wage. However, I believe Stanton would also perceive that her understanding of dignity as constraint, resting on the metaphysical or religious ground of the inter-dependence of all life, (the dharma of natural systems), has not been accepted as the worldview required to perceive scientifically and spiritually the laws of reciprocity and mutual causality that govern all life. This view has not even entered "mainstream" public discourse as a necessary insight, except through limited ideological expression; it certainly has not been realized as the foundation in ideal realism that the Buddha and all illumined beings through human history have in various ways affirmed as necessary for just human development.

Women and men in the United States therefore lack a clear shared vision, as well as a means through social practice to discern subjectivity in practical reasoning, and to recognize how the urgent human needs that women are manifesting reflect oppression in their conditions and the assumptions of structural violence in U.S institutions generally. Reduced and fragmented vision means that the problems of oppression are perceived statically, as human norms, "unfortunate" perhaps but fixed and "real". I believe that people in the U.S. have difficulty engaging with the moral limitation and I-Thou structure that are necessary to revive democracy, and to address injustice at a root level, because of cultural habits that close them from the scientific questions, genuine community experiences, and reverent inner realizations related to apprehension of genuine freedom and equality. This questioning, interacting and experiencing is vital to the fulfillment of dignity as constraint and therefore necessary to respect actual human capacity for transformation and to renew democracy itself.

I will attempt to summarize some of the evidence in support of my views in this closing section below, by reviewing the current situation in U.S. government, education, marriage, public health, science and technology and law. My consistent finding is that dignity as empowerment has not been balanced through a realization of dignity as constraint. The imbalances and problems afflicting women are indicative of this deeper problem of neglect that resides in the "machinery", as Dewey would say[34], of an outmoded democracy. The fact of oppression and gender imbalance in all these domains of the public sphere signals that democracy still needs to be radically re-structured and revived through I-Thou realizations of sociality.

Consider how women are now empowered with the positive right to vote, to become civic leaders, and, although representation in all branches of government is admittedly not equal to that of men, are also empowered by their ability to hold office; in addition, there are now much greater numbers of women who have advanced and excelled in all fields. However, despite this evident empowerment, there is little sense of the matrilineal line that Stanton referred to, of "geniuses, saints and philanthropists who have devoted themselves to art, religion and reform" that girls today might turn to for spiritual and moral guidance and

---

[34] See reference to *Later Works Volume 2*, p. 325 and Bernstein chapter *"Dewey's Vision of Radical Democracy"*

inspiration. This is most likely related to market forces dominating media and influencing its content and also biased school curriculums. Moral, aesthetic and spiritual development requires relation to exemplar role models, from history, present-day life, religion as well as fiction and mythology, who manifest ideal or divine virtue and noble human character; without a way to relate to standards of what is conducive to authentic human progress, people lose the ability to evaluate the merit of their own choices, preferences and habits, and the inspiration. An expanded view of one's larger family of ancestors and contemporaries, and of the human moral imagination, is essential to realization of the unity of life and to dignity as constraint. Especially for U.S. girls surrounded by norms of competition, aggression and personal acquisition, relation to a matrilineal line is vital for transformation of society and girls' future and is necessary for balanced realizations of human dignity as both empowerment and constraint.

Dignity as empowerment is also found in institutions of higher learning, which have opened their doors to women, and, despite on-going and perhaps increasingly subtle problems with various forms of sexual harassment, have allowed women for the most part to study and enter a profession of their choosing. Nevertheless, it must be admitted that pursuit of education, as well as processes of learning, and becoming educated, have been largely reduced to the securing of degrees, certifications, and social capital. Access through education to the full range of learning and life skills needed to realize spiritual and moral standards of independence is not available to either gender. This lack arguably more injuriously affects women and the children they are most often more tasked to raise. Here again is the problem that the ground of unified being supporting dignity as constraint has not been related to practically. How can a woman, or any human being, come to recognize the unity of life as something more substantial than a relatively fleeting realist intuition, if this person does not have the language, daily practices of reverent remembrance, and I-Thou intra- and inter-personal social skills and structures to live in deep accord with that recognition? Dignity as constraint therefore remains unrealized and its creative moral forces remain unable to infuse the grace of wisdom and the scope of planetary caring, into the everyday concerns and norms of so-called "higher" education.

Because U.S. women generally have become more empowered to participate in education and work, the average age of marriage has raised considerably since Stanton's day, as has the number of women with a career and means to an independent income. Divorce, custody and property rights are also considered to be indicators of women's increased levels of dignity as empowerment. But again, there are indicators that empowerment has not been balanced with constraint. There are serious social and economic inequalities afflicting the people of the United States and a serious education divide: over a million students drop out of high school each year and Centers for Disease Control and Prevention reports that in 2015, a total of 229,715 babies were born to women aged 15–19 years, a birth rate of 22.3 per 1,000 women in this age group, with 50 percent of teen mothers never receiving their equivalent of a high school diploma. Lack of adequate nutrition for pregnant women, mothers and children in this group is also a critical issue; food banks and school breakfast and lunch programs mostly offer "staples" like white bread, peanut butter and processed foods with corn syrup solids, sugar and hydrogenated fats, and dairy products from hormone-injected cows, often with these and other products containing added food coloring, artificial flavor and preservatives. The correlation that Stanton saw in her own time, between education level, age of child-bearing and state of health and nutrition, still exists today, and reflects structural deficiencies still present in institutions, despite many improvements in women's attainment of negative and positive rights. It also, most profoundly, reflects a lack of spiritual realization of the meanings of equality and democracy in terms of laws of inter-dependency and mutual support.

The effects of generational poverty and the problems of poor health, addiction and domestic violence in urban ghetto and poor rural communities as well as in struggling lower middle class homes across the country have been left largely unaddressed and have shattered all conventional notions of the word "family". They affect women in these groups seriously and silently due to lack of just representation in governance and the lack of a conception of inclusive and participatory democracy such as Stanton and her fellow suffragists like Matilda Joslyn Gage advocated for in the 19th century. Here one sees just how much the large scale structural inadequacies in all institutions and lack of civic engagement in the renewal of culture and democracy have taken their toll on the institution of marriage in the U.S.

Even seemingly successful married women who have been empowered, through expanded opportunities and affirmative action in the United States, to lift themselves, in many regards, out of impoverished childhood conditions, to delay marriage and to support themselves first independently, still find themselves, despite a huge industry focused on health and physical fitness, to be prone to serious health conditions like breast cancer, fibromyalgia, chronic depression, attention deficit and stress-related injury and illness. Their daughters often suffer at some point from problems like eating disorders, apathy and felt estrangement from family and local place. Professionals in the Western medical system do not engage responsibly in learning that supports holistic integration of health, and deep structural transformation of self and society, instead denying or refusing to address social and spiritual factors in physical, mental and emotional well-being. Expensive surgeries and procedures of all varieties including mandated C-sections are considered highly routine and "normal" as is reliance on invasive testing, use of sedatives and opioids, anti-biotic and steroid treatments and controversial vaccinations: these are profitable for those in the medical profession, and the insurance, bio-tech and pharmaceutical industries, all of which employ I-We constructions of sociality to keep "providers" and "patients" seemingly in different categories, and both removed from the root issues involved in human health crises and needs.

Stanton would certainly recognize that an underlying source of women's troubles today is the annihilation of the ideal of the perfected woman, an ideal that requires one to engage in purposeful actions that unite beauty, truth and goodness in self and world, and to maintain integrity to ecological realities and relationships. This annihilation can be witnessed in popular entertainment, music and video games in which women are routinely portrayed as sexualized commodities or as entirely secular and professionalized, and often either participants in, or victims of, overt or covert violence. The society's problems with environmental degradation are highlighted by U.S. feminists like Terry Tempest Williams, who contends that the bouts with cancer that she and so many of her female relatives experienced are directly related to nuclear fallout local to her home in Utah; all of these kinds of problems, are at root, related to this annihilation of the ideal of perfected woman.[35]

Nature's transcendental beauty has itself been destroyed in so many places; in Appalachia particularly, mountain top removal for coal has left stripped and leveled land, which then, in many instances, has been covered over and converted into locations for corporate style prisons. The rending apart and demolition of beauty, truth and goodness can be found not only in self-serving corporate actions and in the falsifying of legal terminology, (for instance, re-naming hazardous materials from mining, "fill", and then legalizing the presence of "fill" in rivers and streams) but also, in the clusters of uncanny deaths over the years, of innocent Appalachians, many children, living near these sites. The resulting violations in public and ecological health would clearly still indicate to Stanton a violation of "God's law", with the health of women, children and wildlife serving as an empirical normative orientation. It points clearly to the need to respect deeper laws of mutual causality and to institutionalize creative living practices

[35] Williams, along with her mother, grandmothers and aunts all developed cancer, which she believes was a result of nuclear fallout in her home state of Utah.

of ethical law. However, throughout the world such violations exist: indigenous communities located in places like Peru, Russia, and Sweden are threatened and often decimated by mining practices, proof that U.S. citizens, who themselves could reinvigorate their understanding of the meaning of governance, and initiate the regulative practices that could prevent this infringement, are lacking a felt sense of dignity as constraint.[36]

While technology like the internet has opened frontiers in communication and given women a new forum for creative expression and a public way to voice their views, through blogs and websites, this kind of dignity as empowerment, like the example of empowerment through education, can in no way be considered equally available to, or realized, by all. The digital divide is still very real, and girls especially are prone to the unregulated and non-reflective social forces in media, with tragic stories continually coming forward of girls in misery and even committing suicide due to the profoundly cruel statements and uncivil norms on popular forums like Facebook. It is safe to say that Stanton would most likely speak even more firmly and urgently to girls today, concerning their need to develop their powers of mind, sense of place, duty and personhood. She would surely urge them to turn their attention to the "highest good" and the task of "moulding themselves into a grand and glorious womanhood" so that through this standard of excellence and affirmation of transformative development, they could clearly discern what is conducive to their well-being and what brings about their abasement. In her last speech before Congress, *Solitude of the Self*, Stanton made it clear that each individual must be supported through education and law to come into a sanctified and ultimately unmediated relation to Mystery, to an Inaccessible and Transcendent Omniscient

[36] See endnote ix on African-centered conceptual framework for analyzing culture to understand how citizens without a sense of dignity as constraint are deprived of both the logos germ/seed *Asili*, and the vital force, *Utamaroho*, necessary to advance this kind of sensitive and responsible transformative citizen action.

Creator. Her last and most vital affirmation of the need for an intra-personal grounding in I-Thou sociality, which she spoke of in the most practical of terms, desiring only to protect the very vulnerable ontological ground of human experience, would most likely remain her most essential message to people of both genders today, as they attempt to navigate new social terrain like the Internet.

There is a general ethos in the United States, stemming from an immature relation to the history of its colonization of American land and its generally innovative, rebellious and positivist beginnings, that it is somehow possible as an individual in the U.S. to "have it all" and even to attain total levels of self-fulfillment, with the help of life coaches, reductionist "brain-based" insights and pharmaceuticals. For an ambitious and "lucky" woman in the U.S. the "dream" is that all is possible: a successful career, wealth, family, and myriad kinds of liberal and traditional fun within one's cultural peer circle, all somehow free from the need to engage oneself in the fundamental questions of our humanity, to extend concern beyond one's own "tribe" or to acknowledge one's responsibility to participate in transformation of oppressive forms of power and in on-going ethical and spiritual self-cultivation. This is a kind of materialist and desacralized notion of *pleroma* or "full" human development. It is the antithesis of dignity as constraint, and represents a one-sided embrace of dignity as empowerment. It can be argued that this acquisitive conception of progress is the source of all imbalance and inequality, gender-related or otherwise.[37]

---

[37] In 1879, during the same general time period as *Our Girls*, the book *Progress and Poverty* by Henry George was published. In it George directly addressed the schism in the U.S. that was created by false notions of progress that increasingly create divides of inequality among human beings and nations. These notions are linked to false beliefs about property, as attainable through unjust acquisition, rather than integrated labor, and also to erroneous ideas about land ownership that subvert realizations of reciprocal relations, planetary belonging and Nature's bounty.

In the 21st century, U.S. female philosopher and feminist Martha Nussbaum, asks how public culture and institutions can cultivate appropriate compassion (long associated with worship of perfected women and goddesses like Mary and Quan Yin). Nussbaum writes on the power of Greek theater and great literature to awaken these depths of human feeling and critical cognition and to serve in the betterment of society. She sees the need to protect ourselves from emotional ecologies that engender disgust, shame and envy, which are harmful to relationships and indicators of structural oppression in our laws and norms. These structural imbalances and resulting emotional responses effect our perceptions and seriously skew human judgment, therefore thwarting what Stanton would call "full symmetrical development" and hindering transformation within our institutions.

Nussbaum believes that insights of "compassionate imagination" may be embodied in laws and institutions in the 21st century at many different levels and in many different ways. Once institutionalized, they could protect us from the harmful effects of the negative emotions she identifies. For Nussbaum, the ideal of moral benevolence—again, an ancient ideal from goddess traditions in Eastern religion—is the lens through which we should envision how institutions and basic political principles should be designated. I believe her writing on this topic in *Upheavals of Thought* can be understood as an attempt to establish a movement toward dignity as constraint and in this regard is akin to Stanton's call for girls to strive for "perfected womanhood" and to engage responsibly in the duties of citizenship. Stanton, like Nussbaum, hopes for the transformation of power through the restructuring of U.S. institutions and revitalization of its democracy when people are animated by this ideal striving.

Nussbaum and Amartya Sen, an Indian philosopher and economist also living in the U.S. today, have each put forth a capability theory that invites people to think about capability in terms of opportunity to achieve elementary functions. These theories have at heart a commitment to structural egalitarianism that reflects to some degree, I-Thou realizations of human sociality, and so can also be linked in some ways to Stanton's understanding of their being a sacred order in human development that should not be violated, that correlates with flourishing, and that reflects the reality of inherent human moral power and human needs. However, as philosopher Thomas Hurka points out, there is still a problem with the sequence of moral theorizing that Nussbaum and Sen offer. First, he says, it is necessary to develop "objectivist accounts of the good" which I would call integrated accounts that cross subjective, objective and inter-subjective domains of inquiry. In what Hurka calls "Sen-Nussbaum capability theory" good human functioning includes some things like the act of choosing, pleasure and even nutrition, which are only instrumentally good and not necessarily intrinsically good; and there is no way in which all the values put forth are unified and recognized as inherently related to one another.

Hurka points out that Sen and Nussbaum underestimate the centrality of an objectivist account of the good, a moral position which he says was well understood in ancient ethics concerning substantive claims about the good. An example of this kind of centralized and primary integrated account of the good, that clearly influenced Stanton, was Deganawidah's account of the Great Law of Peace, the Great Values, the Sacred Twin Principles, the Great Tree of Justice and practice of the Good Mind, all of which worked in a unified way to help to protect their natural resources and ecology, to establish just and compassionate governing structures and to inspire on an on-going basis, citizen responsibility and engagement in the federalized Haudenosaunee Nation, considered the oldest participatory democracy in the world.[38] Because of this influence, and her own sensitivity and responsiveness to injustice, I believe Stanton was perhaps more personally attuned to the metaphysical and religious ground that truly supports dignity as

[38] For descriptions of these, please see my chapter in *Practical Spirituality and Human Development* 2017, or contact me for full text.

constraint. In *Our Girls* and other writings and speeches related to her sincere reflective activist work for justice and equality, I find that she seems more enlivened by this ground of unity, and expressive of it, than Nussbaum and Sen are today.

For this reason, I maintain that *Our Girls*, Stanton's 19th century popular talk about gender, human development, and democracy, is an especially valuable and potent social medicine for people now, that if received and taken seriously, can connect men, women, boys and girls alike to the true significance of gender equality. Its significance I believe is this: that as each one begins "walking forward" through the "gate" to perception of the unity of life, it becomes possible for each and all to know I-Thou sociality, to experience not only the metaphoric birth of the goddess Minerva, but also to realize on a spiritual level one's inner Joseph. As this promise of real and symbolic inner wholeness is restored to the meaning of gender equality— a promise signifying the possibilities of complementation and integrity, offered by Deganawidah in his declaration of the Sacred Twin Principles of balance — humanity will come to know firsthand the "laws of restoration" Stanton referred to at Seneca Falls.

Like a powerful baptism, remembrance and comprehension of Stanton's message, and of the teachings offered by the great messengers, like Bahá'u'lláh, rising in the spiritual zeitgeist of the 19th century, can awaken and protect a much stronger and more primal human need: the need creatively and morally to name the whole of the humankind as one's family, to develop more deeply one's sense of belonging to a particular tribe, so as to realize one's larger mystical community on the planet. One then relates oneself directly to authentic ideal ethical paths to human belonging and participates in the moral and spiritual renewal of a republican democracy in which healthy peoples and nations, in a sanctified or "ordained" civic way, come to live together entirely free from oppression, tyranny and unnecessary fear. Stanton's remedy indeed represents the promise of this peace that "can only be found through action."

REFERENCES

Abdu l-Bahá (1982). *Selections from the Writings of 'Abdu'l-Bahá.* (Haifa: Bahá'í World Centre, lightweight edition).

Abeysekara, Ananda (2008). *The Politics of Post-secular Religion: Mourning Secular Futures.* New York: Columbia University Press.

Ani, Marimba (1994). *Yurugu: An African-centered Critique of European Cultural Thought and Behavior.* Trenton, NJ: Africa World Press, Inc.

Bernstein, Richard and Molly, Cochran (*eds.*) (2010) "Dewey's Vision of Radical Democracy" *The Cambridge Companion to Dewey.* London: Cambridge University Press.

Beyleveld, D. and Brownsword, R. (2001). *Human Dignity in Bioethics and Biolaw.* Oxford: Oxford University Press.

Brandom, Robert (2008). *Transcription of the Interview with Robert Brandom* (Interviewer: Seddone - Leipzig, G. 30/06/08). Shoichet, A.L. (*ed.*) found at http: //www.filosofia.it/archivio/images/download/multimedia/08_Brandom%20Interview_transcription.pdf

Commager, H.S. (*ed.*) (1938). *Documents of American History.* New York: F.S. Crofts & Co. *American History Online.* Facts on File, Inc.

DeRoo, N. and Manoussakis, J.P. (2016). *Phenomenology and Eschatology: Not Yet in the Now By.* New York: Routledge Publishing.

Dewey, John (1984). *Later Works Volume,* 2, 1925-1953: 1925-1927, *Essays, Reviews, Miscellany, and The Public and Its Problems (Collected Works of John Dewey).* Illinois: Southern Illinois University.

Geredien, Julie (2017). "Practical Spirituality and the Transformation of Power: How the Great Law of Peace and Iroquoian Culture Awakened Social and Spiritual Vision in Early American Suffragettes" *Practical Spirituality and Human Development.* London: Palgrave Macmillan.

Gordon, Ann. (*ed.*) (1997). *National Protection for National Citizens, 1873 to 1880. The Selected Papers of Elizabeth Cady Stanton and Susan B. Anthony,* Volume 3. New Brunswick, N.J.: Rutgers University Press.

Hagan, Willow Michele (1848). *Iroquois Native American Cultural Influences in Promoting Women's Rights Ideologies Leading Up to the First Women's Rights Convention in Seneca Falls on the 19th and 20th July.* Paper. Available at https://centerwest.org/wpcontent/uploads/2015/05/iroquois_native_american_hagan.pdf.

Hallamish Moshe, Transl Ruth Bar-Han and Ora, Wiskind-Elper (1999). *An Introduction to the Kabbalah.* Albany, New York: State University of New York Press.

Haudensaunee Confederacy (December, 2000) "What is the Great Law of Peace?" *Neighbor to Neighbor, Nation to Nation.* Available at www. sixnations. org.

Hewitt, J.N.B. (1926). Women Chiefs, NAA, Hewitt Collection, No. 3577, p.

Husted, Harper (*ed.*) (1881). *History of Woman Suffrage: 1848-1861.* New York: Fowler & Wells.

Jacobson, Nora (2012). *Dignity and Health*. Nashville: Vanderbilt University Press.

Lample, Paul (2009). *Revelation and Social Reality: Learning to Translate What is Written into Reality*. Florida: Palabra Publications.

Macy, Joanna (1991). *Mutual Causality in Buddhism and General Systems Theory: The Dharma of Natural Systems*. New York: State University of New York Press.

Maneck, Susan (1994). "Religion and Women" Albany: SUNY Press. Found at: http://bahai-library.com/maneck_women_bahai_faith

Mann, Barbara A. and Johansen, Bruce Elliott (2000). *Encyclopedia of the Haudenosaunee (Iroquois Confederacy)*. Connecticut: Greenwood Press.

Manne, Kate (2015). Locating Morality: Moral Imperatives as Bodily Imperatives. Paper. http://metaethicsworkshop.web.unc.edu/files/2015/04/Mane-Locating-Morality.pdf

Maritain, Jacques (1944). *The Rights of Man and Natural Law*. London: The Centenary Press.

Miller, Bradford (1998). "Seneca Falls First Woman's Rights Convention of 1848: The Sacred Rites of the Nation" *Journal of Bahá'í Studies*, 8(3). Found at https://bahai-studies.ca/wp-content/uploads/2014/05/8.3-Miller.pdf

Momen, Moojan and Todd, Lawson B. (2004). "Tahirih". *In*: Jestice, Phyllis G. Holy People of the World: A Cross-cultural Encyclopedia. Santa Barbara, CA: ABC-CLIO. ISBN 1-57607-355-6. Found at: https://bahai-library.com/momen_lawson_abc-clio_tahirih

Moomen, Moojan (2001). "The Tablet of Unity (Lawh-i-Ittihad)- A Provisional Translation" *Lights of Irfan*. Wilmette, IL: Irfan Colloquia. pp. 93–98.

Myss, Caroline (1996). *Anatomy of the Spirit: The Seven Stages of Power and Healing*. New York: Random House Harmony Books.

Nussbaum, Martha (2001). *Upheavals of Thought: The Intelligence of Emotions*. Cambridge: Cambridge University Press.

Prentice, Roger (2004). "Spiritualizing Pedagogy: Mystical and Ontological Aspects of Bahá'í- inspired Education." First presented at the Irfan Colloquia Session #58 (English) Louhelen Bahá'í School: Davison, Michigan, USA.

Reid, Herbert and Taylor, Betsy (2009). *Recovering the Commons: Democracy, Place and Global Justice*. Springfield: University of Illinois Press.

Shoghi, Effendi (1944). *God Passes By*. Found at http://www.bahai.org/library/authoritative-texts/shoghi-effendi/god-passes-by/god-passes-by.pdf? cfec7dad

Shoghi, Effendi (1984). *The Advent of Divine Justice*. 4th ed. Wilmette, Ill.: Bahá'í Publishing Committee.

Shoghi, Effendi (1993). *The World Order of Bahá'u'lláh: Selected Letters*. Baha'i Pub. Trust.

Siegel, Daniel (2007). *The Mindful Brain*. New York: Norton & Co.

Smith, Theophus (1995). *Conjuring Culture: Biblical Formations of Black America*. London: Oxford University Press.

Stanton, Elizabeth Cady (18 January, 1892). *Solitude of Self.* Delivered before the Committee of the Judiciary of the United States Congress.

Stanton, Elizabeth Cady (1870). "Declaration of Rights and Sentiments," *Address of Mrs. Elizabeth CadyStanton, Delivered at Seneca Falls & Rochester, N.Y. July 19th & August 2d, 1848.* New York: Robert J. Johnston.

Stanton, Elizabeth Cady (1993, first published 1895). *The Woman's Bible*. Boston: Northeastern University Press.

Stanton, T. and Stanton Blanch, H. (*eds.*) (1922). *Elizabeth Cady Stanton as Revealed in Her Letters, Diaries and Reminiscences*. Vol. 2.

Stout, Jeffrey (2005).*Democracy and Tradition*. Princeton: Princeton University Press.

Temple, M. and Campling, J. (2000). "The New Public *Service* Ethos", *In*: Campling, J. (*eds.*), *How Britain Works*. London: Palgrave Macmillan, pp. 111–132.

Touraine, Alain (1995). Translated by David Macey. *Critique of Modernity*. Oxford: Basil Blackwell.

Vatter, Miguel (March 2013). "Politico-Theological Foundations of Human Rights, The Case of Maritain." *Social Research: An International Quarterly*, 80(1): 233–260.

Wagner, Sally Roesch (2001). *Sisters in Spirit: The Iroquois Influence on Early American Feminists*. Summertown, TN: Native Voices.

Weil, Andrew, MD (1983). *Health and Healing: The Philosophy of Integrative Medicine*. New York: Houghton Mifflin Co.

Chapter 5

Women's Movements and Feminism in India

Deepti Priya Mehrotra

INTRODUCTION

Women's movements and feminism have deep roots in India. We can trace women's resistance against patriarchy to ancient India, for instance Buddhist nuns, *bhikkhunîs*, composed songs, called therigathas, as far back as sixth century B.C. (Tharu and Lalita, 1995: pp 59–69). In these educative songs, they described how they found their own paths to liberation, leaving behind home and family, poverty or wealth. Similarly the bhakti traditions in medieval India had poets like Akkamahadevi, Rami, Meera Bai and Bahinabai, who forged their own paths in life, resisting conventional roles considered appropriate for women, expressing their views in forthright and powerful actions as well as words (Tharu and Lalita, 1995: 77–114).

Feminism, broadly defined, is the understanding that women are oppressed socially and politically, this oppression can be resisted and, ultimately, brought to an end. Women's movements have arisen in India and other parts of the world, giving rise to specific *feminisms*. In this chapter, we will get acquainted with diverse issues taken up, variety of struggles and diverse ideologies – including anti-colonial feminism, liberal feminism, eco-feminism, socialist and Marxist feminism, Gandhian feminism, dalit feminism, radical feminism.

A NOTE ON METHODOLOGY

This chapter draws upon years of intimate knowledge of many aspects of the women's movement in India — as an active participant, as well as an academic. The paper uses a mix of methodologies: including data from oral history, participant observation as well as interactions and observations based on numerous field trips (for instance to Chipko movement areas, campaigns against gender-based violence in Kanpur, protests opposing 'dowry murders' in Delhi, and so on). Along with the experiential trajectory of my own engagement in women's movements, a considerable number of interviews, conducted over the years with diverse feminist activists and other concerned individuals, have formed important source material for the paper.

WOMEN IN ANTI-COLONIAL STRUGGLES

Women were among those who established strong resistance to the colonial British regime in India. These women included women from ordinary families such as Jhalkari Bai, Azizan Bai and Uda Devi as well as members of the elite like Rani Lakshmi Bai of Jhansi, Maharani Jind Kaur of Punjab and Begum Hazrat Mahal of Avadh. Such women played a leading role in confronting colonial power, waging war against annexation of territories, and fighting the First War of Independence, 1857.

During the twentieth century, Preetilata Wadedar, Kalpana Dutt, Madame Bhikhaiji Cama, Sarojini Naidu, Jaggi Devi, Vijaylakshmi Pandit and tens of thousands of other women participated actively in the struggle against colonial rule. These struggles took different shapes, for instance the revolutionary terrorists in Bengal, Nupilans (women's wars against colonialism) in Manpur, civil disobedience and other Gandhian movements across the length and breadth of the country.

Lakshmi Bai of Jhansi was just 18 when her husband, Gangadhar Rao, died, in 1853. Their baby, born when Lakshmi Bai was 16, had lived only a few days; but before Gangadhar Rao's death the couple adopted a 5-year old boy. However, the British refused to accept little Damodar Rao as heir to the throne, and instead proclaimed annexation of Jhansi. Lakshmi Bai refused to submit to this injustice (Devi, 2000). She trained women and men from Jhansi in use of sword, lance, guns and horse-riding, building a strong army composed of citizens from every caste and creed. The women's wing of the army, called Durga Dal, was led by **Jhalkari Bai**, a brave woman from the Kori, weavers', caste. Jhalkari and her husband Pooran were both committed to the cause of independence. During 1857-58, Rani Lakshmi Bai led the army in battle against British forces. They fought courageously, although they could not match British arms and artillery. Jhalkari Bai persuaded Lakshmi Bai to escape from the south gate of Jhansi Fort, distracting the British by herself pretending to be the queen. Jhalkari Bai was martyred, through her sacrifice ensuring the survival of Lakshmi Bai, so that war against the British could continue. Lakshmi Bai kept up the good fight – but was killed on the battlefield a few months later. Lakshmi Bai and Jhalkari Bai are immortalized in folk songs and legends, their memories treasured by the ordinary people of Bundelkhand (Naimishrai, 2015).

Maharani Jind Kaur of Punjab put up strong resistance to the British, after her husband Maharaja Ranjeet Singh's death in 1839. Although the British accepted her as Regent and her minor son Duleep Singh as heir to the throne of Punjab, at the same time they tried to annexe the Punjab through underhand means. Because she was a figure around whom revolutionary sentiments coalesced, the British ousted her from the palace in Lahore, and imprisoned her in Sheikhupura Fort. Even from the Fort, Maharani Jind Kaur contacted soldiers, courtiers, peasants and patriots throughout Punjab, planning a massive rebellion to oust the British. The plan was leaked by a traitor and the British removed Jind Kaur to the Fort of Chunar, near Varanasi. Despite strict security and constant surveillance, this intrepid fighter escaped in disguise, evaded arrest warrants and walked incognito to Nepal, where she took refuge with the royal house. After many years she was allowed to meet her son, who had been exiled to Britain. She related the entire history to Duleep Singh before she died, due to which he became a life-long rebel to the cause of Punjab. His daughter Sophia Duleep Singh became a militant suffragist in Britain, a fighter for women's political rights (Ahluwalia, 2001).

Begum Hazrat Mahal was a brave patriot who led the anti-colonial rebellion in Avadh, rather than her husband, Wajid Ali Shah. Another significant figure in the 1857 resistance was Azizan Bai, a tawaif in the Kanpur cantonment area. **Azizan Bai** actively participated by passing messages between soldiers, and acting as a centre for meetings; when arrested by the British, she refused to divulge any information, preferring instead to be martyred for the cause of independence.

During the first half of the twentieth century, the anti-colonial movement intensified and became widespread, waged by diverse groups espousing various ideologies, from revolutionary terrorism to Gandhian non-violence. Women were active on all the fronts. **Pritilata Waddedar** and **Kalpana Dutt** were revolutionary terrorists from Bengal. Both young women, good students in school and college, joined Jugantar, Surya Sen's group in Chittagong. Pritilata had learnt use of lathi and guns during her college days in Calcutta, as a member of the Deepali Sangh. Both she and Kalpana took part in armed attacks on British personnel and property. In 1932, Preetilata led an ambush on the European Club in Chittagong. British officers and their families were thrown in disarray, as bullets disrupted their revelries. Some of the officers retaliated, joined by the police. The team scattered, and police began to chase the young revolutionaries. Already injured by a bullet, Pritilata decided to take poison rather than face arrest and torture. She was just 22 years old at the time Kalpana Dutt, a couple of years younger than Pritilata, similarly took part in the Chittagong Armoury Raids. Kalpana was arrested and imprisoned for long years. After 1947, Kalpana Dutt became a member of the Communist Party of India, and worked life-long to end injustice and exploitation (Vohra, 1986, 15–36).

Madame Bhikhaiji Cama, an extraordinary Parsi woman, was a militant nationalist who helped build support for the cause of Indian independence throughout Europe. She became a member of the Home Rule Society in England, and in 1907 raised the Indian tricolor for the first time, in the international socialist conference at Stuttgart. In exile for thirty-five long years, the British did not permit her to return to India unitl 1936; she died a few months later (Sethna, 1987).

Jaggi Devi was born to Kurmi Kashi and Dhiraji, both members of the Avadh Kisan Sabha, and later married Baba Ram Chandar, leader of the Kisan Sabha — an inter-caste marriage. Jaggi held meetings with peasant women in countless villages – mobilizing against exploitation by landlords and the British regime, as well as for girls' education, ending sexual exploitation of women, and the custom of child marriage. After 1947, Jaggi brought up her children, including the youngest called Svatantra Bharat, eking out a livelihood from a tiny patch of land. In the '70s she became active again to free India of poverty, corruption and illiteracy, campaigning from village to village, and even coming to Delhi to tell Prime Minister Rajiv Gandhi how the country should be run. She died in 1992, her passion for freedom as strong as ever (Mehrotra, 2005).

Lakhs of women adopted Gandhian non-violent methods — burning foreign cloth and donating jewelry as part of Swadeshi; spinning and weaving; participating actively part in Non-cooperation, Civil Disobedience, and Quit India movements. Aruna Asaf Ali, Ashalata Sen, Satyavati Devi, Sarala Behn, Kamla Nehru, Renana Tyabji, Ratnamayee Devi, Saraladevi Chaudurani, Perinbai Naoroji, Mithuben Petit, Sharadaben Mehta, Usha Mehta, Prabhawati Devi, Ashadevi Aryananayakam and Rajkumari Amrit Kaur were Gandhian activists, working untiringly for social and political change, many facing long prison terms. Kasturba Gandhi was a leader in her own right — Gandhi often said that he learnt the method of satyagraha from Kasturba; she participated actively in the freedom movement campaigns, suffering jail sentences, and engaged in constructive work activities and running of ashram life

Along with Kamladevi Chattopadhyaya, Vijaylakshmi Pandit, Annie Besant, Sucheta Kripalani and others, **Sarojini Naidu** was involved in the anti-colonial struggle and improving conditions for women in India. Sarojini Naidu was a leading member of the All India Women's Conference (AIWC), a women's organization set up in 1927. AIWC became the spokesperson for Indian women, demanding girls' education, voting rights for women, rights to inherit property, end to polygamy and rights of women workers. Its leading members included Lakshmi Menon, Raksha Saran, Kulsum Sayani, Muthulakshmi Reddy, Mithun Lam, Rameshwari Nehru and Hansa Mehta. AIWC is active to date, across the country, as a social welfare organization (Nayar, in Nayar and Mankekar, 2002).

Feminist Pioneers: Women's Education and Empowerment

Savitribai Phule, Pandita Ramabai and Rokeya Shekhawat Hussain were among the earliest women activists in India. They set up educational institutions for girls, and spoke up fearlessly against ill-treatment of women. **Savitribai Phule** learnt reading and writing from her husband Jotiba Phule, and started the first girls' schools in 1948, in Pune, facing abuse and assault. She opposed the caste system along with Jotiba Phule, allowed dalits to use the well in their house, and managed the Satya Shodhak Samaj. She exposed hypocritical morality by taking in pregnant unmarried women – she opened a shelter home for such women and their children; the couple also adopted one such child, Yashwant. In the 1890s Savitri Bai worked for plague victims, herself contracted the disease, to which she succumbed (Dandavate, in Nayar and Mankekar, 2002).

Rokeya Sekhawat Hussain learnt to read and write secretly, from her elder brother, as a child in Bengal. After marriage,

Shekhawat Hussain encouraged her studies. After his death the young widow set up the Shekhawat Memorial Girls' School, a pioneering institution for Muslim girls, still running in Calcutta (Nahar, in Nayar and Mankekar, 2002). Rokeya Shekhawat is often called the first feminist writer in India – in her novel Padmarag she creates an alternative world run by women, a well-ordered, beautiful place, run on scientific lines for the benefit of all (Hossain, Rokeya Sakhawat, 2005).

Pandita Ramabai learnt reading and scriptures from her mother Lakshmi Dongre, who was taught by her iconoclastic husband Anandshastri Dongre. After her parents and elder sister died during famine in Maharashtra, young Ramabai with her brother walked some 3,000 kilometres, to Kashmir and then Bengal, giving religious teachings along the way. In Calcutta Ramabai lectured to packed halls, and Brahmo Samaj leader Keshub Chandra Sen gave her the honorific 'Pandita' as well as 'Saraswati'. Her book 'The High-Caste Hindu Woman' was widely acclaimed, but she was harassed by the orthodox Hindus. She married a dalit scholar, had a daughter Manorama, but lost her husband to illness. Shaken in her Hindu faith, Ramabai adopted Christianity, and opened the first homes for widows in India, Sharda Sadan and Mukti Sadan. She taught skills like literacy, nursing, gardening, printing, spinning, weaving – her goal was to create empowered young women, who could be independent social reformers (Chakravaraty, 1998).

Women such as the early educationists, freedom fighters, members of AIWC were among tho pioneers in India's women's movement. Their ideology was not limited to any specific category; rather it was a mix of anti-colonial feminism, liberal feminism (witness their great belief in education), socialist feminism (evident in their involvement across class, caste and religion), radical feminism (concern with the personal exploitation of women); some were Gandhain feminists, others espoused violent revolution. Each in her own way, these valiant pioneers laid the groundwork for subsequent women's movements – in independent India.

1947 Onwards: Women's Issues in a Free Nation

With independence, women thought a new era had begun, where their rights would be respected, within an enlightened and prosperous country. Women leaders worked in refugee camps during the riots which accompanied Partition, while social workers like **Mridula Sarabhai** went across the borders to bring back abducted women, to their natal families and communities, a painful exercise, fraught with trauma (Butalia, 1998).

The new Constitution, drafted by Constituent Assembly members including **Durgabai Deshmukh**, promised equality between women and men. The government took steps to improve economic conditions across the country, thinking it would impact women's work and livelihoods.

However, by the 1970s it was found that women's conditions had barely improved. The *Report of the Committee on the Status of Women* (1974-75) showed low status of women in terms of work, education, security, political participation and economic well-being. This helped galvanize a strong women's movement.

Eco-feminism at the grassroots: Chipko movement

In 1972, women from the hills of Uttarakhand launched a movement against deforestation, rampant due to destructive development policies. When private contractors came with axes, women of Reni village, district Chamoli, led by **Gaura Devi**, hugged the trees saying, "First kill us, then cut our trees!" They knew the significance of forests in protecting the soil, water and clean air, evident in slogans like 'Kya hain jungle ke upkar, mitti pani aur bayar'. The environmental movement snowballed over the next few years, with ordinary rural women across Uttarakhand rising up in defence of their forests, such as Sudesha Devi in Tehri Garhwal. Veteran Gandhians such as Vimla Bahuguna, Radha Bhatt, Chandi Prasad Bhatt and Sundarlal Bahuguna helped spread and consolidate the movement. Many of the women leaders active in the Chipko movement had studied in an extraordinary school, Lakshmi Ashram, run on Gandhian lines in Kausani, where they had been inspired to work life-long for the welfare of common people of the land (Bhatt, undated).

Chipko became a world-famous eco-feminist movement, raising issues of global relevance. In India, it sparked off action against deforestation across the country, such as the Appiko movement in the Western Ghats. Chipko also diversified into movements against destructive mining, and big dams, — the Tehri dam; and several big dams currently on the anvil. Women are at the forefront of such environmental movements – local women as well as social workers like Medha Patkar and Chittaroopa Palit who devoted their lives to the Narmada Bachao Andolan.

Violence against Women

Dowry and Domestic Violence

The 1970s saw a spate of movements protesting violence against women. One of the major issues was wife-murder, popularly termed 'dowry death'. Daily newspapers reported deaths by burning: kerosene stoves bursting was generally reported as the cause. However, *Mahila Dakshata Samiti* investigated the murder of a young woman, Hardeep Kaur, while **Subhadra Butalia**, a Delhi University teacher and member of *Stree Sangharsh*, gave witness in court, settling the matter against the in-laws. After this case, 'accidental death' was widely questioned. *Stree Sangharsh*, an autonomous women's group, enacted a street play on dowry, Om Swaha, to huge crowds (Butalia, 2002). Activists across the country, such as the *Chhatisgarh Mahila Jagriti Sangh* in Raipur, adapted the play, helping create awareness and build a national campaign. Women's groups came together to form the Dahej Virodhi Chetna Manch, a joint platform for action against dowry and dowry deaths (Jagori, 1988).

Activists formed Saheli, Karmika,Shaktishalini, and other groups such as Awaz-e-Niswan in Mumbai, and Sakhi Kendra in

Kanpur, to provide counseling and legal aid to women facing dowry harassment and other forms of gender-based violence. **Shah Jehan Begum**, a working class woman who had lost her eldest daughter Noor Jehan, to the dowry menace – ran the shelter home, Shaktishalini, over nearly two decades. Grief-stricken, shaken to the core to find her daughter killed by in-laws, Shah Jehan Begum had spontaneously organized a demonstration at the local police station, in Nangloi, west Delhi (in 1976), protesting police inaction, refusing to bury the corpse until the police registered an F.I.R. Aided by lawyer Nandita Haksar, Shah Jehan Begum fought in court for long years but failed to obtain justice; she determined that "what has happened to my daughter must not happen to any other woman." Satya Rani Chaddha, who too had lost her daughter to dowry murder, ran Shaktishalini with Shah Jehan Begum, the two, with their team, providing succor to thousands of violated women.

Amendments were made to the Dowry Prohibition Act (1961). In subsequent years women filed lakhs of cases under Section 498A (domestic violence within first seven years of marriage). A number of complainants withdraw their cases, leading some people, including the Supreme Court, to falsely conclude that the cases were false. Research by Tata Institute of Social Sciences indicates that, in fact complainants withdraw cases due to extreme family pressure for out-of-court settlement (Dave, Ajgaonkar, Pradhan and Chakraborty, 2017).

Women's organizations are besieged with women coming with burns, marks of beating, torture and abuse. Sustained efforts of women's groups and feminist lawyers like Indira Jaisingh and Flavia Agnes, led to passage of a specific law – Protection of Women against Domestic Violence Act (2005), which recognises physical, mental, emotional and economic violence; and provides for immediate relief to abused women. Family courts have been constituted to fast-track such cases, with provision for legal aid and a role for social workers. However, the issues are still not understood by law enforcement agencies: implementation continues to be extremely lax, and court judgments often reek of misogyny, reflecting the patriarchal mindset of judges.

Rape and Sexual Harassment

In the 1970s women's organizations pointing out how widespread was the issue of rape. When Rameeza Bi was gang-raped by policemen in Hyderabad and her husband killed, 20,000 people protested, led by the *Progressive Organisation of Women.* In Maharashtra a minor girl called Mathura was gang-raped by policemen, but the court exonerated them, saying the girl was already sexually active. Lawyers including Lotika Sarkar and Upendra Baxi wrote an open letter to the Supreme Court pointing out that sexual history of victims is irrelevant in case of rape. In Bombay women set up the *Forum Against Rape*, subsequently renamed *Forum Against Oppression of Women* (FAOW); in Bangalore the women's group *Vimochana* was active on such issues; and in Delhi *Stree Sangharsh* investigated mass rape of women in Santhal Parganas. Issues of custodial rape were also exposed, and amendments made in rape laws (Indian Penal Code sections 375-376) (Kumar, 1993). However, social norms remain harsh and law enforcement weak.

In the 1990s Bhanwari Bai, a government employee in Rajasthan's Women's Development Program, was gang-raped by high-caste men. When the Jaipur High Court ruled that "high-caste men could never commit such a crime", women's groups castigated the patriarchal mindsets of the judges; Bhanwari Bai showed exemplary courage in continuing the battle for justice. In 2012 the gang-rape cum murder of Jyoti Singh, a young student in Delhi, sparked off a powerful women's protest, led by university students, supported by women's organisations. The group Jagori intensified its "safe city" campaign, along with other women's groups, demanding strong measures for women's security. A high-level commission brought out a report which spelt out the case for police reforms as well as specific changes in laws regarding violence against women (Verma, 2013).

Marital rape is still not recognized by Indian law. Given the high prevalence of intimate partner violence, marital rape is indeed a serious issue. However, learned judges have opined that recognizing marital rape would lead to breakdown of the institution of marriage – exposing their own regressive mindsets.

The issue of sexual harassment was taken up during the 1980s and '90s by Delhi University colleges such as Indraprastha, Miranda House and St. Stephen's. In 1981 a gang of hoodlums came into St. Stephen's and harassed women. Subsequently women students organized a massive campaign, mobilizing women from over twenty colleges, demanding measures for security, including Sexual Harassment Committees, women-only buses, plainclothes policewomen; students also held feminist self-defence classes and the first-ever program on sexual harassment on Indian television.

Sexual harassment remains a burning issue. Sexual Harassment in the Workplace (Prevention, Protection and Redressal) Act, 2013, provides for strict action in cases of sexual harassment of women in their workplace.

Over the past few years, young women have formed organizations such as Pinjra Tod (in Delhi) to take up cudgels for the right of women to mobility and self-determination, demanding respectful hostel rules, appropriate arrangements for security, and the need to change misogynist mindsets that those in power routinely exhibit. Such initiatives are fighting the everyday violence women face – including sexual harassment that has become a routine occurrence in universities and workplaces, villages and cities, all across the country.

Women and Work

The proportion of women workers is lowest in the organised sector, and high in the informal sector — where work as well as income are irregular: in occupations such as vegetable vending, maidservants, piece-rate home based workers — rolling agarbattis, bidis, folding paper bags, stitching, assembling plugs, making costume jewelry, and so on. Home-based piece-rate work, characteristically exploitative in nature, absorbs maximum women are working – for they manage home and family along with this paid work... and because they are isolated from other women workers, there is no opportunity for negotiating better wages. They are usually paid a pittance, middle-men and capitalists siphoning off huge profits (Mies, Bernholdt-Thomsen and Werlhof, 1988).

Women's work in the household is naturalized, considered to be performed out of love; in fact women generally have little option. Women in different parts of the world including India have sporadically raised the demand 'wages for housework' – protesting against the widespread devaluation of such work. Men in south Asia, especially middle and upper class men, resist performing menial household tasks. Educated women are questioning this attitude, yet progress on this front is slow, and uneven.

Women in the organized sector do have some work security, income and legal rights. The Factory Act (1948) provides that women have to be given advance notice before change in shift timings, protection from hazardous jobs, crèches facilities, separate toilet facilities and canteen; the Maternity Benefits Act (1961) assures women maternity leave of six months for their first two children; the Equal Remuneration Act (1976) prescribes equal pay for equal or similar work. Most of these laws are not implemented properly, due to laxity of employers, enforcement agencies and Labor Departments.

Women workers have organized themselves into self-help groups, unions and organizations such as the Self-Employed Women's Association (SEWA). SEWA has unionised lakhs of women, typically informal sector workers, and struggles for their right to livelihood, working conditions, health care, and social welfare. The SEWA Bank is globally recognised. SEWA was started by **Ela Bhatt** in Gujarat, subsequently sprouted branches in several states, which grew into autonomous state-level SEWAs. Similarly there are many unions of working women, and mixed unions, specific to various occupations, such as the Garment Workers' Association, Tea Plantation Workers' Association, Nurses' Unions, Teachers' Unions, and so on. National women's organizations All India Democratic Women's Organisation (AIDWA) regularly takes up the cause of women workers, across diverse occupational sectors in different states (Karat, 2005); so does the National Federation of Indian Women (NFIW) (Chakravartty and Chotani, 2014).

Sex workers have formed the National Network of Sex Workers (NNSW) which has members from 12 Indian states. Veena [name changed], a sex worker from Maharashtra, asserts their rights as workers – she says, "We earn our living by working, as you earn your living by working. We bring up our children, as you bring up your children." She objects to patronizing attempts to `rehabilitate' sex workers, noting that there are positive and negative aspects to most occupations. Through her income, she has single-handedly managed to educate both her children – her daughter is studying to become a doctor (Interview with Veena, 2017). Rather than heaping moral judgment on sex workers, the women's movement has been actively struggling for their rights, including legalization and proper working conditions which will support their struggles for dignity, safety, health and income.

Feminist Health Movement

Feminist groups such as Chetna (in Gujarat), Sama and Action India (in Delhi) work to improve the conditions for women's health. Feminist activists such as Gouri Choudhry and Gyanvati (senior members of grassroots organisation Action India) point out the urgency of prioritising women's health in budgets and within the public health system. Women's groups emphasize need for non-hazardous contraceptive methods, safe abortion, respectful childbirth, and attention to overall health including women's mental health (Interviews with Gouri Choudhry and Gyanvati, 2015). Depression is a typically women's disease, particularly post-natal depression – such diseases need to be understood within the context of women's lives, patriarchal families and society (Davar, 2001).

The women's health movement has looked seriously into traditional women's knowledge – indigenous healing methods, home remedies; everyday nutrition; and midwives' expertise in childbirth. Childbirth educator Janet Chawla of the NGO Matrika recommends that the best of traditional methods should be combined with the best of modern medicine, to create optimal options for women (Chawla, 2006).

Women and Governance

In the arena of governance, a major step forward was the passage of 73rd and 74th Constituional Amendments in 1992, providing for 33% representation of women within Panchayati Raj institutions. Initially many elected women representatives – Panches or Sarpanches — were unaware of their powers and duties, and allowed their husbands to fill in for them – in formal meetings and activities. However, women's organizations and NGOs like *Aagaz Foundation, Hunger Project, Urmul Trust* and *Mahila Manch-U.P.* undertook systematic training of elected women representatives (Tripathi, 2009). Once the women realized the potential of their post, they took matters in their own hands (Interview with Neelam Chaturvedi, 2009).

Research studies in West Bengal, Maharashtra, Karnataka, Madhya Pradesh and elsewhere indicate that the presence of women in Panchayats has led to: markedly less corruption and far greater attention to people's issues such as drinking water, food security, schools and Anganwadi centres, rural employment, housing, poverty alleviation and infrastructure including construction of roads. States such as Maharashtra have increased the quota for women in Panchayats, to 50%. The active leadership of women is changing the face of local governance, although of course established corrupt forces are busy trying to disrupt the new order.

The Women's Representation Bill, providing for 33% reservation for women in Lok Sabha and Vidhan Sabhas, has not been passed although women's organisations have unanimously raised the demand during the past two decades. Women's representation in state and central governance continues to be abysmally low. The powerful nexus of male politicians, adept in the ways of power and corruption, wish to continue ruling the roost. None of the political parties has consistently supported the Women's Representation Bill, although most have paid lip service while in the opposition, and *all* women in Parliament, to whichever party they may belong, have from time to time offered unstinted support to the Bill. The stiff opposition to this Bill is a major indicator of the tenacious hold of patriarchy in this country.

Peace, Justice and anti-Militarism

Women's organizations like *WISCOMP* (Women in Security, Conflict Management and Peace), and the *Meira Paibis* work relentlessly for peace. WISCOMP and *Aagaz-e-Dosti* actively bring together young people from India and Pakistan in friendly learning spaces, to become harbingers of peace. WISCOMP works on peace education within schools as well.

Meira Paibis are women's groups in Manipur, who work ceaselessly to prevent atrocities by armed forces; and battle against alcoholism and drug abuse. They oppose the Armed Forces Special Powers Act (AFSPA) which has been operative since 1980. **Irom Sharmila**, a young activist, undertook a fast demanding withdrawal of AFSPA, drawing global attention to the militarism and atrocities in Manipur; she continued her fast for sixteen long years (2000-2016). She would say, "I am a rational human being. My fast is for justice and peace" (Interview with Irom, 2007). Human rights groups have documented untold atrocities on ordinary citizens, in Manipur as well as Nagaland – including killings, rape and torture. The Extra-Judicial Victims' Families Association (EVFAM) – formed by widows of young men killed in fake encounters – has filed a case in the Supreme Court of India listing over 1500 extra-judicial encounters. Preliminary findings, based on detailed investigation of a few of the dalleged encounter killings, indicate that these were indeed extra-judicial killings (fake encounters); all the cases are being investigated now. This is a major victory for ordinary citizens, against unlawful exercise of power by the state. Ordinary women have taken up cudgels, in the interests of justice and peace (Mehrotra, 2009).

Dalit Feminism

Dalit feminism is a powerful, positive force on the socio-political horizon. Dalit women have also formed their own organizations such as the *All India Dalit Mahila Andolan*. These organizations are struggling to improve the conditions for dalit women, in society, protesting atrocities and violation of rights by upper class men. The deadly nexus of caste and gender structurally disempowers dalit women, placing them in conditions of endless abuse and torture, at the hands of their own men as well as upper-caste patriarchy (Rao, 2005).

Dalit feminists point out that dalit women suffer double discrimination – they bear the double burden of patriarchy and caste domination. They suffer exploitation as agricultural workers or landless peasants, at the hands of upper-class landowners and other feudal powers. Dalit women suffer domestic violence within their own homes, as do women from other castes; they are also expected to carry out hard labour in traditional menial occupations such as sweepers and sanitation workers. Dalit women's groups are actively involved in spreading awareness and taking effective action, on all these fronts.

Women's movement in India demands gender-just personal laws for all, arguing that different personal laws deny the right to equality as well as justice. India has different personal laws for different communities, thus women from Hindu, Muslim, Christian, Parsi, tribal etc communities enjoy dissimilar rights pertaining to marriage, divorce, property inheritance, guardianship etc.

Particular legal cases have exposed the extreme vulnerability of women due to different and gender-unjust personal laws. Shah Bano, an elderly woman in Madhya Pradesh, filed a case for maintenance from her husband, a wealthy lawyer who had summarily divorced her; the court granted the right, to her and via the judgment to other Muslim women as well. **Mary Roy**, from Kerala, filed for inheritance of parental property, which she finally won, thus improving inheritance rights for all Christian women. Mary Roy, a divorcee, took care of her aged parents, but after their death her brother threw her out of the parental home (Shah and Gandhi, 1992).

In August 2017, the Supreme Court outlawed triple talaq (talaq-e-biddat ie husband's unilateral right to divorce by uttering the word talaq three times at one sitting). The most heartening fact about this case is that it was filed by Muslim women – Shayara Bano who is a victim of triple talaq, and *Bebaak Collective* as well as *Bharatiya Muslim Mahila Andolan*– women's organizations for, of and by Muslim women.

Senior lawyer Indira Jaisingh has argued that the triple talaq judgment should pave the way for abolishing separate personal laws altogether, and provide all women with the right to equality before the law. Economist Bina Agarwal makes a strong case for uniform laws of inheritance for all Indian women, irrespective of religion, as a necessary step towards equality between the sexes (Agarwal, 2016).

Pre-natal Sex Determination

With the advent of pre-natal sex determination techniques, women's groups such as *Forum against Oppression of Women* (FAOW) in Bombay were amongst the first to raise the issue, as far back as the 1980s. The Indian state took cognizance of the issue in 1994, passing the PCPNDT Act (Pre-Conception, Pre-Natal Diagnostic Techniques Act), under which sex-selective abortion is a crime.

The census of India shows sharply declining 'child sex ratio' (girls per 1,000 boys, age 0-6 years) – it was 945 in 1991; 927 in 2001; and 914 in 2011. Despite the law, sex-selective abortion (commonly called 'female feticide') is rampant, especially in north and north-western India. It is a notoriously difficult crime to investigate, and very few arrests have been made under the law. Several women's organizations have identified and exposed doctors who conduct the tests: activists who are pregnant act as decoys, police in tow to apprehend the criminal doctors red-handed, within their clinics.

Alternative Families and Alternative Sexualities

The patriarchal family is being questioned, and changed – in many ways. Alternative family structures are gaining recognition – including single parent families – usually single mothers caring for their children, but also a small proportion of single fathers taking responsibility for their children. Women are asserting their right to remain single – something traditional society is unwilling to accept. Young people are sometimes choosing their own partners – and facing social pressures to conform to the arranged marriage system.

Research on single mothers and women-headed families indicates that while these women may be terribly overworked, they also experience a sense of autonomy and scope to take their own decisions. They may be unwed, divorced, separated or widowed – may have gone through traumatic times – yet often learn to create a new balance in life, which is actually more harmonious than the previous. Single mothers with small children require support structures which society and state should help build up; they typically have less income than when they were married, yet focus more on the education of their children; also the children develop relatively flexible gender roles and ability to cross gender-based work boundaries.

People are also choosing to create households with friends, or live-in partners; and crossing barriers against same-sex relationships. Alternative sexualities are now openly discussed, with a strong LGBTQ (lesbian, gay, bisexual, transgender, queer) movement in the country. Groups such as *Labia, Sangini, Nazariya and Sangath* provide space for LGBTQ persons to meet, share and discuss issues they face — and ways to challenge social discrimination as well as archaic laws.

Disability issues have also come to the fore, with women's groups like Tarshi and Crea taking up sexuality, disability and related issues, setting up educational and training resources on these subjects. The Adolescence Education Program is also running in a few thousand schools, to provide life-skills based sexuality education to the young generation (NCERT, 2011).

Feminist Research, Art and Media

Research, art and media are essential dimensions of women's movements. With the mainsprings in activist movements, feminist scholarship and teaching is facilitated by autonomous institutions such as Center for Women's Development Studies (CWDS), Women's Studies Centres, Gender and Women's Studies courses in various universities, as well as the Indian Association of Women's Studies.

Feminist art by artists such as Sheba Chhacchi, Nalini Malani and many others also extends the nuanced understanding of women's experiences, and gender issues. Within the women's movement there has been tremendous creative outpouring in the form of wonderful posters, flip-charts, resource material, books and booklets, graphic stories as well as songs, plays and films. Media including journals, newspapers, television and internet-based social media are all essential modes through which women's issues are being communicated for spreading awareness, as well as encouraging diverse views and perspectives.

IN CONCLUSION: PERSONAL AND POLITICAL JOURNEYS

The women's movement in India is part of a global ferment, challenging women's secondary status, and paving the way towards equality, justice and freedom, through a wide variety of struggles. Feminist activists are at the forefront of social change, yet the first requirement is change within oneself – for we are all moulded within patriarchy. Perhaps the most interesting and exciting facet of feminism is the personal journeys that each of us engages in – creating a wealth of stories of change, creating a million new paths towards empowerment. The personal journey is at the same time political – change is most graphically expressed as a process flowering in multiple dimensions.

REFERENCES

Agarwal, Bina (2016). Gender Challenges, Volume 2 Family, Property and the State, OUP, New Delhi.

Ahluwalia M.L. (2001). Maharani Jind Kaur, Singh Brothers, Punjab

Bhatt, Radha undated. Kumaoni Striyon ki Saahas Yatra, Bageshwar.

Butalia, Subhadra (2002). *Gift of a Daughter,* Penguin, New Delhi.

Butalia, Urvashi (1998). The Other Side of Silence: Voices from the Partition of India, OUP, New Delhi.

Chakravartty, Gargi and Chotani, Supriya (2014). Charting A New Path: Early Years of National Federation of Indian Women, People's Publishing House, New Delhi.

Chakravaty, Uma (1998). Rewriting History: The Life and Times of Pandita Ramabai.

Chawla, Janet (2006 ed.) Birth and Birth-givers: The Power behind the Shame. Shakti, New Delhi.

CSWI, Towards Equality – Report of the Committee on Status of Women in India, Government of India, 1974.

Dandavate Pramila, Nayar Sushila and Mankekar Kamla Women Pioneers in India's Renaissance. Ministry of Information and Broadcasting, Government of India, New Delhi, pp. 49–53.

Davar, Bhargavi (2001). Mental Health from a Gender Perspective. Sage, New Delhi.

Dave, A., Ajgaonkar, V., Pradhan, R. and Chakraborty, RM. (2017). 'In search of justice and care: How women survivors of violence navigate the Indian criminal justice system. *Journal of Gender-Based Violence*, 1(1): 79–97. DOI: 10.1332/239868017X14900133026601.

Devi, Mahasweta (2000). The Queen of Jhansi, Seagull, Calcutta. Translated, Sagaree and Mandira Sengupta.

Hossain, Rokeya Sakhawat (2005). Sultana's Dream and Padmarag: Two Feminist Utopias, Penguin, New Delhi. Translated Barnita Bagchi.

Jagori (1988). "Nukkad Nukkad Angan Angan". New Delhi.

Karat, Brinda (2005). Survival and Emancipation: Notes from Indian Women's Struggles, Three Essays Collective, New Delhi

Kumar, Radha (1993). The History of Doing an Illustrated Account of Movements for Women's Rights and Feminism in India 1800-1990, Kali for Women.

Mehrotra, Deepti Priya (2005). Kisanin Jaggi Devi: A Passion for Freedom, Indira Gandhi National Center for the Arts.

Mehrotra, Deepti Priya (2009). Burning Bright: Irom Sharmila and the Struggle for Peace in Manipur, Penguin, New Delhi.

Mies Maria, Veronica Bernholdt-Thomsen and Claudia Von Werlhof (1988). Women: The Last Colony, St. Martin's Press.

Nahar, 'Rokeya Shekhawat Hussain', in Nayar and Mankekar. Women Pioneers in India's Renaissance. Ministry of Information and Broadcasting, Government of India, New Delhi, pp. 61–69 80).

Naimishrai Mohandas, Veerangana Jhalkari Bai and Radhakrishna (2015). Paperbacks, New Delhi.

Nayar Sushila (2002). Naidu Sarojini (1876-1949) in Nayar, Sushila and Mankekar Kamla. Women Pioneers in India's Renaissance. Ministry of Information and Broadcasting, Government of India, New Delhi, pp. 61–69.

NCERT (2011). National-level Assessment of the Adolescence Education Program. New Delhi, unpublished report.

Rao, Anupama (2005). Gender and Caste. (*eds.*), Philipose Pamela and Bishnoi Aditi. Women Unlimited, New Delhi.

Sethna, Khorshed Adi (1987). Madame Bhikhaiji Cama. Ministry of Information and Broadcasting, Government of India, New Delhi.

Shah, Nandita and Gandhi, Nandita (1992). The Issues at Stake: Theory and Practice in the Contemporary Women's Movement in India, South Asia Books, Bombay.

Tharu, Susie and Lalita, K. (1995). *Women's Writing in India*, 1: 600 B.C. to the Present, OUP, New Delhi.

Tripathi, Vishvambhar (2009). Learning to Lead: Exploring Leadership Education in the Context of Elected Women Representatives in Village Panchayats 2008-09. Aagaz Academy, Bhopal.

Vohra, Asha Rani, "Krantikari Mahilaein", Ministry of Information and Broadcasting, Government of India, New Delhi, pp. 15–26.

INTERVIEWS CONDUCTED BY THE AUTHOR:

- Veena, Kathmandu, 2017
- Uma Chakravarty, New Delhi, 2016
- Gouri Choudhry, New Delhi, 2015
- Gyanvati, New Delhi, 2015
- Neelam Chaturvedi, Kanpur, 2009
- Irom Sharmila, 2007
- Shah Jehan Begum, New Delhi, 2006
- Sundarlal Bahuguna, Tehri, 1992
- Jaggi Devi, Daudpur Kunda, Pratapgarh, 1989
- Radha Bhatt, Kausani, 1989
- Sudesha Devi, Rampur, Tehri Garhwal, 1988
- Vimla Bahugunaa. Silyara, 1988
- Chandi Prasad Bhatt, Gopeshwar, 1987

Chapter 6

Gender Equality in Islam and Muslim Women in India: An Agenda for Reforms

ABDULRAHIM P. VIJAPUR

Islam is one of the great religions of the world, whose followers are found in every country and continent. As an egalitarian belief system it introduced the concepts of universal brotherhood and non-discrimination among Muslims on the ground of sex or race. Islam gave the women fundamental rights and championed all movements to improve the status of women, at a time when societies were overtly traditional and socially underdeveloped. This paper attempts to examine the following questions: Does Islam provide for gender equality? To what extent this equality of sexes is found in practice in Islamic societies? Are there any deviations from the scriptural precepts of gender equality? What reformative measures have been undertaken in Muslim countries to improve the status of women by enacting laws? What has been the picture of India in this regard? Answers to these and related questions are explored in this paper.

ISLAMIC IDEALS AND PRECEPTS

Both the Quran and the Prophetic traditions elevated the status of woman and gave her human, civil, social and economic rights never previously given by any religious system. The Muslim woman has an independent personality, equal to man in religious duties, in the right to education, in reward for her deeds as well as in defending her beliefs. She has complete independence and total control over her possessions. Islam gave her equal legal capacity with the man. This means that she has the ability to enter into all kinds of contractual arrangement and to conduct business on her own without the need for her husband's consent. Such a legal right, given in the 7th century, is yet to be achieved by the married woman in some contemporary societies where the husband has a certain right to oversee his wife's affairs. *French women did not achieve this legal right until* 1965.

In inheritance, the woman, as a daughter, gets half of her brother's share, but under other circumstances she gets as much as or even more than other men in the family. Women's share in property varies depending on the circumstances. In Chapter 4, Verse 7 of the Quran identifies four circumstances:

1. *Higher share for* males: The son takes twice as much as his sister, if the deceased is their father.
2. *Equal shares for males and females*: "The female takes an equal share to that of the male if the deceased is their son who has children of his own: 'And to parents (of the deceased) a sixth each of the inheritance, if he has children'".
3. *Equal shares*: Are given to males and females (brother and sister) who are distant heirs: 'to each of them twain (the brother and sister) the sixth'.
4. *Higher shares for the females than men*: The female who is the daughter (with no siblings) of the deceased takes half and his father takes one sixth. And if there be only one (daughter) then the half, and to the parents of the deceased a sixth each.

Thus Quranic prescription is based on the principle of equity. Higher shares are usually given to those whose needs are greater so that they may discharge their financial responsibility. A woman as a daughter is under the care / responsibility of her father, as a sister under the care of brother, as a wife under the care of her husband. The often made criticism that Islam does not treat women equal to men in the matters of inheritance is unjustified. Critics always base their remarks looking at the first situation and ignore the three other situations where she gets as much as or even more than males. Many critics are either unaware of the other situations or are biased. Moreover, it should be noted that Islam gave right to property to women twelve centuries before England adopted it legally. *Hindu women got this right only in 1955-56 when Hindu Code Bill* (comprising four Acts – the Hindu Marriage Act, 1955, the Hindu Succession Act, 1956, the Hindu Minority and Guardianship Act, 1956 and the Hindu Adoptions and Maintenance Act, 1956) *was adopted by Parliament.*

Muslim woman has other rights too. She cannot be forced into marriage by her family or guardian; she has to give her consent. If the marriage was solemnised during childhood she can repudiate it on reaching puberty. She can retain her maiden name after marriage, if she so wishes. She has the right to demand the power of divorce plus the power at the time of the marriage contract to disallow polygamy by her husband.

Muslim woman was also given equality in the principle of jihad (religious war). Many women participated in battles during the time of the Prophet Mohammad. One Muslim woman, Nasiba bint Ka'b, defended the Prophet with her sword and arrows in the battle of 'Uhad'. Another example of brave woman can be found in Umayyati bint al-Gafariyya, whose courage at the battle of Khaibar was praised by the Prophet. After the victory, the Prophet presented her with a necklace, as a counterpart of the military decorations of our day. She wore it throughout her life, and it was buried with her in accordance with her will. In everyone one of the Prophet's wars of conquest, women generally worked alongwith men and succoured the wounded.

It is also interesting to note that until the third century of Islam and even later women enjoyed with men the right to pray in the mosques. Khaliph Omar is said to have appointed a reader of Quran especially for them at public worship.

In sum, woman in Islamic teachings/theory enjoys a higher status in comparison to her counterparts in other religious traditions and systems. The Prophet declared many times that "Paradise lies under the feet of the mother". In his last public address he advised Muslims to "treat their women well and be kind to them".

Varying Practices and Modern Reforms

Throughout the Islamic world, there has been a considerable gap between scriptural dictates and actual practice. As a result we find many discriminatory practices toward women. Due to these discriminatory practices, Islam has been criticised on the ground of polygamy, divorce laws, veiling and seclusion of women and the generally prevailing unequal treatment of women as compared to men. Moreover, there are varying practices of applying gender equality in different regions of India. In fact, we find divergent practices in different countries and different schools of Islamic law (*Shariah*). These discriminatory practices can be removed by reforming and reinterpreting *Shariah* in the light of contemporary socio-political thought and the huge corpus of international human rights law.

Though Islam does permit plurality of wives not exceeding four, it is only on the condition of strict equality of treatment among them. But the practice shows that this condition is not followed universally by majority of Muslims in the world. God warns in the Quran that "If you fear you will not be able to deal justly with them, then marry only one" (Chapter 4, Verse 4). In another place, He cautions: "You are never able to be fair and just between women, even if it is your ardent desire" (Chapter 4, Verses 3 and 129). Polygamy is not a general rule; it is only a necessary and emerging provision for the preservation and fostering of high social values (involving marriages of widows or orphans) and for safeguarding society against promiscuity. This permission has undoubtedly been abused, but many Muslim States are seeking to eradicate such abuse through legal regulation of the institution of marriage. For instance, Egypt changed its marriage laws in 1920, 1923, 1929 and in 1956 it abrogated the *Shariah* courts. In 1931 Egypt restricted the solemnization of child marriages by precluding the court from hearing any claim of marriage whatever if the husband had not reached the age of 18 and the bride the age of 16 at the time of litigation. Furthermore, the court could not hear any disputed claim of marriage unless that marriage contract had been registered. Earlier, in 1923, it had made a criminal offence for a Registrar to register a marriage in a case where the bride was not above 16 and the bridegroom above 18.

Similarly, Tunisia, Morocco, Algeria, Iraq and South Yemen have enacted new provisions governing personal laws. Syria, Morocco, Pakistan and Iran have also severely restricted polygamy noting the impossibility of fulfilling the Quranic injunction that multiple wives be treated equally. Tunisia and Turkey have gone the farthest in directly outlawing polygamous marriages. In Lebanon, Jordan, Egypt and Morocco the woman can insert in her marriage contract the right to divorce if her husband should take a second wife.

Regrettably, no serious attempts have been initiated in India to reform family laws with a view to improving the status of women. Such initiatives should come from the leaders, theologians and cross-section of people of the Muslim community. Government initiative will be misconceived by the community as a step towards Uniform Civil Code.

Though the Quran commands that the wife alone shall receive the dower (*mahr*) payable by the husband, which was paid in pre-Islamic period to her father, in many cases in India it is hardly paid in practice.

Originally, divorce laws were fair. Out of three kinds of divorce, two were to be initiated by women. First, a wife may seek from a court a *judicial separation* on grounds of deficiency, mischief, fear of temptation arising due to long absence of the husband or inadequate maintenance. Second, a wife can seek divorce by redemption (Khul) on grounds of deep-seated animosity. But the most commonly practiced system is divorce by the husband – independently of the intervention of his wife or of court – leading to misuse. In the majority of divorce cases husband plays a dominant role. The tightening of divorce laws were the later developments. Moreover, the Quran prescribes that this kind of divorce will not be effective until the "waiting period" (*Idda*) is over. Prior to Islamic era a husband could discard his wife at a moment's notice. The Quran now virtually suspended the effect of the divorce until the expiry of *idda*, which was to last until the wife had completed three menstrual cycles or, if she proved pregnant, until the delivery of the child. This period is primarily designed, according to the express terms of the Quran itself, to provide an opportunity for reconciliation, and during it the wife is entitled to receive maintenance from the husband. In fact, the husband is required to pronounce *talaq* (divorce) thrice to his wife with a gap of one month each between these utterances. The practice of triple *talaq* in one breath, which prevails in India and other Muslim countries, goes against this Quranic precept.

The basis of discrimination against women is generally attributed to Quranic injunctions / verses. A literal or restrictive interpretation of these verses reduces women to a lower status. Let us cite these verses: "*Men stand superior to women* in that God has preferred the one over the other, they have authority over the other, they have authority over women *because they spend their wealth to maintain them.* Good women are obedient.... As for those from whom you fear disobedience, admonish them and send them to beds apart and *beat them*, but if they obey you, take no further action against them [italics added]" (Quran, 4: 34). Veiling of women is supported through verses 30-31 of Chapter 24, and verses 53 and 59 of Chapter 33.

In the 7th century Arabia and other places women were economically dependent on men for their survival and security. In such a social and historical context the Quranic pronouncement of men's superiority was rationalized. Women were then considered as wards of men. Applying his evolutionary principle of interpretation Ustadh Mahmood Taha, the leader of reformist movement in Sudan, who was executed by former Sudanese President Numeri, says that now the male guardianship over women should be terminated as women are no longer economically dependent on men these days. This Quranic verse (*i.e.*, 4: 34) should be set aside as having served its purpose and should not be applied to the contemporary societies.

As regards the veiling it should be said that it was a pre-Islamic practice in many societies – from Greece to Persia and the Byzantine Empire. One verse of the Quran (24:30-31) tells women to veil their bosom and hide their ornaments. "Ornaments" was later taken (by the early interpreters of Quran from Persia) to mean everything except the hands, feet, and perhaps the face, though this interpretation makes no logical or linguistic sense. In addition, if everything was to be veiled, there would be no point in ordering bosoms veiled separately. Another verse tells them to draw their clocks tightly round them so that they may be recognized and not annoyed. And these are the only words taken to refer to veiling. Thus, it appears that the veiling and the harem system were later developments that arose in certain Muslim countries as a result of social conditions and local traditions. Whatever are the causes of their developments, such practices have nothing to do with the principles of Islam.

The gap between precepts and practices is quite glaring with respect to women's inheritance rights. It must be noted that except for the Arab populations which was responsible to develop *Shariah* under the guidance of the Prophet, for other peoples (who became Muslims later) *Shariah* posed serious problems; because it's basic concepts were often wholly alien to the traditional structure of their societies. Despite being Muslims they could not strictly adhere to *Shariah*. Local customs determined the inheritance rights of woman. For instance, the Berber community of North Africa does not provide inheritance to women. Berber customary law of this nature is applied to almost half of the Muslim population of Morocco in all civil matters. In Java and Sumatra, inheritance rights continued to be regulated by the customary matriarchal law. In western Nigeria Shariah is scarcely applied. It is interesting to note that certain Arab tribes of the Yemen never relinquished their established customary law under which, inter alia, women did not enjoy any property rights.

In the Indian sub-continent, the Ismailite Khojas, the Bohoras and the Kutchi Memons continued, after their conversion to Islam from Hinduism, to be governed by the Hindu law of succession, and thus retain the power, in contravention of *Shariah*, to will away the whole of their estates.

In almost every region of India customarily Muslim women were not given share in landed property. It was a prerogative of males only. Muslim males resented when attempts were made to enforce Shariah rules on giving inheritance rights to women. When the Federal Assembly was debating the adoption of Muslim Personal Law (*Shariah*) Application Act, 1937, there was strong opposition to it from the landowning classes of Punjab on the ground that the bill would ruin agriculturists. Though the Act was passed, this abrogated prevailing customs or usage concerning inheritance rights, among others, it explicitly excluded from its purview agricultural land, the devolution of which would continue to be governed by local customs. While the Act meant to extend women's property rights, it hardly served that purpose. Thus the Act served the political purpose of affirming Muslim identity, without antagonizing the powerful Punjabi landlords.

After Indi's independence, legal reforms were initiated in the subcontinent. The Pakistani Parliament initially passed the West Punjab Muslim Personal Law (*Shariat*) Application Act of 1948, which included agricultural land in its purview. In 1962, it passed the West Pakistan Muslim Personal Law (*Shariat*) Application Act, which was applicable to the whole of West Pakistan, except the "Tribal Areas" in North West Frontier Province. It made women legally entitled to inherit agricultural property as full owners.

The Bangladeshi (formerly East Pakistani) Muslims were not affected by legal reforms in West Pakistan. Here the 1937 Act of India was in force. Here despite the absence of subsequent amendments (or even before the passage of 1937 Act), *Shariah* applied also to agricultural land.

In India too, the 1937 Act has continued to be applicable even after independence. It is gratifying to note that in Tamil Nadu and Andhra Pradesh the Act was amended in 1949 to include agricultural land, in 1963, Kerala did the same. In Assam, Maharashra, Gujarat, and West Bengal, there was no strong preference of custom even before the Act was passed; hence in these states the *Shariah* rules could be applied to agricultural land as well. But in several states of north-west India such as Uttar Pradesh (which included till recently Uttrakhand region too), Punjab, Himachal Pradesh and Haryana, the Act has not been amended to include agricultural land. Despite the land reform laws, customary law still govern the succession of such land. Thus, in these states severe gender inequalities still persist as far as succession of landed property among Muslims is concerned. Muslim intelligentsia and leaders (both political and theological) should mobilize public support to amend / reform the 1937 Shariah Act to remove gender inequality.

Empowerment of Muslim Women: Towards Reforming Muslim Personal Law

Mahatma Gandhi once said "one step for women, ten steps for nation". "Human Development, unless engendered, is endangered", proclaimed the 1995 UNDP's *Human Development Report,* which was released on the eve of Fourth World Conference on Women: Action for Equality, Development and Peace, held at Beijing, China.

These two profound statements highlight the importance of women's empowerment. Empowerment means to give somebody the power or authority to act. Therefore, empowerment of women means that the women have the power or capacity to regulate their day-to-day lives in the social, economic and political fields. This will enable them to move from the periphery to the centre stage. The main motive behind women's empowerment is to protect their rights, to enrich their quality of life and involve them in decision making process at all levels, particularly in those decisions, which are related to their lives and families. Empowerment of Muslim women involves: higher literacy level and education, better health care for them and their children, awareness about their reproductive rights, implementation of *Shariah* law to give inheritance rights, abolition of triple *talaq*, a practice followed in India in contradiction of Quranic dictum, punishing those demanding dowry (as it is against *Shariah*), ensuring the payment of *Mehar* (dower) to women at the time of marriage, encouraging their participation in local and urban governments as elected representatives.

Some of the reforms/measures suggested above require reforms of Muslim Personal Law. Initiatives in this regard should come from the Muslim community itself. If the Government, a political party or Supreme Court advocates such modest reforms, it will be taken by the community leaders, both religious and political, as interference in their personal laws and threat to their identities, which are protected by the constitution. Moderate Muslim intellectuals and women's groups from the Muslim community should initiate debate and discussion in this direction. The Women's NGOs and Hindu women's organizations should not insist on the need of drafting Uniform Civil Code, rather the approach of all should be to advocate reforms in all personal laws of different communities so as to make them gender just. Changes made in all family laws as a result of the initiatives of the respective communities to reform their personal laws will be more acceptable to them than the uniform laws which may threaten their distinct cultural identities.

FURTHER READINGS

Agnes, Flavia (1999). Law and Gender Inequality: The Politics of Women's Rights in India (New Delhi: Oxford University Press, 1999).

Ahmed, Anees (2001). "Reforming Muslim Personal Law", *Economic and Political Weekly*.

Ahmed, L. (1992). Women and Gender in Islam Historical Roots of a Modern Debate (New Haven: Yale University Press).

Ali, Shaheen Sardar (2000). Gender and Human Rights in Islam and International Law – Equal Before Allah, Unequal Before Man? (The Hague: Kluwer Law International).

An-Na'im, Abdullahi Ahmed (1990). Toward an Islamic Reformation: Civil Liberties, Human Rights and International Law (New York: Syracuse University Press, 1990).

Ansari, Iqbal A. (1979). "Muslim Personal Law in India". *Journal of Muslim Minority Affairs*, 1(2): 86-96.

Chavan, Nandini and kidwai, Qutub Jahan (2006). Personal Law Reforms and Gender Empowerment: A Debate on Uniform Civil Code (New Delhi: Hope India).

Choudhury, Cyra Anila (2008). "(Mis) Appropriated Liberty: Identity, Gender Justice and Muslim Personal Law Reform in India", *Columbia Journal of Gender and Law*, Vol. 17, 2008 (Also can be accessed at: www.ssrn.com).

Derrett, J. and Duncan, M. (1968). *Religion, Law and the State in India* (London).

Esposito, J.L. (1983). *Women in Muslim Family Law* (Syracuse: Syracuse University Press).

Fayzee, A.A. (2003). *Outlines of Mohammedian Law*, 4th edition (Oxford University Press).

Hassan, Riffat (1968). "Are human rights compatible with Islam? The Issue of the Rights of Women in Muslim Communities", available at >www.iemed.org/documents/novesrealitats/Strawson/a.pd

Jaising, Indira (*ed.*) (1996). *Justice for Women – Personal Laws, Women's Rights and Law Reform* (Mapusa, Goa: The Other India Press).

Jones, Justin (2010). 'Signs of Churning': Muslim Personal Law and Public Contestation in twenty-first Century India". *Modern Asian Studies*, 44(1): 175–0200.

Kazi, S (1999). *Muslim Women in India* (London: Minority Rights Group International).

Larson, G.L. (*ed.*) (2001). Religion and Personal Law in Secular India: A Call to Judgment (Indiana University Press).

Mahmood, Tahir (2002). *Muslim Law of India* (New Delhi: Lexis Nexis Butterworths).

Menski, Werner (2008). "The Uniform Civil Code Debate in Indian Law: New Developments and Changing Agenda". *German Law Review*, 9(3).

Metcalf, Barbara (2007). "Putting Muslim Personal Law in Perspective", Center of Advanced Studies on India, University of Pennsylvania, (This paper can be accessed at: www.casi.ssc.upenn.edu/iit/bmetcaff.)

Parashar, Archna (1992). Women and Family Law Reform in India: Uniform Civil Code and Gender Equality (New Delhi: Sage Publications).

Rahman, Fazalur (1983). "Status of Women in the *Quran*", *In*: Nashat, G. (*ed.*), *Women and Revolution in India* (Boulder: Westview Press).

Subramanian, N. "Legal Pluralism, Legal Change and Gender Inequality: Changes in Muslim Family Law in India", www.profs-polisci.mcgill.ca\subramanian\papers.

Upadyay, R. "Muslim Law: Should it be Politicised?"<www.saag.org.papers7\paper666.html>

Vijapur, Abdulrahim P. (1993). "The Shariah is not as Immutable as it Seems", *Indian Express*.

......., "Is Shariah Immutable or Dynamic? – The Scope for Reformation", 21st *Century Trust News* (London), January 1994. Also published in *The Muslim World League Journal* (Makka, Saudi Arabia), 21(9), March 1994 and an extended version in *New Quest* (Poona), No. 104.

World Bank (2001). *Engendering Development: Through Gender Equality in Rights, Resources, and Voices* (New York: Oxford University Press).

Chapter 7

Gender and Personal Laws in India

ABHA CHAUHAN

In many parts of India, different religious and cultural communities are governed by separate personal laws which in many ways are gender discriminatory and become obstacle to the achievement of women's equal rights and gender justice. The constant diktats of khap panchayats or declaration of fatwas, particularly in the realms of marriage, desertion, divorce, maintenance, property rights etc. make women's condition deplorable and vulnerable. Where legislation has codified male privileges, women remain unable to gain access to inheritance or property and face other restrictions – from purdah to honour killings. The effective application of personal laws is also hindered by the extent to which they lie in various states of codification and impairs women's ability to access objective and independent legal assistance. This paper attempts to understand the origin and growth of personal laws of different religions and the legal position of women in some of the religions and communities in India. It shows how women are denied justice and discriminated against due to lack of gender insensitivity in formulation and codification of personal laws and their implementation. It also focuses on the efforts being made on women's part to resist such oppressions. The Personal Laws of Hindus, Muslims, Christians and Parsis have been analyzed along with the recent changes from a gender perspective.

INTRODUCTION

Neither laws nor their practice are neutral processes. The recognition of this standpoint in gender studies has increased the awareness of how laws help in sustaining the unequal power-relations between women and men at every level. Their lack of implementation further accentuates existing social inequalities. Different religious and cultural communities all over India are governed by separate personal laws which discriminate against women and are hindrance to gender equality and justice.

India has been a home of many world religions like Hinduism, Islam, Christianity, Zoroastrian, Buddhism, Jainism and Sikhism for a long time. Hinduism, Buddhism, Jainism and Sikhism – the so-called Indic religions were born here. Christianity, Islam, Judaism, Zoroastrianism, and the Bahai faith arrived in India from abroad at different points of time during the last two millennia (Madan, 2004). The Hindus constitute 79.80 percent of India's 1.25 billion population, the Muslims 14.23 percent, Christians 2.30 percent, Sikhs 1.72 percent, Buddhists 0.70 percent, Jains 0.37 percent, the 'others' account for 0.66 percent of the population, while 0.24 percent did not state their religion (2011 Census). Among the 'others' are mentioned tribal people who adhere to their own traditional faiths and Zoroastrians and the Jews. Constitutionally, reference to Hindus was construed as including a reference to persons professing the Sikh, Jain or Buddhist religion (Article 25, 2 [b]).

India is a secular, democratic, republic and its Constitution guarantees equality to all people irrespective of religion, race, caste, creed, sex or place of birth (Article 15). It allows freedom to all to profess, practice and propagate religion (Article 25 [1]). Secularism is defined as equal treatment to all religions and therefore, despite the efforts of many people to work towards implementing the Uniform Civil Code (UCC) at the time of framing of the Indian Constitution, it could only be made into a Directive Principle (Article 44). So far, not much effort could be made in the direction of UCC, and all major religions in India are allowed to continue with their own 'personal laws' to govern civil matters. Most of these laws, which are religion specific, discriminate against women. Time and again efforts have been made to undo this imbalance, sometimes with limited and other times with greater achievement.

Earlier, various attempts were made to bring reforms in the personal laws and improve the legal rights of women within these. Despite an overall commitment to non-interference in religious matters during the British rule, the spheres of family and personal law were reformed to a certain extent throughout the latter half of the 19th and early 20th centuries. In particular, the members of the major communities, the Hindus and Muslims, were progressively Hinduised and Islamised respectively. This process brought them closer to the law according to textual authorities and simultaneously reduced the importance of customary laws. The two minor religions, the Parsis and the Christians, were also subjected to reforms of their marriage, divorce, property and inheritance laws, though the Parsis were more successful than the Christians owing to the reform initiatives taken by the community leaders.

Though these efforts resulted in the process of bringing uniformity within the major religions, customary laws of many communities, some of which were women friendly, were curtailed. The period between 1850 and 1930 thus witnessed the elimination of a wide range of customs, which diverged from the Anglo- Hindu law as the standard of proof required was very high. Unless it could be proved that the custom was ancient, certain, obligatory, reasonable and not against public policy, it had a very little chance of survival.

The only customs, which were saved from the crushing effects of the British courts, were the customs of the agricultural people in the Punjab and matrilineal practices of the Malabar region. Otherwise a legal Hinduism, as well as Islam and Christianity wherever prevalent were imposed upon the communities with diverse customs. Many of the customs that were crushed favoured women (Agnes, 1999:52), like provisions of simple rules of divorce and remarriage contrary to the more formal and difficult methods that were introduced later as a part of codification of different laws.

PERSONAL LAW AND WOMEN IN INDIA

Personal laws refer to a large range of religion-based family laws governing marriage, separation, inheritance, maintenance and adoption. They govern certain issues of marriage and inheritance in particular. These laws tend to define, control, and in many cases limit the rights of women within and outside families. It has been felt by most Indian feminists that retention of a plurality of personal laws in the name of 'protecting religion' was detrimental to the social and legal status of women (Nair, 1996: 180). By the first decades of the 20th century, the gradual expansion of the legislative process to include wider sections of the Indian elite produced a number of initiatives aimed at modifying personal laws, though not necessarily with the aim of improving women's rights.

By the 20th century, the demands began to be raised by most women organizations like All India Women's Conference (AIWC), the Women's India Association and the National Association of Women. All those who took active part in the broader national movement argued and contested for more equitable laws (Nair: 1996: 197-99). In the case of Hindu law reform, a small band of liberals in the Parliament, rather than the mainstream Congress nationalists, sowed the seed of change. In fact, among the Congress there were several who opposed the change. In the Muslim case, it was the Ulema rather than the Muslim League or Congress that took the lead in reforming Muslim Personal Law, for reasons to do with its political aspirations.

At the same time, the demand for codification of law was being articulated by the women's movement. By 1934, the 'All India

Women's Conference' (AIWC) even passed a resolution advocating the establishment of an unofficial committee to investigate and reform Hindu law. Basing themselves on the Karachi Congress Resolution (1931) which guaranteed sex-equality, the women's sub-committee called for a Uniform Civil Code to replace the separate personal laws, although this could remain optional for a short transitional period.

Therefore, what were called 'personal laws' at the time of Independence were often seriously modified laws pertaining to various religions. Inherent in these personal laws was the sanctioned discrimination against women. However, on the one hand, codification and reform of personal law continued and on the other hand, demand for the UCC gained grounds around the time of independence (1947) and subsequently during the enforcement of the Constitution of India (1950).

Dr. B.R. Ambedkar as a framer of the Constitution protested in vain against the retention of personal laws. Women in Parliament, notably Rajkumari Amrit Kaur and Hansa Mehta agitated vociferously against the provisions in Article 25 of the Constitution meant for granting freedom of conscience and free profession, practice and propagation of religion. With liberal nationalists like Minoo Masani, they insisted on a Uniform Civil Code (UCC) as they considered many activities carried on in the name of religion like *purdah*, polygamy, caste disabilities, animal sacrifice, dedication of girls to temples etc. as greatly disadvantageous for women (Nair, 1996: 219).

The members of AIWC also continued their efforts for ensuring the inclusion within independent Indian Constitution of guarantees relating to women's rights under personal law. The well-reasoned demands made by these women like Hansa Mehta, Rajkumari Amrit Kaur and Lakshmi Menon for a Uniform Civil Code as a justiciable right was disregarded when the matter was finally relegated to unenforceable status under the Directive Principles of State Policy. The argument for a clause in the

Constitution which guaranteed freedom of religious propagation and practice, most vociferously opposed by women members, was finally included due to the insistence of members of the Minorities Committee (Ibid: 200-201). Rather than UCC, the first task was seen to be the codification of personal laws to bring about gender justice as far as possible. To begin with, the Hindu code Bills that aimed to codify and reform *Hindu* personal law in India were passed in the 1950s.

The Bills weathered opposition from a range of groups in Parliament, conservative hardliners, independent Hindu fundamentalists, the Hindu *Mahasabha*, the Sikhs, some Muslims and even a few women parliamentarians. Women Members of Parliament like Renuka Ray and Durgabai Deshmukh, and the Congress campaigned long and hard to have the Hindu Code Bill passed in its entirety, insisting that it could only be an interim measure before a UCC was passed. But they were faced with the formidable opposition of the orthodox and even some liberal Hindu social groups. This was to the extent that Ambedkar, the then Law Minister who introduced the Bill and prepared and circulated its drafts resigned in protest. Later, after the general elections (1951-52) with the efforts of the first Prime Minister of India, Jawaharlal Nehru the provisions of the Hindu Code Bill were finally introduced in 1955-56 into the Indian Parliament in a piecemeal manner (not as one single Bill) and with many modifications.

Changes in the Hindu Personal Law

Earlier the rights of most Hindu women were governed by the *Mitakshara* and *Dayabhaga* systems of law. While the latter was the leading authority in Bengal the former was recognized as an authority in the rest of British India. Under these laws the man enjoyed absolute rights over all property, whether ancestral or self-acquired. The earliest effort to effect changes in the Hindu *Mitakshara* law was made through the 'Hindu Law of Inheritance (Removal of Disabilities) Act' of 1928 and the 'Hindu Law of Inheritance (Amendment) Act' which further extended the right to property granted by the 'Caste Disabilities Removal Act' of 1850 and put women in the line of succession (Nair, 1996: 198). Further advancing the claim of women to property was the 'Hindu Women's Right to Property Act' of 1937, a very important piece of legislation known as the Deshmukh Act after the liberal author of the Bill.

The changes in the Hindu Personal Law after independence of India were encompassed in four Acts: The Hindu Marriage Act (1955), the *Hindu Succession Act* (1956), the Hindu Minority and Guardianship Act (1956), and the Hindu Adoptions and Maintenance Act (1956).

The main purpose of the enactment of *The Hindu Marriage Act of 1955* was to amend and codify the law relating to marriage among Hindus that brought uniformity among them. It laid down conditions for a Hindu marriage, specifically making bigamy punishable, and fixing the age of marriage at 18 and 15 for men and women respectively. However, in 1978, the Child marriage Restraint Act was amended raising the minimum marriage age of men and women to 21 and 18 respectively. *The Hindu Marriage Act* also spelled out the conditions under which divorce was permissible. It was still difficult to prove desertion, cruelty and adultery and only in 1976 was the law further amended to make divorce by mutual consent possible. Among communities where divorce had been practiced without cumbersome procedures and long waiting periods, often to the advantage of women, the law resulted in making divorce expensive and difficult for the poorer classes. Although customary divorce was accepted in the final form of the Bill, it could not be 'immoral' or 'opposed to public policy', thereby leaving wide scope for individual judges to interpret these phrases (Nair, 1996: 225).

The state introduced *The Special Marriage Act of 1954* to provide for inter-religious as well as same faith marriages for the people of India and all Indian nationals in foreign countries. The Special Marriage Act, 1954 replaced the old Act III, 1872 and has 3 major objectives: to provide a special form of marriage in certain cases;

to provide for registration of certain marriages and; to provide for divorce. Persons married under the Act have their division, maintenance and succession governed by the rules under the *Indian Succession Act of 1925* and the *Special Marriage Act of 1954*.

The Hindu Succession Act of 1956 was introduced to amend and codify the law relating to intestate or unwilled succession among *Hindus*. It laid down a uniform and comprehensive system of inheritance and applied to persons governed by both the *Mitakcara*and *Dâyabhâga* schools as one Act. In this way it codified the multiplicity of laws concerning the property rights of women and considerably broadened them. It permitted Hindu female to hold any property possessed by her as her absolute property with full power to deal with it or dispose of it. It also entitled the widow to succeed to the property of her husband. Daughters, including adopted daughters, could claim a share in the father's property (though not in ancestral property). But unlike the son 'the daughter did not get an immediate interest in the joint family property....She was only entitled to inherit a part of the property that constituted the share of the father once he died' (Ibid.).

Therefore, despite considerably broadening the spectrum of women's rights, *The Hindu Succession Act* 'codified a power structure which continued to exclude women from having a direct control over assets', and although all female heirs of the first degree were given a right to demand partition of the estate, 'the retention of the concept of coparceners or the nucleus of a Hindu undivided family gave a better deal to the son' (Ibid: 225-26). *The Hindu Adoption and Maintenance Act of* 1956 entitled a female Hindu who is single to adopt a child herself and in her own right. It also made provisions for the maintenance of an estranged wife and for an illegitimate child to claim support from the father during his lifetime. But, the Act recognized the father as the natural guardian of legitimate children in respect of their person and property, while the mother the natural guardian of the illegitimate child.

However, even though the codification of Hindu Personal Law did bring about drastic changes in making the legal position of women better, these were more closely related to the Anglo-Hindu law of *Mitakshara* and *Dayabhaga* and in many cases undermined the privileges women enjoyed under various customary laws. Though some of the most glaring discrepancies in the legal position of Hindu women were reformed through the *Hindu Marriage Act of 1955* and the *Hindu Succession Act of 1956*, a few like those related to coparcenary rights, where daughters did not have claims to ancestral property, continued. It was only after the 2005 amendments to the *Hindu Succession Act* that daughters were granted the right of coparcenary and could claim a share of Hindu joint family property and ask for its partition. Under the *Hindu Succession (Amendment) Act, 2005* the daughter of a coparcener shall by birth become a coparcener in her own right in the same manner as the son, and the daughter has the same rights in the coparcenary property as she would have had if she had been a son.

It was in 2005 itself that agricultural land came under the purview of the *Hindu Succession Act, 1956*. So far, the reforms of Hindu law that had given women a right to inherit property did not apply to the most prevalent and valuable form of property in India, that is, agricultural land. Tribal women, who were excluded from the benefits of the Hindu law reforms, have begun to move courts to challenge the exemptions. In May 2013, a group of tribal women form Kinnaur district in Himachal Pradesh challenged the constitutionally of a colonial law that recognized customary practices that prevent women form inheriting ancestral property.

Women from the Oraon and Ho communities of Jharkhand had earlier challenged the constitutionality of the Chotanagpur Land Tenancy Act, 1908 which limited the right to cultivate forest land to male descendants. In *Madhu Kishwar and others v. the State of Bihar and Others* Case, the petition challenged certain provisions of this Act which provide for succession to property in the male line, on the premise that this is discriminatory against women. The Supreme Court held that these provisions violated women's right to livelihood recognized in Article 21 of the Constitution asking the state of Bihar to amend the law.

Tribal leaders and officials expressed concern that allowing female inheritance would lead to the alienation of tribal land. The Supreme Court, while upholding male rights to succession, held that female heirs of the last male tenant could hold and use the land as long as they were dependent on it for their livelihood (Cotula, 2006: 60). Thus the Court provided an economic solution to tribal women without striking down tribal laws. It can therefore be said that certain customary laws are also discriminatory, as in this case where tribal women were deprived of their land rights. It is important therefore, that they make use of the new provisions to claim and receive equal rights like men.

Muslim Personal Law

The *Koran* is believed by Muslims the world over to be the last revelation of God given to Prophet Muhammad and is the highest source of jurisprudence. The Koran was unique for its time in specifically delineating basic rights, as well as duties for women, and in stressing that women are the spiritual equals of men. In addition to the Koran, further interpretation and guidance is given by the *hadis,* or saying made by or about Prophet Mohammad and written down by his followers. The Koran and *hadis* form the basis of Islamic law, guiding all aspects of life. Yet, no set of laws could fit all the changes that were occurring even in the time of Prophet Muhammad and subsequently.

In past centuries as in the present, there have been differences among Muslim communities to the extent to which they believe Islamic law or *Sharia* should be applied strictly or interpreted to meet the needs of Muslims in their particular social and cultural circumstances. *Sharia* deals with many topics addressed by secular law, including *crime*, *politics*, *economics* and personal matters. Human interpretations of *Sharia* (*fiqh*) vary between *Islamic sects* and respective *schools of jurisprudence*, yet in its strictest and most historically coherent definition, *Sharia* is considered the infallible law of *God*.

There are four sources of Islamic law- the *Koran, Sunna, Ijma* and *Qiyas*. The *Koran*, the divine revelation (the word of God), is the highest source. It is compiled from memory after the Prophets' death from the version of Osman, the third Caliph. It contains about six hundred verses but not more than two hundred verses deal with legal principles and only eighty verses deal with law of personal status. As the Prophets' successors, the Caliphs took up the responsibility of adjudication of disputes among the people and while drawing upon the *Koran*, they continued the application of the ancient Arab system of arbitration and customary law. The second source of Islamic law is *Sunna* or tradition. The word *Sunna* means 'trodden path'. Earlier the term was applied to the custom and practice of pre-Islamic tribes and the early Muslims of seventh century AD and later it denoted practice and precedents of the Prophet – *Hadis*. As a source of law *Hadis* is as binding as the principles of the Koran. By the eighth century, *Sunna* became the ideal and established doctrine of the ancient schools, expounded by it representatives. In the present context, *Sunna* could either mean the living tradition of the schools or the traditions of the Prophet (Agnes, 2004: 29-30).

The third and equally binding source is *Ijma*, which is an agreement among legal scholars of any generation. This is based on accepting the provisions of the change with the altering times and that the new facts require new decisions. In developing Islamic law by consensus, the doctrine of *Ijtihad* meaning one's own reasoning to deduce a rule of Shariat law, was developed. However by the ninth century this liberty to reason was restricted and *Ijtihad* was considered as the privilege of great scholars of the past. The fourth source of Islamic law is *Qiyas* which is reasoning by analogy. It does not involve laying down new principles but merely a rule of interpretation (Ibid).

There are two broad sects of Islam, the Sunnis and the Shias. The four recognized Schools of Sunni law, to which 85 percent of the world's Muslims belong, are *Hanafi, Hanbali, Maliki* and *Shafii*. Most of the Muslims in India and in South Asia are Sunnis belonging to *Hanafi* School. The Shia School of *Ismaili* sect is the dominant majority in Persia. The most important Shia Schools of law are *Ithana Ashari* and *Ismaili*. In India, the *Bohras* and *Khojas* are Shias belonging to the *Ismaili* sect. The laws of the two main sects and their sub-sects vary a great deal from each other. The *Maliki* School is the most favourable to women and is followed in North Africa where women enjoy greater rights. The *Shafi* School comes next (Agnes, 2004: 30).

Islam came to India through the trade routes of the Arabs *via* the Arabian Sea. Some of these traders settled down along the Malabar Coast in 8th century and adopted the local customs and practices like the *Mopillas* of Kerala and did not follow the *Shariat* law. The *Shariat* was first introduced to the Sultanates of Afghan and Turkish rulers and entered India around the 12th to the 13th century AD. The Muslim Sultans who invaded India were *Hanafis* and relied upon the *Ulemas* to be the religious and legal arbitrators. The Moghul emperors too were *Hanafis* and the *Qazi* appointed by them administered the *Hanafi* law. It is through this channel that the *Shariat* was established in India.

The dramatic political alliance and cleavages of the early 20th century and the gathering force of the Congress and the women's movement, produced new pressures for reforms of Muslim Personal Law as well. The All India Muslim Personal Law Board (AIMPLB) was constituted in 1973 to adopt suitable strategies for the protection and continued applicability of *Muslim Personal Law* in India. The two important reforms of this period, the *Muslim Personal Law (Shariat) Application Act, 1937* and *TheDissolution of Muslim Marriage Act, 1939* succeeded in Islamising Indian Muslim law, as well as defining and limiting some of the rights women had enjoyed under customary law, without a commensurate change that would make them equal to Muslim men (Nair, 1996: 191-92).

A movement was launched by the *Jamiat-al-Ulema-i-Hind* in 1930s, which eventually led to the passage of the North West Frontier Province (NWFP) *Shariat Act of 1935* which superseded custom as a source of law. The NWFP Act was a significant legislation – it clearly laid down all the areas in which Muslims were subject to the *Shariat* and provided for the possibility of reform through legislative intervention. It used the words 'Muslim Personal Law' and '*Shariat*' interchangeably thereby irrevocably linking religion to personal law. The Bill purported to improve the status of women as it was regarded in the customary law as 'disgraceful' where women did not have rights of inheriting family property. As the Bill was opposed by a certain section of society, a modification in the Act was made and it became the *Muslim Personal Law (Shariat) Application Act of 1937*, an Act to make provision for the application of the Muslim Personal Law (*Shariat*) to Muslims in India. Keeping in mind the larger political agenda of unifying Muslims and keeping the feudal landowners satisfied, an amendment was made to keep agrarian land holdings out of the purview of the Bill which resulted in the subversion of women's rights (Agnes, 2004: 70). Thus the *Act of 1937* stated that notwithstanding any custom or usage to the contrary, in all questions (save questions relating to agricultural land) regarding intestate succession, special property of females, including personal property inherited or obtained under contract or gift or any other provision of Personal Law, marriage, dissolution of marriage, maintenance, dower guardianship, gifts, trusts and trust properties, and *wakfs* (other than charities and charitable institutions and charitable and religious endowments) the rule of decision in cases where the parties are Muslims is to be the Muslim Personal law (*Shariat*). Within this enforced uniformity, women stood to gain very little and the benefits largely remained symbolic.

However, like the Hindu Succession Act, 1956 which specifically exempted tenancy rights in agricultural land, the 1937 *Shariat* Act explicitly excluded from its purview all agricultural land depriving women of the rights in all kinds of property (Chowdhry, 2009: xv-xix). In the states of north-west India, the succession rules relating to agricultural land held under tenancy have a different order of devolution than the personal laws specify and are applicable to all religious groups. Here the specific rules of devolution in tenurial laws show a strong preference for agnatic succession, with a priority for agnatic males (Agarwal, 1994: 216). The *Muslim Personal Law (Shariat) Application Act,* 1937 that abrogated the prevailing customs in favour of the Muslim Personal law giving property rights to women under the Islamic law was not extended to the state of Jammu and Kashmir (J&K) depriving women of the rights inherent in the law. This became possible only when The *Jammu and Kashmir Muslim Personal Law (Shariat) Application Act, 2007* was enforced in the state bringing all Muslims of the state within one purview.

Similarly, the changes were brought about in Muslim Personal law through the enactment of the *Dissolution of Muslim Marriages Act,* 1939. This Act provided Muslim women a statutory right to divorce within their religious boundaries. It intended to consolidate and clarify the provisions of Muslim law relating to suits for dissolution of marriage by women married under Islamic law. It was a landmark reform in the history of Islamic (mainly *Hanafi*) law in India, though it did not affect the Muslim men's right to unilateral divorce (Agnes, 2004: 70-71).

The *Muslim Women (Protection of Rights on Divorce) Bill 1986*, a controversially landmark legislation was passed by the Parliament to protect the rights of Muslim women who have been divorced by, or have obtained divorce from, their husbands and to provide for matters connected therewith or incidental thereto. The Act, in effect replaced the legal right of a Muslim woman to maintenance from her husband with total dependence on her family. This is related to what became famous as the 'Shah Bano Case' and generated a lot of controversy that still persists in some form or the other even today. The judgment was following a precedent of making Shah Bano Begum, a 60 year old woman by making her eligible to claim maintenance on divorce from her husband under Section 125 of the Code of Criminal Procedure (Cr PC).

However, its timing and the observations on Muslim law by the judges led to the widespread outcry by organizations such as the All India Muslim Personal Law Board (AIMPLB). The Central Government sought to contain conservative opinion by enacting the Muslim Women (Protection of Right to Divorce) Act 1986 which effectively nullified the Shah Bano judgment and legislated the Muslim law that required the husband to only make a 'fair and reasonable provision' for maintenance within the *iddat* period of 3 months after the divorce as per the Muslim law.

In 2001, Daniel Latifi, Shah Bano's lawyer held that the 1986 Law had to be read in conjunction with the rights to equality and to life with dignity in the Constitution and confirmed that the lump-sum granted to a divorced women had to be sufficient to maintain her for life. Over the last two decades, resolute Muslim women and sympathizing judges have interpreted the 1986 law to hold that 'reasonable and fair' provision during the *iddat* had to be sufficient to maintain the divorced women for the rest of her life. Since the 1980s, courts have continued to rule on questions of Islamic law and pick interpretations that have favoured women, with little opposition from Muslim leaders.

Since its foundation in 1973, the AIMPLB has emerged as the main spokesperson on the question of Muslim Personal Law which is also consulted by the Government. Over the last decade, it has been criticized because of its domination by Hanafi Sunni Ulema from the Darul Uloom Deoband. This led to the creation of 'All India Shia Personal Law Board'. The 'All India Muslim Women's Law Board' (AIMWLB) was formed in January 2005 to adopt strategies for the protection and continued applicability of Muslim Personal Law in *India*, with a particular focus on women's issues like *marriage*, *divorce*, and other *legal rights*. In July 2013, Mumbai's first Sharia Court was set up to settle civil and marital disputes in the Muslim community. This is to be followed by setting up of similar courts in other cities.

The 'All Sharia Women Court' started functioning in Pune since 2013 with an aim to redress the grievances of Muslim women in the city. Set up here by *Bharatiya Muslim Mahila Andolan* (BMMA), the first all-women Sharia Court deals with various family issues, including marital discord, divorce as well as property related disputes (The Hindu, October 5, 2013). The *Bharatiya Muslim Mahila Andolan* (BMMA) was inaugurated in January 2007 as a mass organization of Muslim women from across the country to become an alternative progressive voice of the community to raise their socio-political and economic concerns and fight for the citizenship rights of the Muslims emanating from the Constitution. It continues to facilitate an organized initiative to bring about gender just reforms in Muslim family law by strengthening the drafting of the codification of Muslim law. The BMMA has supported a ban on the practice of *'triple talaq'* (verbal divorce). It also recommended that polygamy be made illegal in Muslim Personal Law in India.

Both, the AIMWPLB and BMMA created new model *nikahnama* which provided more egalitarian provisions on women's rights. The BMMA released a draft on June 23, 2014, 'Muslim Marriage and Divorce Act' recommending that *polygamy* be made illegal in *Muslim Personal Law* of India. NGOs such as Awaaz-e-Niswan in Mumbai are engaged in the advocacy of women's rights and the spread of legal awareness through Islamic scriptures and reinterpretations of the *Sharia*. The women's groups also assist women with their daily interactions with law like helping secure custody rights or guarding women against domestic violence. Women like Bader Sayeed, D. Sharifa Khanam and Jaibunisha from Tamilnadu are waging an unusual war within faith to free women from the practice of arbitrary triple *talaq* (divorce) and the vexatious issue of derisory alimony (Rohit De, 2013).

In 2002, in a landmark ruling *Shamim Ara's v. State of Uttar Pradesh* case the court invalidated arbitrary triple *talaq*. It held that the husband did not have a unilateral right to triple *talaq*, he had to provide good reasons for the divorce and had to first go through attempts at reconciliation. The Supreme Court verdict commented that in order to be valid, *talaq* has to be *pronounced* as per the Quaranic injunction and that none of the ancient holy books or scriptures mention such form of divorce. This landmark ruling and many other similar ones however, did not receive wide media attention nor were they discussed in public forums (Agnes, 2016). In a recent case, which got a huge media coverage, when Shayara Bano's husband gave her triple *talaq* after 15 years of torturous marriage in October 2015, she approached the Supreme Court in 2016 seeking declaration of *talaq-e-biddat*, polygamy and *nikah hallala* illegal. The Supreme Court in its judgment in August 2017 delivered the verdict declaring *talaq-e-biddat* or instantaneous triple *talaq* as unconstitutional.

Christian Personal Law

Until the 19th century, the converted Christians followed the local customary practices of pre-conversion traditions in respect of property, inheritance and marriage rituals. The concept of a distinct Christian Personal Law evolved only during the latter half of the 19th century with statutory enactments introduced by the British and the Portuguese. The enactment, *The Indian Christian Marriage Act* (ICMA) of 1872, provided for the solemnization and regulation of Christian marriages. The primary aim was to extend this to the British and other Europeans the beneficial provisions of the English statue (Agnes, 1999: 144).

The subsequent British enactments liberalized divorce and by 1937, adultery, cruelty, desertion and insanity were made into independent grounds of divorce in England. But in India there were no corresponding attempts to modernize the Christian family laws. Thus, there have been unequal grounds for men and women regarding divorce among Christians. A landmark judgment by Kerala High Court was given in mid 1995, making it possible for a Christian woman in Kerala to seek divorce on any one of the grounds of cruelty, desertion or adultery. This judgment brought the Kerala Christian women on par with the women of other communities and showed the way for an amendment at the central level that would be applicable to all Indian Christian women.

In matters of succession, the Christian subjects of British India were governed by the provisions of *Indian Succession Act* of 1865. The rights of Christian (and Parsi) women to separate property were further expanded by the *Indian Succession Act of* 1925 which gave equal property rights to daughters and sons and the same rights over property to the surviving spouse. In 1929, the *Indian Succession Act* was further amended to stress the separation of interest in property acquired before marriage and each single partner's full powers of disposal after marriage. Altogether the Act did not apply if one of the partners was non-Christian (Non-Parsi or Non-Jew) at the time of wedding. Also, even after conversion, communities continued to follow the pre-conversion laws regarding succession. Most Christian communities followed the rule of coparcenary or joint Hindu family property.

The Syrian Christians of Kerala, even at Independence remained under the purview of the *Travancore Succession Act of 1916* and the *Cochin Succession Act of* 1921, governed by their distant set of personal laws. Under both *Travancore and Cochin Succession Acts*, the woman was disadvantaged, especially regarding the share in the intestate's property which was very limited.

Thus, Christians continued to be governed by the discriminatory provisions of the uncodified Hindu law, which denied daughters a share in the parental property. These persistent inequalities have been challenged, especially in the landmark *Mary Roy v. State of Kerala* Case in 1986. Mary Roy was denied her share in the family property worth lakhs of rupees and decided to go to the Supreme Court to challenge the *Travancore Syrian Christian Act* (1916) as a violation of her constitutional right to equality. She won a significant victory when the Supreme Court declared that the *Travancore Act* was struck down with effect from 1951, *i.e.,* the date when the princely State of Travancore and

Cochin joined the Indian Union. It declared that the Christians in the former State of Travancore are governed by the provisions in Chapter 11 of Part V of the Indian Succession Act 1925 since the extension of Part B States (Laws) Act 1951. Though, those who stood to lose from the inevitable changes opposed it, many women like several nuns in Kerala gained from this decision as they could state their claim for share in the ancestral property (Nair: 1996: 229).

Among the several discriminatory provisions of their personal laws, the narrow and constrained ground of divorce has caused the greatest hardships to Christian women. Under Section 10 of the *Indian Divorce Act,* the husband can obtain a divorce on the ground of adultery, whereas the wife has to prove an additional ground either of cruelty or desertion. Since adultery is difficult to prove and not all husbands who treat their wives with cruelty or desert them also commit adultery, Christian women faced great hardships till the amendment of 2001. Till then, Christian woman could not claim more than one-fifth of her husband's income as alimony. The reforms of 2001 brought in a significant change in the legal status of Christian women, though lot still needs to be done to bring gender parity.

Parsis and Personal Law

After settling down in India in the seventh century, the Parsis adopted the local language and customs, while maintaining their distinct identity. The adaptation of the institution of local Panchayat for administration of their affairs is an important indicator of this adaptation. In 1778, the *Bombay Parsi Panchayat* was granted recognition and a lawfully constructed Panchayat came into effect in January 1787.

By 1885, the Parsis wanted to have their own law and wanted their laws to be protected. After following various steps, two Bills were finally enacted. These were the *Parsi Intestate Succession Act, 1865* and the *Parsi Marriage and Divorce Act of 1865.* Thus

Parsis finally succeeded in securing a separate law for themselves. The Parsi marriage and divorce law incorporated the provisions of the English matrimonial statute, which transformed the Christian marriage status to a dissoluble contract. Following the Christian model, the Parsi marriages were made monogamous and adultery was made into a ground of divorce. Through these statutes, the Parsi also secured legal recognition for their customary arbitration forum of the panchayat and the community obtained a hold over matters of marriage and divorce within the Anglo-Saxon court structure.

In 1925, when the *Indian Succession Act* was enacted, the *Parsi Intestate Succession Act* was incorporated in this Act. However, though the *Indian Succession Act* did not discriminate between male and female heirs, the Parsi inheritance laws, continued to do so and females continued to inherit half of the share of their male counterparts. When reforms were initiated in the family laws of Hindus and Muslims, the Parsis also initiated a process of reform. The changes suggested by a Draft Bill of the 'Council of the Parsi Central Association' to improve the position of the widow and daughter the statute and allotment of share to parents, were incorporated into the *Indian Succession Act* in 1939.

The *Parsi Marriage and Divorce Act* became redundant in the course of time in the context of the changes coming about in English family laws between 1865 and 1930 and Parsis started their efforts to reform their own laws. The Parsi Panchayats, Parsi Associations, *Parsi Anjuman* and the Parsi jurists all over India played important roles in the process of introducing the Bill that was passed in March 1936. The reforms expanded the scope of dissolving the marriage by introducing several new grounds – non-consumption of marriage, insanity, pre-marriage pregnancy, grievous hurt and desertion.

The eighties witnessed the emergence of a new women's movement in India and reform in personal laws. Among the Parsis, the process was initiated by the Board of Trustees of the *Bombay*

Parsi Panchayat. Amendment to marriage laws in the form of *Parsi Marriage and Divorce (Amendment) Bill* came into force in 1988 through which grounds for divorce were liberalized and divorce by mutual consent was introduced. The amendment to succession laws could be enacted only in 1991, by which the discrimination between female and male descendants was abolished. This way the Parsis, through the process of reforms initiated from within the community could bring about separate law for them though these did not reflect complete gender equality.

However, an issue that has moved to the Supreme Court (initiated by a Parsi woman Goolrookh Gupta who married a non-Parsi) from the South Gujarat town of Valsad is all set to become a landmark case on the rights of Parsi women who marry outside the community to retain their parental religion. The Gujarat High Court in its verdict in 2012 said that even if a woman is married under the Special Marriage Act, 1954 she automatically takes on the religion of her husband. This shows that despite the liberal changes, women have to fight a long struggle (Rohit De, 2013).

CONCLUSIONS

Family and personal laws in India are intrinsically related to various major religions in the country. In the ancient time the Hindu laws were guided by the scriptures, which in turn gave space to the customary practices of the people. The intervention however, by the legal courts was limited and caste *panchayats* and *sangh* continued to play important roles. Mughal rule also did not interfere in the local customs considering them family matters, though Islamic law became the part of Mughal court proceedings. During the colonial rule interventions were made by the State in the realm of family law, primarily at the pretext of doing away with the barbaric customs of the indigenous people and in the process established Anglo-Saxon jurisprudence. Thus, the application of Hindu and Islamic laws was transformed through processes of translation, interpretation and adjudication by the

British judges and came to be described as Anglo-Hindu and Anglo-Mohammadan law.

In the process of streamlining the pluralistic society several customary rights of women were crushed, as they could not meet the legal requirement set by the British courts to prove a custom. The colonial interventions also facilitated the construction of distinct and mutually hostile religious communities of Hindus and Muslims, to be governed by their respective personal laws.

During the national freedom struggle, there were attempts to restore women's rights. The primary aim of the two legislations enacted in 1937, The *Hindu Married Women's Right to Property* and the *Application of Shariat Act* was to restore the property rights subverted through the legal precedents set by the British courts. But within a changed socio-economic and political context these legislations brought in only marginal respite. It is seen that efforts were made before and after independence on two fronts almost simultaneously. One, to reform the personal laws and the two, to introduce uniform civil code that would do away with the inequalities perpetrated in the name of religion. The Constitution with its mandate of equality brought visions of gender justice and the nineteen fifties saw arguments and debate around the *Hindu Marriage Act, 1955* even though its introduction in many ways compromised women's rights located within various customary laws.

During the decades that followed, inroads were made into uniform laws where the objective was more to protect the patriarchal interests of Hindu and Muslim men. The Hinduisation of the *Special Marriage Act* in 1976 and the denial of rights to divorced Muslim women through enactment of the *Muslim Women (Protection of Rights on Divorce) Act 1986*, following the Shah Bano controversy, are two concrete example of this trend. The role of judiciary and later opening of the gates of temple at Ayodhya, demolition of Babri Mosque (1992) and the new economic order of the early nineteen nineties making life for the poor and women difficult, further vitiated the atmosphere and increased communal divide providing thereby reasons, especially by the minority communities to resist changes in the personal law.

In the present context, it can thus be stated that the Uniform Civil Code which was sought for in earlier debates and efforts, has almost become a forbidden territory. However, what is being undertaken now by all major religious communities is the codification of their personal laws so as to make them more gender –equal and gender-just. Various religious community leaders, jurists and women's organizations are making several efforts to bring about changes in personal laws of various religions.

Thus the need of the hour is to bring about reforms within the personal laws of different religions and that too mainly through the efforts from within the community. Besides this, it is also possible to enact uniform legislations in specific areas of family law without invoking the controversy of majority-minority politics. The *Dowry Prohibition Act, 1961,* and the subsequent amendments to it; the law against child marriage (predated Independence), which made child marriage punishable across communities and to which subsequent amendments were made in 2005; the *Medical Termination of Pregnancy Act, 1971*, introduction of new offence of cruelty to wives under S. 498 (A) IPC in 1983, the *Family Courts Act, 1984* and Pre-Natal Diagnostic Techniques (PCPNDT) Act, 1994 are indicative of this possibility.

The enactment of *The Protection of Women from Domestic Violence Act, 2005* which gives rights to maintenance, custody and residence to women of all communities apart from providing for protective orders against violent acts, is another example of such an effort. Yet more recent Act is the *Sexual Harassment of Women at Workplace (Prevention, Prohibition and Redressal) Act, 2013* that seeks to protect women irrespective of their caste, class, religious and regional background, from sexual harassment at their workplace.

The demands are also made for law dealing with the division of marital property and with 'honour crimes'. Therefore, the reforms of the personal laws and simultaneous initiatives in the specific realm of family law would go a long way in improving the condition of women in India within different religions.

The emerging scenario suggests that legal reform has little impact on the lives of women in the absence of legal awareness and networks of support that can help them access these rights. It also reveals that legal reforms without a corresponding change in social values can have adverse effects. The role of women's movement and women's organizations has been quite strong and effective in these.

The need of the hour is to do away with discriminatory laws across communities and to give equal rights to women within the family, which most personal laws do not. The reforms had to be two pronged. First, there have to be certain uniform laws across communities if they were acceptable to women; and second, the effort should be to get rid of the discriminatory aspects of certain personal laws. The fundamental basis of reform had to be on the principles of secularism, democracy and equal rights.

REFERENCES

Agarwal, Bina (1994). *A Field of One's Own: Gender and Land Rights in South Asia*. Cambridge: Cambridge University Press.

Agnes, Flavia (1999). *Law and Gender Inequality: The Politics of Women's Rights in India*. New Delhi. Oxford University Press.

_________. 2004. *Women and Law in India: An Omnibus*. New Delhi. Oxford University Press.

_________. 2016. 'Muslim Women's Rights and Media Coverage'. *Economic and Political Weekly,* 51(20).

Chowdhry, Prem (2009). 'Understanding Land Rights of Women', *In*:Chowdhary, Prem (*ed.*), *Gender Discrimination in Land Ownership* (xv-xxxv). New Delhi: Sage Publications India Pvt. Ltd.

Cotula, Larenzo (2006). *Gender and Law: Women's Rights in Agriculture.* Rome. Food and Agriculture Organization of the United Nations.

De, Rohit (2013). 'Personal Laws: A Reality Cheque'. *Frontline.*

Dube, Leela (1997). *Women and Kinship: Comparative Perspectives on Gender in South and South-East Asia.* New Delhi. Vistaar Publications.

Government of India (2011). *Census Data: Religious Composition*. New Delhi, Office of the Registrar and Census Commissioner of India.

Madan, T.N. (2004). 'Religions of India'. *In:* Das, Veena (*ed.*), *Handbook of Indian Sociology*. New Delhi, Oxford University Press. New Delhi.

Nair, Janaki (1996). *Women and Law in Colonial India: A Social History.* New Delhi. Kali for Women.

PTI (2013). 'All Women Sharia Court Starts functioning in Pune'. *The Hindu: Business Line*.

Chapter 8

Politicizing the Feminine: Sociological Analysis of Gender Issues

B.K. Nagla

INTRODUCTION

The female subject has been seen as the eternally feminine "source of life, power and energy". Feminist reader looks towards politics of gender. As we know that our gender identities are a product of the essentialization of our historic roles in society. The problem of historical and cultural forces is responsible in the shaping of gender relations. Sexed sexual human beings in hierarchical relations of power are more likely to liberate through the accumulation of gendered essence. Women are considered inferior only when they have less power; and men are considered superior only when they have more power. These are judged when we say "What should I be?"

The idea of this paper is globalizing the feminine is a practice, not merely preference. In this context, the major questions arise in our minds are: How we view the world is incredibly significant to how we live in the world? How we understand the categories of "Women", the female, the feminine and the feminist is crucial to whether or not we materially remain in them?

To answer these questions for feminist understanding of women as globally recurring subjects, we have tried to look in this paper towards history of feminist theorising which lie into three kinds of essentialism of women:

1. Relationship between the concepts of sex and gender.
2. Certain modes of feminist thought stressing the uniqueness of particular culture and societies in shaping the identities of women.
3. How the knowledge is the manifestation in the lives of actual women. This would reflect the symbolic representation of women.

We maintain the discussion of political rather than the liberal use of the term "essentialism".

The present paper explores the ways in which gender has been politicised in feminist theories and to investigate how these conceptions bear upon issues of female empowerment.

Context

THE past years have seen the publication in books and journals of a number of articles discussing and for the most part deploring the issues related to feminist movement — the intellectual and political impetus behind women studies.

The structuring of gender relations has always been reflected in the division of labour between the sexes. With the development of industrial societies the eighteenth and nineteenth centuries, this was manifest in the development of ideology of 'separate spheres', in which women specialised in domestic work and men in market work; women's sphere was the home, men's public life (Davidoff and Hall, 1987). This ideology was uncritically reflected in the writings of early sociologists. For example, Durkheim argued: 'Today, among cultivated people, the woman leads a completely different existence from that of the man... the two great functions of the psychic life are... dissociated, [in] that one of the sexes takes care of affective functions and the other of intellectual functions' (1964: 60)[1]. The Marxist division of labour between production of use values for home consumption, and exchange values for markets, disappears for rural women who produce both (Nickols and Srinivasan, 1994).

ETYMOLOGICAL MEANING OF THE WORD GENDER

Looking up the etymological genealogy of the word "gender' in the context of contributing this keyword to a German Marxist dictionary, historian of science Donna Haraway starts her entry as follows:

> The root of the English, French, and Spanish words is the Latin verb *generare,* to beget, and the Latin stem *gener-,* race or kind.... the substantatives "Geschlecht," "gente," and "genero" refer to the notion of sort, kind and class... the modern English and German words, "gender" and "Geschlecht," adhere closely to concepts of sex, sexuality, sexual difference, generation, engendering, and so on, while the French and Spanish seem not to carry those meanings readily. Words close to "gender" are implicated in concepts of Kinship, race, biological taxonomy, language, and nationality. (Haraway, 1991: 130).

Indeed, as she goes on to sum up, "'gender' is at the heart of constructions and classifications of systems of difference" (ibid., p. 130). Conclusions of a similar nature have been echoed in other studies as well. The French philosopher Derrida, commenting on Martin Heidegger's near silence on these matters, distinguishes between "the geschlecht" and "Geschlecht", where Geschlecht can connote "sex, race, family, generation, lineage, species, and genre/ genus."

Gender is not only richly intertwined with other meanings when investigated along etymological and linguistic lines. In the context of exploring "the science question in feminism," Sandra

Harding (1986), among others, has emphasized the symbolic meanings associated with gender____ meanings that she feels undergird more specific conceptions of gender identity and gender relations. Gender symbolism, as she calls it, is analytically so crucial because

Gender difference is the most ancient, most universal, and most powerful origin of many morally valued conceptualizations of everything else in the world around us.... As far back in the history as we can see, we have organised our social and natural worlds in terms of gender meanings within which historically specific racial, class, and cultural institutions and meanings have been constructed. Once we begin to theorize gender____ to define gender as an analytical category within which humans think about and organise their social activity rather than as a natural consequences of sex difference, or even merely as a social variable assigned to individual people in different ways from culture to culture____ we can begin to appreciate the extent to which gender meanings have suffused our belief systems [and] institutions. (Harding, 1986:7).

John (1996) examines the effects of Harding's comments in greater detail in her writing of Discrepant *Dislocations: Feminism, Theory, and Postcolonial Histories.*

In her extensive study of the relationship between feminism and anthropology, published in 1988, Henrietta L. Moore first points to the uniqueness of the discipline:

Feminist anthropology is more than the study of women. It is the study of gender, of the interrelations between women and men, and the role of gender in structuring human societies, their histories, ideologies, economic systems and political systems. Gender can no more be marginalized in the study of human societies than the concept of "human action" or the concept of "society." It would not be possible to pursue any sort of social science without a concept of gender.

BIOLOGICAL SEX AND PATRIARCHAL GENDER

One of the first radical feminist to insist that the rots of women's oppression are buried deep in patriarchy's sex/gender system was Kate Millett. In her *Sexual Politics* (1970), Millett argued that sex is political primarily because the male-female relationship is the paradigm for all power relationships: "Social caste supercedes all other forms of inegalitarianism: racial, political, or economic, and unless the clinging to male supremacy as a birthright is finally foregone, all systems of oppression will continue to function simply by virtue of their logical and emotional mandate in the primary human situation." (Millett 1970: 25).

CONCEPTS OF SEX AND GENDER

The term 'gender' scarcely appears in the academic writings of the first half of this century. The notion seems to have guided wide currency only with the coming into being of the sex-gender distinction. By the seventies, this conceptual distinction had found general acceptance within the sociology in particular and social sciences in general. Before moving to the debate of sex-gender, we would like to comprehend the concept of sex and gender by making distinction between the two.

We begin by taking into account the distinction between sex-gender as discussed by Ahuja Agrawal (1997).The sex-gender distinction is modelled upon the more general distinction between nature and culture, or that between the biological and the social. 'Sex' is what makes a male or female, and 'gender' is what constitutes an individual as masculine or feminine in a given society. Furthermore, sex accounts for those aspects of being a man or a woman which are universal, that is, which are found to be constant cross-culturally. Variations, on the other hand, are accounted for by gender. It is this difference that explains the possibility of a male being feminine and a female being masculine within a given social framework. Thus, that which is regarded as masculine in one society may be treated as feminine in another, and *vice versa*.

Since these are gendered categories which are socially constituted. As two domains of human existence, sex and gender are thus viewed as ontologically separate in this frame work. This, however, does not imply that gender has no relation with sex. On the contrary, sex is seen as providing the raw material out of which gender is construed (see Mead, 1963, 1968; Oakley, 1972; Rubin, 1975).

Thapan (1994) made an attempt to intermesh the *cultural* and the *biological* with the *personal* and the *private* in order to understand femininity. The *public*, as she sees it, includes cultural and material forces which impinge upon a women's *private* self, her-self identity, and more importantly, her perceptions of her body. The public has a particular, as well as several different, views of femininity that enhance female subordination in one way or another and the private affirms this subordination essentially by submitting to it. The public *in this context* is the culture of a particular society in terms of the visual and social images. In India, the manner in which this culture is presented as well as appropriated would of course vary according to class and age differences, community and regional differences, religious differences, and differences relating to urban and rural areas.

Currently, there is no agreed usage for the term 'gender'. Recent work on the sociology of gender draws attention to the controversial gender issue within feminism. This is important in a number of significant ways. Davies (1996; 663-666) views in three ways: First, there is a move to regarding gender not as an attribute but as a relation (Scott: 1986; Connell: 1987). Insisting on the relational equality of gender provides dual challenge. On the other hand, it affirms gender as a social construction, thus drawing attention away from the behaviour of particular men and women towards historically and culturally constructed masculinities and femininities which are one resource, among others, from which subjectivities, identities and behavioural regularities emerge. On the other hand, it challenges both those who have studied only women and those who, have worked on masculinity to ensure that a relational focus is sustained. Secondly, there is a focus on gender relations as power relations that take a binary form, a form in which women (or rather the qualities that women represent) are constructed as 'devalued Others', as carriers of qualities that thereby remain unacknowledged and denied (Hartsock, 1990; Jay, 1991; Bologh, 1990). Thirdly, there is an acknowledgement that gender understood in these ways can be seen to operate at multiple levels; it gives meaning to, and affects, the formation and reproduction of organisations and institutions as well as having an influence of the level of interactions and identities (Acker, 1990.1992; Alvesson and Billig, 1992; Savage and Witz, 1992; Mills and Tancred, 1992). A particularly important derivative from this is that gender relations are not fixed. Active processes at different levels are necessary to sustain gender-relations; such relations can thus be challenged, dislodged and transformed in the process of their daily reproduction.

CONCEPTS OF MASCULINITY AND FEMININITY

Much at present remains controversial in this particular turn of thinking about gender. One central problem derives from the need to give content to the concepts of masculinity and femininity - something that is usually achieved by reference to the attachment/separation problematic developed by feminist psychologists. John Gallos captures the essentials of the arguments of a number of influential writers in this field in a brief passage where she explains:

> [D]evelopment for men has meant increased autonomy and separation from others as a means of strengthening identity, empowering the self, starting a satisfactory life course. . . . For women, attachments and relationships play a central role in both identity formation and concepts of developmental

maturity - - . , colouring hoe women see themselves, their lives, their careers, and their ongoing responsibility to those around them. . . . (1989: 115-6).

Feminism

Although the word 'feminism' evokes Western stereotypes for many Indian scholars (Kishwar, 1990), Indian women are credited with having resisted patriarchal oppression for more than 2,000 years (Tharu and Lalita, 1993). The coalescence of isolated resistance into a *movement* in India in the 19th century emerged at about the same time as in the US (Donovan, 1985) and Europe (Anderson and Zinsser, 1988). Explanations of this synchrony are beyond the parameters of this paper.

Theorising Gender

The scope of a social theory of gender is not easily defined. There are a number of speculative abstractions that appear to define it, such as the 'dialectic of sex' (Firestone, 1980); 'relations of reproduction' (Centre for Contemporary Cultural Studies, 1978); and the astonishing new science 'dimorphic' (Strober, 1976). But these are more slogans for a particular way of theorising than specifications of what is being theorised.

The practice of categorising theories as a method of inquiry into feminist projects is more common in the West than in India. In India, crystallizing issues and activism has been more urgent. However, the need for theorising to comprehend and guide activist work comes at the conclusion of a major review of issues (Gandhi and Shah, 1991).

It is better to accept that the social theory of gender is not a tightly-knit logical system. It is, rather a network of insights and arguments about connections. For instance, one argument connects the dynamics of industrial capitalism and its sexual division of labour to the structure of the family (*e.g.*, Zaretsky, 1976), while another connects the structure of the family to the production of femininity (*e.g.,* Chodorow, 1978). The scope of the theory of gender at any given time is defined by the reach of this network of arguments.

Connel (1985) views that the network firmly connects the following issues: the social subordination of women, and the cultural practices that sustain it; the politics of sexual object-choice, and particularly the oppression of homosexual people; the sexual division of labour, the formation of character and motive, so far as they are organised as femininity and masculinity; the role of body in social relations, especially the politics of childbirth; and the nature of strategies of sexual liberation movements. The field defined by this network has no name in common use, though terms like 'patriarchy' and 'sexual politics' are useful in pointing to sizeable parts of it. Young *et al.* (1981) speak of 'the social relations of gender', a precise but somewhat awkward term. "Gender relations' is perhaps the most practical name for the whole network.

A social theory of gender is implied and required by current sexual politics. Its scope cannot be defined *a priori*, but can be defined practically by the reach of network of arguments generated by feminism, gay liberation, psychoanalysis and some branches of academic sociology and psychology. The work of the feminist scholars testifies to the diversity of feminist theories. They agree on one point however: that the gender, the socially constructed definitions of what it means to be a woman and a man, is a fundamental category of any analysis of social life. Here, we describe briefly four major feminist theories as discussed by Kachuck (1995). They are mainly liberalism, essentialism, Marxism/ socialism. And postmodernism. Feminist liberalism identifies women as a class entitled to rights as women, but leaves economic and social structures intact, with no way to redress inequitable distributions of social goods among women-and men. The essentialists' useful attention to hitherto unappreciated qualities of women is gravely flawed by failing to notice artefacts of their status in a patriarchal society. Their analyses present women as biologically, socially, and/or psychologically determined. While the essentialists recognise gender power relations, women's agency to change their status emerges in impractical programmes.

The postmoderns provide important caution against privileging some women at the expense of others. When they insist on prohibiting all truth claims as equal threats of dominance, women's demands for relief from oppression can only be seen as no more justified than that of their oppressors. The endless deferral of conclusions, as a critic suggests, can be seen as constructing a 'feminine' space where intellectuals aggressively play out tentative ideas.

Feminist socialism seems the most promising of the theories. It overcomes the limitations of the others. Feminist socialists view the essentialist and radical feminist definitions of patriarchy as generative of human oppression as being anti- theoretical. The concept of liberal assumption of natural substrata of mind, entitling an elite group to control those who deviate. The vision of the end of capitalism offers hope of eliminating not only gender but all oppressions by eradicating hierarchical social structure. The economy is an important pillar of social arrangements but does not stand alone. What is needed are feminist syntheses of economy with its dimensions of consciousness, sexuality, procreation and child rearing, and cultural phenomena that are at least partially independent of the economy, such as race, religion, and ethnicity. The relationship of individuals to the community needs to be thought out. Finally, to fulfil the promise, a political programme is necessary.

Broadly, accounts of gender relations that have attempted some synthesis of this field have been of two types (Connell, 1985). One emphasises the social construction of the categories of gender, the ways they are learned, inhabited, and transmitted. It speaks of 'sex roles', 'stereotypes', and 'socialisation'. In terms of academic social science it stems from the work of Margaret Mead (1950), Talcott Parsons (Parsons and Bales, 1953) and Mirra Komarovsky

(1946, 1950). This approach has enjoyed a huge revival in social psychology, sociology and allied disciplines since about 1970. The other tendency takes men and women for most purpose as already-constituted categories, and focuses on the relations of power and exploitation between them. It speaks of 'sexual politics', 'oppression', and 'patriarchy'. Its intellectual sources are less specific, though a number of the important ideas were crystallised by Simone de Beauvoir (1949). There is much less academic writing in this vein than in the 'sex-role' vein, but the ideas are widespread in the movement publications of women's liberation and gay liberation.

Feminism's Identity Crisis

Thapan (1994) broadly identifies two main themes in women's research in India. "Situations of gender asymmetry . . . constitute one definite framework adopted in a large number of studies on women". The main focuses of such studies are the "structural and material arrangements underpinning such inequality". The second focus can be seen in those researches concerned with "defining the 'feminine' space in cultural and symbolic terms". This approach tends to make little reference to the notion of gender asymmetry (Niranjana, 1992:401).

Niranjana argues that in the first kind of studies, the conflicting situations encountered by women in the modernising process range from dowry, desertion, sexual exploitation and violence against women, problems of single and working women, education and land rights, the role conflicts among working women. The socio-economic asymmetries generated and sustained within this context are moreover perceived as contributing to the subordinate status of women. These studies also offer a critique of the process of development itself to the extent that they argue that an understanding of the material basis of women's subordination and its intersection with the ideological is necessary in order to analyse women's status. There has thus been reassessment of the developmental process and a debate on science, technology, ecological destruction, and its impact on women. (See for example, Shiva, 1988; Agarwal, 1989). The women's movement clearly recognises the fact that women are in a sense 'victims of development' and has attempted to transcend this characterisation by drawing on the strength, knowledge and experience of women in fashioning an alternative world-view.

Next, we consider the symbolic-culturist view of conceptualising the feminine. In cultural terms, femininity has been examined in India primarily in terms of the socialisation of the girl child into different roes to be performed by her in her multi-faceted but mainly home-bound life. These include the good daughter, the virtuous wife, the obedient daughter-in-law, the nurturant mother, and if circumstances allow, the working women (see, for example, Dube, 1988). Significant to such analyses is the view that there are innate, unchanging and eternal components of femininity.

Sex and Law

Confronted with the challenge of rationalising and accommodating profound difference among women, in both character and ideology, feminism has always been issue of conflicting ideas about sexuality and gender which lead to conflicting vision of law and social policy. If men and women are naturally and consistently different in terms of character, temperament and moral sensibility, then the law should treat them differently, as it has through most of our history, with labour legislation that protects women, for example, or with laws preferring women in custody disputes: Special protection for women, not equal rights, becomes a feminist goal.... But if men and women do not conform to masculine and feminine character models, if sex is not a reliable predictor of behaviour, then justice requires a sex-neutral approach to law which accommodates different people's different characters and experiences....

Kaminer (1994) describes the debate about sex and gender in his article on 'Feminism's of identity crisis. In academia this has been dubbed the "sameness-difference" debate, though no one on either side is suggesting that men and women are the same. Advocates of laws protecting women suggest that men and women tend to differ from each other in predictable ways, in accord with gender stereotypes. Equal-rights advocates suggest that men and women differ unpredictably and those women differ from one another unpredictably....

In the 1980's the feminist academics, especially postmodernists who could take both sides in the debate of sex and law, in celebration of paradox and multiculturalism. On one side, essentialism_ a belief in natural, immutable sex difference___ is anathema to postmodernists, for whom sexuality itself along with gender, is a "social construct". Sensitivity to race- and class-based difference among women also militates against a belief in a monolithic feminine culture: From a postmodern perspective, there is no such category as "women". Taken to a logical conclusion, this emphasis on the fragmentation of the body politic makes postmodern feminism an oxymoron; Feminism and virtually all our laws against sex discrimination reflect the presumption that women do in fact constitute a political category. On the other side, to the extent that postmodernism includes multiculturalism, it endorses tribalism, or identity politics, which for some feminists entails a strong belief in "women's ways". Thus the theoretical rejection of essentialism is matched by an attitudinal embrace of it.

Outside academia, debate about sex and justice are sometimes equally confused and confusing, given the political and ideological challenges of affirmative-action programme and the conflicting demands on women with both career aspirations and commitments to family life. Feminists often have to weigh the short-term benefits of protecting wage-earning mothers (by mommy-tracking, for example) against the long term costs of a dual labour market. Sometimes ideological clarity is lost in complicated strategy debates. Sometimes ideological conflicts are put aside when feminists share a transcendent social goal, such as suffrage or reproductive choice. And sometimes one ideological strain of feminism dominates another. In the 1970s equal-rights feminism was ascendant. The 1980s saw a revival of protectionism (Kaminner, 1994).

Female sexuality as located within a libidinal economy it participates by virtue of her collective historically and culturally identity. It has been observed that the history of female oppression under the structures of patriarchy. Metaphysically speaking, woman is what woman has, and without it she is not woman. The female subject as the eternally feminine "source of life, power and energy". Feminist reader looks towards politics of gender. French version of "feminine" refers to femaleness or femininity. Sex and gender are theoretical constructs. Sex is a biological category whereas gender is a socio-cultural category. Female body is represented in culture.

To show feminine "From Plato to Freud has been perceived in terms of matter, physics, the passion, the emotions, the irrational-characteristics traditionally associated with nature. Patriarchal values are consciously imported into language (historically-culturally conditioned existence). Masculinity and masculism into man result a kind of essentialist which refer to the "unconscious determinants of patriarchal culture" than the conscious reasoning behind them.

As we know that our gendered identities are a product of the essentialization of our historic roles in society. The problem of historical and cultural forces in the shaping of gender relations. Sexed sexual human beings in hierarchical relations of power are more likely to liberate through the accumulation of gendered essence. Women are considered inferior only when they have less power. These are judged superior only when they have more power. These are judged when we say "What should I be? How should I be "?

Policy maker patiently listens to the idealist. But idealists and realists don't mix each other. What are innovative are the accounts of gender relations? Hegemonic conceptions of "Woman", and emancipatory practices offered by several feminist writers: Kumkum Sangri; Sudesh Vaid; Christine Sylvester, and Chandra Talpade, Mohanty deal with this dualism.

The idea of this paper is politicising the feminine is a practice, not merely a preference. In this context, the major question arises in our minds are:

How we view the world is incredible significant to how we live in the world? How we understand the categories of "woman", the female the feminine and the feminist is crucial to whether or not we materially remain in them?

To answer these questions for feminist understanding of woman as globally recurring subjects, we have to look towards history of feminist theorising which lie into three kinds of essentialism of women:

1. Relationship between the concepts of sex and gender. Sex is a biological category. Gender is a social function.
2. Certain modes of feminist thought stressing the uniqueness of particular culture and societies in shaping the identities of women.
3. How the knowledge is the manifestation in the lives of actual woman. This would reflect the symbolic representation of women.

All three examples refer to a form of reductionism. They are associated with similar problem of identity. We maintain here the discussion of political rather than the literal use of the term "essentialism". Our primary interest is to explore the ways in which gender has been politicised in feminist theories and to investigate how these conceptions bear upon issues of female empowerment. If being a feminist means engaging in ethical discourse. In the history of feminism. There have been responses to the constructed identity of woman- as not men that posit woman as able to "hold out against oppression and constitute herself as a superb, equal, hence impossible subject, untenable in a real social framework.

Female accounts reveal as eternally different or physiologically superior to man, and have served as a means by which the inferior status of woman within various patriarchies has been questioned. This type of feminist is challenge to the legitimacy of male power. On the other, ontological constructed woman-leaving her to sink or swim in the totalizing sea of masculist identity, in a body politic, the politics of gender is kept submerged. Radical feminism rectifies this situation. Woman an innate identity confronting this structure of male domination with female qualities equal to or essentialized into maleness. For example, women are more peace loving, soft-headed, irrational pacifists.

Therefore, she may gain, she will not know freedom. This is the politics of feminism. Masculinist ways of understanding the world, for if woman are essentially different from men, and are subordinated gendered positions because of this differences then women must assume the strategies, tactics, and (in essentialist terms) the identities of men in order to acquire - But this is logically impossible. However, we should not confuse biological and cultural position of women.

Legal and institutional reform will allow women a place in the dominant project of western culture. If women step into public realm, cultivated in private realm, will eventually cease to exist, since women will effectively become men. Yet it was Simon de Beauvoir who said that in order to become truly free, women must become men.

If biologically category discredited, cultural category offered the politics of contemporary feminism. Feminists of non-western and non-white backgrounds have criticised mainstream feminist notions of "woman" as the "universalization" of the experiences of essentially white, western and middle class women. The concept of subjectivity is an ethical issue. Cultural feminism is a critique of actual of women. In this approach to feminism, discursive constructions of "womanhood" are deconstructed in the interests of demystifying the feminine and radical politicising gender to the extent that gender itself is rendered a meaningless category.

Now we look at critical feminist theory of international relations which is an epistemological issue and post-modern feminist view. The question of problematic identity of women and the actual lived experience of women exist as being "the critical method" in feminism (epistemological traditions). Post-modernist feminists believe in the possibility of a more comprehensive knowledge about the world achievable through an epistemological that would allow for greater objectivity and truth. They asserts the impossibility of such knowledge *i.e.*, discourses, derives no meaning from itself but in relation to other discourses.

The issue of subjectivity into debates about being and not being refers to the Ethics and Aesthetics, theory and Reality. To understand how choices are made not arbitrariness but logically argue privilege of opting out of discussion making. (This is the assertion as given by Derrida's theory of deconstruction which is not a negative metaphysics, *e.g.*, Feminist objectivity encompasses the idea of knowledge located in particular time and place at the conjunctions of specific social and cultural precisely with the problem. Several issues reflect deep political concerns in feminist theorising. However, the ontological question is here of subjectivity and the essentialist, relativist, and nihilist implications of epistemology, notion of the colonisation within feminism of non-feminist work by the assumption of white western women.

Nationalist models of reformist and development implications of- patriarchal practices and political economy, religion, law, culture all related to the question of politics of social change. In the history of emancipation-historiography should be seen and contextualization- related with race, class and nation should be analysed.

Finally, gendered based notion of the individual reflects social-psychological expectations. The idea of social contract is related with looking after children, motherhood. It changed in context to political economy. The politics of emancipation is a life politics. Social arrangement is a security dilemma. But critical feminist thinking are concerned with the colonising effect and western conception of woman.

Identities of men and women are conceptualised in social and material conditions, hence these gender relations are reduced to an oppositional politics between men and men. Thus, gender becomes a category of construction in "Womanising" practices and theorising women. Hegemonic "western" feminism's and the formulation of autonomous, geographically historically and, culturally grounded feminists are concerned for strategies. The first is one of the deconstructing and dismantling and the second one of the building and constructing.

REFERENCES

Acker, J. (1990). "Hierarchies, Jobs, Bodies: A Theory of gendered Organizations". *Gender and Society*, 4: 139–58.

Acker, J. (1992). "Gendering Organizational Theory", *In*: Mills, A.J. and Tancred, P. (*eds.*), *Gendering Organizational Analysis*, London: Sage.

Agarwal, Anuja (1997). "Gendered bodies; The Case of the 'third gender' in India". *Contributions to Indian Sociology,* 31(2): 274–279.

Agarwal, Bina (1989). "Rural Women, Poverty and Natural Resources: Sustenance, Sustainability and Struggle for Change". *Economic and Political Weekly,* 24(43).

Alverson, M. and Billing, Y.D. (1992). "Gender and Organization: Towards a Differentiated Understanding". *Organization Studies*, 13: 73–103.

Anderson, Bonnie and Zinsser, Joan (1988). *A History of their own: Women in Europe from prehistory to the present*, Vol. 2, New York: Harper and Row.

Bologh, R.W. (1990). *Love on Greatness: Max Weber and Masculine Thinking: A Feminist Inquiry*, London: Unwin Hyman.

Chodorow, N. (1978). *The Reproduction of Mothering*, Berkeley: University of California press.

Connell, R.W. (1985). 'Theorising Gender'. *Sociology,* 19(2): 260–272.

Connell, R.W. (1987). *Gender and Power*, Oxford: Polity.

Davidoff, L. and Hall, C. (1987). *Family Fortunes*, London: Hutchinson.

Davies, Celia (1996). "The Sociology of Professions and the Profession of Gender". *Sociology*, 30(4): 661–678.

De Beauvoir, S. (1949). *The Second Sex*. Harmondsworth: Penguin.

Donovan, Josephine (1985). *Feminist theory: The Intellectual Traditions of American Feminism*. New York: Ungar.

Dube, Leela (1988). "On the Construction of gender: Hindu girls in patrilineal India", Chanana, K. (*ed.*), *Socialisation, Education and Women*, New Delhi: Orient Longman.

Durkheim, E. (1964). *The Division of Labour in Society*, New York: Free press.

Firestone, S. (1980). *The Dialectic of Sex*, New York: Bantam.

Gandhi, Nandita and Shah, Nandita (1991). *The Issues at Stake: Theory and Practice in the Contemporary Women's Movement in India*, New Delhi: Kali for Women.

Hartsock, N. (1990). *"Foucault on Power: A Theory for Women"*. *In*: Nicholson, L.J. (*ed.*), Feminism Postmodernism, London: Routledge.

Jay, N. (1991). "Gender and Dichotomy", *In*: Gunew, S. (*ed.*), *A Reader in Feminist Knowledge*, London: Routledge.

John, Mary E. (1996). *Discrepant Dislocations: Feminism, Theory and Postcolonial Histories*. Delhi: Oxford University Press.

Kachuck, Beatrice (1995). *"Feminist Social Theories; Theme and Variations'. Sociological Bulletin*, 44 (2): 169–193.

Kishwar, Madhu (1990). "Why I do not call myself a Feminist'. *Manushi*, pp. 2–8.

Komarovsky, M. (1946). "Cultural Contradictions and ex Roles'. *American Journal of Sociology*, 52: 184–189.

Komarovsky, M. (1950). "Functional Analysis of Sex Roles'. *American Sociological Review*, 15: 508–516.

Mead, M. (1950). *Male and female*. London: Gollancz.

Mead, M. (1963). *Sex and Temperament in Three primitive Societies*, New York: William Morrow and Co.

Mead, M. (1968). Male and Female: A Study of the Sexes in the Changing World, New York: William Morrow and Co.

Nickols, Sharin Y. and Srinivasan, Kamala (1994). "Women and Household Production", *In*: Borooah, Romy (*ed.*), *Capturing Complexity: An Interdisciplinary Look at Women, Households and Development,* New Delhi: Sage Publications, pp. 102–122.

Niranjana, Seemanthini (1992). "Discerning Women: Variations on the theme of gender". *The Indian Journal of Social Science*, 5(4).

Oakley, A. (1972). *Sex, Gender and Society*, London: Temple Smith.

Parsons, T. and Bales, R.F. (1953). *Family, Socialisation and Interaction Process*, London: Routledge and Kegan Paul.

Rubin, Gayle (1975). "The traffic in Women: Notes on the Political Economy of Sex". *In*: *Toward on Anthropology of Women*, Reiter, Rayna B. (*ed.*), New York and London: Monthly Review Press, pp. 157–200.

Savage, M. and Witz, A. (*eds.*) (1992). *Gender and Bureaucracy*, Oxford: Blackwell.

Scott, J.(1986). "Gender: A Useful category of Historical Analysis". *American Historical Review*, 91: 1053–75.

Shiva, Vandana (1988). *Staying Alive: Women, Ecology and Survival in India*. New Delhi: Kali.

Strober, M.H. (1976). 'Toward Dimorphics: A Summary statement to the conference on occupational segregation'. *Signs*, 1: 293–302.

Thapan, Meenakshi (1994). *Femininity and Culture: An Agenda for Research*, (Occasional paper), IDPAD, Hague-ICSSR, New Delhi.

Tharu, Susie and Lalita, K. (*eds.*) (1993). *Women Writing in India,* New York: Feminist Press.

Wendy, Kaminer (1994). "Feminism's identity Crisis', *Span*, pp. 32–33; 41–42.

Young, K., Wolkowitz, C. and McCullagh, R. (1981). Of *marriage and the Market*, London: CSE Books.

Zaretsky, E. (1976). *Capitalism, the family, and Personal Life*, London: Pluto.

Chapter 9

Interrogating the Feminist Methodology in Social Sciences: Towards an Interdisciplinary Insight

Ashish Saxena and Vijaylaxmi Saxena

Feminists believe that women have been subordinated through men's greater power, variously expressed in different arenas. Theoretical and conceptual frameworks for work on women and gender in development affect the entire research process. Over last few decades the contributions of feminist scholars to social science and humanities research have been very significant. Feminist interrogation of various disciplines has involved critical engagement with conventional research methods and approaches, and the sources for research in various disciplines. Gender research methodologies are essential for furthering the goal of equitable social and economic development. Measuring change on the basis of gender-sensitive frameworks is essential to monitoring the process of development for gender equality and gender equitable results - at all levels and in all contexts.

INTRODUCTION

This paper outlines and assesses the arguments for a distinctively feminist methodology in an interdisciplinary framework. In general parlance, "feminism" is a movement, and a set of beliefs, that problematize gender inequality. Feminists believe that women have been subordinated through men's greater power, variously expressed in different arenas. They value women's lives and concerns, and work to improve women's status. "Feminist research" as a broader category includes any empirical study that incorporates or develops the insights of feminism. Simultaneously, feminist studies use standard research methods, or they may involve explicit attention to methodological critique and innovation.

Theoretical and conceptual frameworks for work on women and gender in development affect the entire research process, from the issues considered at the research formulation stage, to the questions asked when conducting research, to the elements considered important to project planning and implementation, and finally the ways in which indicators are developed to measure success in both the research and programme evaluation processes. Because of this, it is important to explore the connections between shifts in development theory and gender research, to fully understand the methodologies used for research on gender issues today.

From the early days of the women's movements of the 1970s, feminists have tried to intervene in the ways that the social sciences think about and do research. They have attempted to transform the methodologies and epistemologies of their disciplines. Central to these projects have been concerns about whether and how customary approaches to knowledge production promote or obstruct the development of more democratic social relations. To feminist and non-feminist scholars alike, the concept of feminist methodology long has been a puzzling, somewhat troublesome notion. Non feminists tend to view such an approach as "unscientific,' 'ideological," or "biased" (Eichler, 1980), while some feminists find themselves uneasy about the vagueness and ambiguity associated with the term. In fact, the notion of feminist methodology has suffered from comparisons with traditional scientific methodologies by appearing to be too amorphous and indefinable. It is the contention of this analysis, however, that such comparisons are useless in that the concept itself does not represent another type of methodology but rather an alternative to methodology as currently practiced in our largely sexist research institutions. Further, such comparisons obscure the interplay between the epistemological ideas and the technical practice of feminist methodology by highlighting the differences in methodological techniques across (and even within) disciplines, and ignoring over-arching similarities in the methodological assumptions of feminist researcher.

Feminist methodology grows out of an important qualitative leap in the feminist critique of the social sciences: the leap from a critique of the invisibility of women, both as objects of study and as social scientists, to the critique of the method and purpose of social science itself. This is the leap from 'sociology about women' to 'sociology for women'. Feminist methodological critiques have been made on several interrelated levels: philosophical, moral, and practical. The philosophical level involved a critique of positivism: the pretence of value-free science and presumption of objectivity conceived of as a set of procedures or an achievement, rather than a process (Gorelick, 1989).

Over last few decades the contributions of feminist scholars to social science and humanities research have been very significant. They have offered new perspectives and methods in researching women's lives and in analyzing the structures and ideologies that mediate women's everyday existence. Feminist interrogation of various disciplines has involved critical engagement with conventional research methods and approaches, and the sources for research in various disciplines. But there is yet to be a systematic documentation and reflection on what constitutes feminist research, on the feminist use of various research techniques, tools and methods, how these have offered possibilities for rethinking research within various disciplines and also on the interdisciplinary aspects of doing feminist research. The "feminist standpoint" research representing reality from women's experience has helped to reconstruct the domain of conventional research with the use of a wide variety of qualitative research methods such as participatory observation, consciousness-raising methods, in-depth interviews, group diaries, documenting oral narratives and testimonies, photography or "talking picture" techniques, etc.

Feminist attempts to intervene in the ways that social science think about and practice their epistemologies and methodologies have been more successful in some disciplines than in others. To begin with, a methodology is a theory and analysis of how research should be conducted (Harding, 1987). Methodologies are often confused with epistemologies, theories of knowledge, and research methods, which are the actual tools used to carry out research. From a gender perspective, researchers have noted that 'traditional' methodologies, epistemologies, and methods are not scientifically 'objective' but the opposite: they generally ignore women's knowledge by showing bias towards the male perspective. In response to this, methodologies used for research on women in development were developed from critiques of particular sex, class, and race biases found in 'traditional' research methodologies as well as dominant perspectives of development.

There are several commonly agreed upon characteristics of research methodologies using a gender perspective (UN-INSTRAW, 2006)

- Consideration of the hierarchical power relations between men and women that tend to disadvantage women throughout the research process - this involves recognizing both gender inequality in the everyday lives of women and men, and also the gendered nature of the research process itself.
- Integration of diversity, including the differing ways that race, ethnicity, class, caste, sexuality, age, and (dis)ability, affect gender relations, with special attention to the voices of the marginalized, into all levels of the research process.
- Analysis of the relationships between and among all research parties (including the researcher/s).

- Common use of qualitative methods considered 'non-traditional' in the physical and social sciences and in research for development in particular.
- Adaptation of quantitative methods to take into consideration 'hard-to-measure' aspects such as women's empowerment, and sensitive items such as gender-based violence.

THE IDEAS OF FEMINIST METHODOLOGY

Women's Studies have lived with casual and unexamined understandings of interdisciplinarity. Generally the term has implied structural descriptions of women's studies programs and departments, in which faculty and students with an array of disciplinary training and what the academy calls "majors" come together to explore common questions.

In 1978, Mies set forth methodological guidelines for feminist research that proposed that the hypocritical "postulate of value-free research, neutrality and indifference toward the research objects, has to be replaced conscious partiality" toward the oppressed, engagement in their struggles change, and the creation of a form of research that fosters conscientization of both the researcher and the researched (Mies, 1983) These guidelines set the dominant formula for research practice The dogmas of positivism - its hands-off approach, its clinical fastidiousness about mutual contamination, its insistence that research must precede change, that indeed change is the business of politicians and not scientists- were overturned. Similarly, beginning in 1974, Smith argued that sociology as currently practiced expressed unreflectively the distortions of a male ruling-standpoint. She urged that instead research must be done "from the standpoint of women," taking "the everyday world as problematic" and beginning women's ordinary, everyday experience (Smith, 1974; 1979). Smith specifically cautioned against confining the inquiry to the world of experience (Smith, 1974; Smith, 1979). Some later feminist methodologists, however, have argued for a social science that is "inductive rather than deductive" (Reinharz, 1983; 172), that "focuses on processes rather than structures" (p. 168), and is "interested in generating concepts *in vivo*, field itself' rather than using "predefined concepts" (p. 168). According Reinharz, whereas the validity criteria of "conventional or patriarchal" science are "proof, evidence, statistical significance [and] replicability," validity criteria of feminist science are "completeness, plausibility,. Understanding, [and] responsiveness to readers' or subjects' experience; study cannot, however, be replicated" (Reinharz, 1983; 171). The role of researcher is to "give voice" to hitherto silenced groups and facilitate own discoveries (Kasper, 1986).

Regardless of the discipline, at least four characteristics are found in all types of feminist methodology. The first involves recognition of the large gaps in our knowledge created by researchers who ignore women and women's concerns or consider them trivial or uninteresting research topics (Epstein, 1981; Schulenburg, 1979; Shapiro, 1981). Thus, a crucial feature of feminist methodology is its focus of research on women's worlds in order to understand women's experiences in a given culture, historical time period, or social position. A second feature of feminist methodology is its emphasis on the importance of the feminist researcher (Bernard, 1979; Dye, 1979; Berndt, 1981). This entails recognition of a methodological bias in the fact that women are now, and have always been, severely underrepresented in all three disciplines (Howard, 1978). This bias is created because male researchers studying women's worlds are frequently unable to understand women empathically. Opinions range from those scholars who believe that only women should study other women (Rohrlich-Leavitt, 1975). A third feature of feminist methodology, present in all three disciplines, is the constant awareness of the need to reformulate existing concepts so that they may be meaningfully applied to women. This often involves demonstrating how particular conceptual formulations exclude women by definition, or has little relevance to women's lives. Interesting to note is that in all three fields, the concept of power has received considerable attention, including extensive critique and reformulation. By redefining power in less-coercive terms as the "ability to do or effect something and final feature of feminist methodology is an explicit awareness of the kinds of research questions that are asked and how these influence nature of research results. First, feminist methodology implies an understanding of how research questions are molded by cultural gender assumptions. Feminist sociologists, for example, have pointed out that defining the sociological research problem often entails pejorative labeling of those who violate traditional gender prescriptions (Committee on the Status of Women in Sociology, 1980). Previous sociological research, for instance, has emphasized the problems of female-headed households and single-parent families, without adequate exploration of the problems associated with two-parent families. Feminist historians have questioned the use of oppression models of women's history, which examine the ways women have been denied rights, power, and influence.

Feminist Methodologies - The Struggle for Egalitarianism

Feminism implies an approach to inquiry and continues to make a major contribution to the social sciences. There is a distinctively feminist methodology. There is no doubt that the growth in influence of feminism in the social sciences over the past few decades has increased the salience of gender within those fields. This variable had not been completely neglected previously, but it had been given relatively little attention in comparison with others like class and ethnicity. This is true in three respects. First, relatively little research had focused on gender differences, and the experiences and perspectives of women and girls had been neglected. Secondly, in research on all topics the significance of gender as an extraneous variable had been underplayed. A result was the tendency to generalise from research on boys and men to human behaviour in a way that neglected potentially significant gender differences. Even more notably, awareness of the effects of gender difference on the research process itself was almost completely absent before the influence of feminism.

Not surprisingly, a key feature of feminist methodology is taken to be a central concern with gender. It is claimed that human social relations of all kinds are heavily structured by differences in the social position of women and men, and most important of all by differences between them in power. From this point of view, gender is a crucial issue in all areas of social life and must be taken into account in any analysis. Thus, the ubiquitous significance of gender and gender asymmetry exists; Common feature of feminist methodology is validity of personal experience (as against the masculinist) emphasis on scientific method. Feminist literature often takes the form of experiences. One of the major tasks of feminist research, explore the experience of women, this experience its own term; Further, that the relationship between researcher and researched should be a reciprocal one, 'hierarchical' distinctions between researcher and researched should be broken down. Lastly, many feminists define a central goal of their research as the emancipation of women, rather than the production of valid knowledge *per se*. view, feminist research is necessarily a process of conscientisation for both researcher and researched, and is to be judged in terms of its success in this respect.

In this context, it would be relevant to explore: (i) How and why certain research methods have come to be privileged over others by feminists researching women's lives and what values these add to feminist theorizing; (ii) How research methods like participatory research, participatory rural appraisals, etc, have been able to modify these techniques to suit their needs and what are the advantages and disadvantages of using these new research techniques in doing gender studies; (iii) How and in what ways feminist researchers have been able to overcome the conventional quantitative and qualitative divide and how have perspectives evolved as regards the integration of both methods in feminist research strategies.

Towards Interdisciplinary Aspect of Feminist Methodology

Feminists do not agree on whether some research methods are more feminist than others. Some feminists, arguing that prevailing quantitative methods have been used against women, advocate for more qualitative, interpretive approaches (Mies, 1983; Reinharz, 1983; Smith, 1987; Stanley and Wise, 1983; Westkott, 1979). Other feminists are indignant at the implication that qualitative methods are more feminist than quantitative methods; they believe that any method can be feminist. Research methodology encompasses all aspects of inquiry. It entails agenda, epistemology, and ethics, as well as methods. Participants in the qualitative-quantitative debate should distinguish among these aspects of methodology. Harding (1987) suggests that what are distinctive about feminist inquiry is not methods (techniques we use to gather and analyze data) but how we know what we know (epistemology) and how we apply theory to our agenda.

Like outsiders to this body of writing, feminist methodologists themselves often rely on competing or simply unarticulated assumptions about what does (or should) hold this body of work together, and those working to develop feminist methodology sometimes seem to write at cross-purposes. This seems especially true in writing on feminist uses of "qualitative" and "quantitative" methods.

In the early 1990s, the use of quantitative approaches in feminist research was far from rare. What set these approaches apart from their non-feminist counterparts was the researchers' attention to the ways in which key concepts were operationalized, the careful matching of statistical techniques to research questions, the transparency with which the researchers presented their data and analysis, and the focus of the analysis on disenfranchised groups and salient policy issues. A review of current writing on feminist quantitative research reveals the continuation of these trends along with new advances and insights in applying quantitative analysis as a feminist method. This body of scholarship shows that, while the gulf between qualitative and quantitative methods is still wide, it is often feminists who have sought to bridge it through their collaborative impulse, their critical stance, their search for more inclusive and nuanced ways to measure complex social phenomena, their location on the continuum of political activism, and their desire to create research that can be used to promote social change.

Our original analysis of feminist approaches to social science research in women's studies revealed some commonalities, which we articulated as guiding principles of feminist methodology: first, the necessity of continuously and reflexively attending to the significance of gender and gender asymmetry as a basic feature of all social life, including the conduct of research; second, the centrality of consciousness-raising or debunking as a specific methodological tool and as a general orientation or way of seeing; third, challenging the norm of objectivity that assumes that the subject and object of research can be separated from each other and that personal and/or grounded experiences are unscientific; fourth, concern for the ethical implications of feminist research and recognition of the exploitation of women as objects of knowledge; and finally, emphasis on the empowerment of women and transformation of patriarchal social institutions through research and research results. Today the spectrum of epistemological and methodological positions among feminists is much broader—a healthy sign of the vitality of feminist studies. There has never been one correct feminist epistemology generating one correct feminist methodology for the interdisciplinary field of women's studies. Feminist scholars work within, against, and across epistemologies, often combining elements from different perspectives. Innovative methods are derived from successful efforts to reconcile differences and even from those efforts that conclude that certain epistemological differences are irreconcilable.

Feminist social scientists have developed distinctive methodological approaches that fit the feminist goals of opposing inequality and research that empowers women, validates their experiences, and improves their daily lives. Despite the consensus on these methods, most feminists avoid using them, especially those methods that challenge inequality most: including action in research, using participatory approaches, critiquing the academic power structure. Some fear that feminist methods undermine scientific standards, but concern stems from a limited, positivist perspective on science. A social practice perspective implies that positivism is only one socially constructed interpretation of the basic standards of good evidence and open debate. Feminist methodology suggests standards that are equal or superior.

This community, and the very idea of "feminist sociology," are products of the "'second-wave'" women's movement that began in the 1960s and early 1970s, and has grown and differentiated in the years since through conflict, institutionalization, and co-optation (Ferree and Martin, 1995; Roby, 1992). Feminist sociologists are committed to both feminism and social science, and they use the tools of the discipline to "talk back" to sociology in a spirited critique aimed at improving the ways we know society.

Until the early 1970s, the field of women's history was characterized by two competing approaches. On the one hand, use of "oppression" models emphasized the subjugation of women and portrayed them largely as passive victims effectively restrained from participating in the creation of culture (Lougee, 1977). An example of this approach, as cited by historians, is the work of Simone de Beauvoir in The Second Sex, as well as Shulamith Firestone's - The Dialectic of Sex (Carroll, 1976). While acknowledging the importance of obtaining information regarding women's subordination, contemporary women's historians have criticized the oppression model for emphasizing women's victimization and ignoring the ways in which women did exercise power (Lerner, 1969). One such development in feminist methodology has been the appearance of relational analysis, first proposed by historian Joan Kelly-Gadol (1976). Such an approach goes beyond examining women's access to power by focusing on the relative position of men and women in the same class. Standardizing the historical time period as well as social class reveals variations in the position of women and their access to different opportunities and privileges. Even so, the underlying model assumes that "women as a group cut through male class systems," and thus relational analysis relates women's and men's history by assuming that societal developments may have radically different consequences for the two sexes (1977: 813).

Anthropological research on women has been hindered by a number of factors. First, cultural prohibitions have limited male anthropologists' access to women, so that often only data on the male sectors of a culture is obtained and reported (Friedl, 1975). Second, even when women informants are available, their activities have been ignored or trivialized by many ethnographers (Reiter, 1975). Third, with women less accessible, anthropologists often have relied on the reports of men about women's roles, attitudes, and behavior. Unfortunately, this method is seldom reliable since it actually elicits men's perceptions of women's worlds, and these perceptions usually are influenced by notions of male superiority (Rohrlich-Leavitt *et al.*, 1975). Thus, anthropology is subject to a double male bias: first, the bias brought by the researcher to the analysis; and second, the bias of the culture being studied. This has led many feminist anthropologists to re-examine the claims made by earlier ethnographers and their male informants about the roles, values, and behavior of women (Shapiro, 1981). Another feature of feminist methodology in anthropology is its emphasis on comparative analysis as a way to examine the variations in women's position and role behavior across different cultures. This focus on the comparative method also has stimulated the growth of inter-disciplinary regional and area studies on women that are necessary for comparative research. Feminist scholars have concentrated on developing appropriate cross-cultural frameworks, especially indices of female status, to apply in comparative analyses. This comparative approach has uncovered wide variations in female power, even between societies considered culturally similar. Attempts to develop such frameworks have led feminist anthropologists to scrutinize the construction of classification schemas used in comparative research.

Lenore Weitzman's book, The Divorce Revolution (1985), is feminist research that helps to explain gender inequality, gives women's experience, and contributes to social change. She studied changes in divorce laws and documented how they put women economic disadvantage compared to men. Her quantitative analysis changing economic situations of a random sample of 228 divorced and men showed that men, on the average, became better off financially divorce, while women became much worse off and often lived in poverty.

A very different type of study by Pamela Fishman (1978) shows micro analysis of conversation can clarify gender inequality, women's experience, and encourage social change on a personal level. Her article, "Interaction: The Work Women Do," is based on three heterosexual couples who agreed to tape-record several hours of their conversations home. Her analysis shows how the men's and women's different conversation styles helped to construct and maintain male dominance.

Nancy Kleiber and Linda Light's (1978) study of a feminist health collective, illustrates the usefulness of participatory methods and a critical, reflexive orientation to the research process. The participatory research tradition has developed useful models of how to translate some of the goals of feminist methodology into practice.

Overall the feminist methodology was about "Giving voice", a progressive development in the history theory. It went beyond criticism of the use of "mainstream" social a tool of oppression and began the quest for a liberatory social the more radically empiricist forms of the feminist critique have limitations, which threaten to encapsulate feminist social science specific milieu being studied and even preclude understanding milieu being examined. For example, use of such techniques as participant observation, and oral history helps to describe the perceived by the persons studied, but it may remain confined within perceptions and thus not be able to provide them with much that already prevails in society.

CONCLUSIONS

To end the oppression of women we need a political movement and a social science that gives voice to women. But because of the multifaceted structure of oppression, giving voice is not enough. To understand the different milieus in which women experience their oppression and to trace their connections with each other, we need a social science produced by women of various social conditions (race, class, sexual preference, nationality, or ethnicity), a social science that reveals the commonalities and structured conflicts of the hidden structures of oppression, both as they are felt and as they are obscured. The quest for such a science confronts and comprises a dynamic tension among the researcher and the researched, struggle and science, action, experience, method, and theory.

Gender research methodologies are essential for furthering the goal of equitable social and economic development. Measuring change on the basis of gender-sensitive frameworks is essential to monitoring the process of development for gender equality and gender equitable results - at all levels and in all contexts.

Rather, a methodology based on plea of many determinations implies a cumulative social science that merely additive. The visions of each subgroup of women must refocus re-vision the knowledge of all. The field is continually decomposed reconceptualized at deeper and more complex levels of understanding, always giving primacy to the vision. Such a science may imply an amazing goodwill, transcending opposing interests, for example, between white employers and "their" maids. That the idea of such a cumulative social science may seem to ignore conflict, conflicts are real, however. The problem of creating a women's social encompassing the consciousness and diverse conditions of different is similar to and related to the problem of creating a non-oppressive women's movement.

Ironically, the academic power structure poses a more formidable barrier to feminist methodology. Because of the hierarchical structure of universities, researchers who use methods that seriously challenge inequality will tend to punished or marginalized. Feminists probably can do little to change whole structure in the short run, but we can create more democratic, participatory structure.

REFERENCES

Allen, P. (1973). Free space. *In*: Radical Feminism, (*eds.*), Koedt, A., Levine, E. and Rapone, A. New York: Quadrangle, pp. 271–79.

Bernard, Jessi (1979). "Afterword." *In*: Sherman, J. and Beck, E. (*eds.*), The Prism of Sex: Essays in the Sociology of Knowledge. Madison: The University of Wiscon sin Press.

Berndt, Catherine H. (1981). "Interpretation and 'Facts' in Aboriginal Australia." *In*: Dahlberg, F. (*ed.*), Woman the Gatherer. New Haven: Yale University Press.

Dye, Nancy Schrom (1979). "Clio's European Daughters: Myopic Modes of Perception." *In*: Sherman, J. and Beck, E. (*eds.*), The Prism of Sex: Essays in the Sociology of Knowledge. Madison: University of Wisconsin Press.

Epstein, Cynthia Fuchs (1981). "Women in Sociological Analysis: New Scholarship Versus Old Paradigms." *Soundings*, 64: 149–162.

Ferree, M.M. and Martin, P.Y. (*eds.*) (1995). Feminist Organizations: Harvest of the New Women's Movement. Philadelphia: Temple Univ. Press.

Friedl, Ernestine (1975). Women and Men: An Anthropologist's View. New York: Holt, Rinehart and Winston.

Gorelick, S. (1989). Contradictions of feminist methodology. *Gender Soc.*, 5(4): 459–77.

Hammersley, M. (1992). 'On Feminist Methodology'. *Sociology*, 26: 2: 187–206.

Harding, S. (*ed.*) (1987). Feminism and Methodology, Bloomington: Indiana University Press.

Kelly, Joan (Joan Kelly-Gadol) (1976). "The Social Relation of the Sexes: Methodological Implications of Women's History." *Signs* 1: 809–824.

Kasper, A. (1986). A feminist, qualitative methodology: A study of women with breast cancer. *Qual. Sociol.*, 17(3): 263–81.

Lerner, Gerda (1969). "New Approaches to the Study of Women in American History." *Journal of Social History*, 4: 333–356.

Light, Linda and Kleiber, Nancy (1981). Interactive research in a feminist setting: The Vancouver women's health collective. *In*: Anthropologists at home in North America, (*ed.*), Messerschmidt Donald. New York: Cambridge University Press.

Lougee, Carolyn C. (1977). "Review Essay: Modern European History." *Signs* 2: 628–650.

Mies, Maria (1983). "Towards a Methodology for Feminist Research." *In*: Theories of Women's Studies, (*ed.*), Bowles Gloria and Renate Duelli-Klein. Boston, MA: Routledge and Kegan Paul, pp. 117–139.

N-INSTRAW (2006). 'Gender Research Guide', United Nations International Research and Training Institute for the Advancement of Women, www.un-instraw.org/en/index.php?option=content&task=view&id=1051&Itemid=247

Oakley, A. (1981). Interviewing women: A contradiction in terms. *In*: Doing Feminist Research, (*ed.*) Roberts, H. London: Routledge & Kegan Paul, pp. 30–61.

Fishman, Pamela (1978). Interaction: The work women do. Social Problems.

Reinharz, S. (1983). Experiential analysis: A contribution to feminist research. See Bowles & Duelli Klein, pp. 162–91.

Reiter, Rayna (1975). "Introduction." *In*: Reiter, R. (*ed.*), Toward an Anthropology of Women. New York: Monthly Review Press.

Roby, P. (1992). Women and the ASA: Degendering organizational structures and processes, 1964-1974. *Am. Sociol.*, 23(1): 18–48.

Rohrlich-Leavitt Ruby, Sykes Barbaraand Weatherford Elizabeth (1975). "Aboriginal woman: Male and female anthropological perspectives." *In*: Reiter, R. (*ed.*), Toward an Anthropology of Women. New York: Monthly Review Press.

Schulenburg, Jane Tibbetts (1979). "Clio's American Daughters: Male History, Female Reality." *In*: Sherman, J. (*ed.*), The Prism of Sex: Essays in the Sociology of Knowledge. Madison: The University of Wisconsin Press.

Shapiro, Judith (1981). "Anthropology and the Study of Gender." *Soundings*, 64: 110–129.

Smith, Dorothy E. (1979). "A Sociology for Women." *In*: The Prism of Sex: Essays in the Sociology of Knowledge, (*ed.*), Sherman, Julia A. and Evelyn, Torton Beck. Madison, WI: University of Wisconsin Press, pp. 135–87.

Stanley, Liz and Wise, Sue (1979). "Feminist Research, Feminist Consciousness and Experiences of Sexism." *Women's Studies International Quarterly*, 2: 359–374.

Westkott, M. (1979). Feminist criticism of the social sciences. *Harvard Education Review*, 49(4): 422–30.

Weitzman, Lenore (1985). The divorce revolution: The unexpected social and economic consequences for women and children in America. New York: Free Press.

Chapter 10

Gender Justice and Social Reform: Vision of Sardar Patel

Neerja Singh

The country is treading in darkness on one foot and that too of a male. They are being constantly hammered that they have to shoulder the burden of the house as far as possible. He has not been taught to accept that. In social and national spheres women have some rights and responsibilities. That is why we are lagging behind. Women in one way are extremely courageous. Men do not endure the miseries to the extent women do. In India misery is destined in women's fate and she smilingly endures them. She is not aware of her rights. The society fears that if she is educated she would have knowledge of her rights and will shake off the privations. But that fear is uncalled for. What is good for man is good for women also. The society adopts a partisan attitude between a male and a female. It pardons a male but a woman is permanently censured and disgraced, if she commits a blunder. So long as women are not sufficiently educated and inculcated with national spirit, till then there will be no prosperity.

-Sardar Patel

INTRODUCTION

One of the reasons for the Congress 'Right' being dubbed as such has been the inadequate understanding or misunderstanding of their social vision and perspective. Their approach to social issues has often been viewed as epiphenomenal or peripheral to their core concern of anti-imperialist struggle. In this chapter an attempt will be made to study their social vision and its place in their overall perspective of the movement.

The Congress 'Right', as would be clear in the subsequent discussion, were deeply concerned with the social ills which were retarding the growth of Indian society and making it decrepit. For the success of the anti-imperialist movement a healthy social foundation was an essential precondition. The anti-imperialist movement would liven up the dormant political consciousness of the masses, and strong social foundations would make acceptance of anti-imperialist ideology an easy process. They, therefore, wanted the Congress to seriously take up social issues such as child marriage, untouchability, women's rights and education, rural indebtedness, dowry, widowhood, conversion, purdah, cleanliness and personal hygiene in particular and the social degradation caused by the dominance of Brahmanism and ritualism in general.

The Congress 'Right' were believers in the efficacy of tradition. They were modern in their ideology and perception but traditionalist in their treatment of issues. This aspect of their approach was not understood by the 'revolutionaries' who were persuaded greatly by their own narrow confines of ideology.

The understanding of social issues by the Congress 'Right' was quite advanced in perception and ideology. Their approach was indigenous and ingenuous, pragmatic and realistic, progressive and purposive. They talked of tradition not for its preservation as such but for progressive change in the social structure without any sharp and abrupt rupture. This aspect of the 'Right' will become more pronounced in the course of discussion of the social issues in the succeeding pages.

Born in a peasant caste which was deeply embedded in the bhakti tradition and Swami Narayan cult, Patel was opposed not only to Brahmanical social order but also to ritualized Hinduism, and its various rites of passage associated with birth and death. He believed in plain speaking and was forthright and frank in expressing his view, and was highly critical of Brahmanical order and its imposition and perpetuation of the caste system:

> I do not believe in any caste or community. The whole of India is my village and men of all communities are my friends and relations. All are children of the same God. After a man dies does anyone ask if the corpse is that of a Brahman or a Chamar!

While referring to the Guruvayur movement Patel blamed the Brahmins for practicing falsehood and deceit in the name of protecting Hindu religion. According to him,

> Hindu religion is at present divided and it now exists only in any outward show, such as applying religious sectarian mark on the forehead, glimpses of deities and in undertaking religious tours of sacred places of pilgrimage. But the true Hindu religion consists in practicing control of the senses, abstaining from sensual pleasures and in realization of Supreme Being *i.e.*, God.

Patel's vision of free India was, "In free India there can be no distinction of caste, creed or religion or of classes, resulting in the domination of one section over another. There may be rich and poor, happy and unhappy, but there can be no difference in stature between one citizen and the other.

The strength of Hindu society was, however, seen by Patel in its ability to adjust itself to the changing conditions. Strongly criticising those who gave the cry of Hinduism being in danger, Patel said:

> Do not be led away that Hinduism is in danger. Hinduism can never be in danger in India. Have we not produced men of religion all over India? What did Shankracharya do? When he died how young he was! But did he raise the cry that Hinduism was in danger? Religion is a matter between man and his maker. If you forget your citizenship and talk of

> religion it is a cloak. Therefore when I hear some people talking about Hinduism in danger I feel that they are going a wrong way. Do not indulge in scaremongering for selfish ends. Do not employ wrong methods for catching votes or forming the parties. It is a very dangerous game. After all, we too want to serve our own people.

Endowed with a robust sense of peasant pragmatism, Patel abhorred show of any kind of religious duplicity. In his speeches at Dharmshala, Kashindra, Baila and Chaloda in Ahmedabad district on 2 January 1935, he criticized religious hypocrisy and evils of the caste system. He cautioned the rural population that unless they did away with such evils, 'true Swarajya' would be elusive:

> Religion is confined only to the religious signs on the body, glimpses of the deity and outward behaviours. We commit sins for as long as 25 years and go to Ganges in a year for bathing. Are people absolved of sins by taking a bath in the Ganges in a year? I therefore advise you for your own benefit to learn to live like members of the same family in the villages because where there is unity, there is peace and where peace exists eternally it becomes an abode of God.

The Right-wing leaders largely accepted the constructive programme of Gandhi and through it they tried to expand the area of influence of anti-imperialism. Their speeches against ritualism, untouchability and social obscurantism were intended to serve the twin purpose of spreading the Gandhian ideology of swarajya and inculcating the spirit of social reform. Patel reminded the farmers that there could not be any caste or religious distinctions amongst them. He said,

> Farmers who till the land, whether small zamindars, farmers or agricultural labourers are essentially farmers, regardless of the caste and the religion to which they belong. All are in the same boat; they will sink or swim together. Nature does not recognize any differences on the basis of caste or religion;

Nature smiles or frowns on everybody in the same manner. All the farmers find themselves in the same economic trouble.

Patel wished every member of scheduled caste to feel that he was superior to the Brahman. Exposing the hollowness of the caste system, he held caste Hindus responsible for the plight of untouchables:

> Many superstitions and hypocritical practices are rampant among the farmers and they are all there in the name of religion. We reject our Harijan brothers whose services are needed not only in agriculture but also in things nobody else is able to do and we hurt them, all in the name of religion. This is a sin. When a person we call an untouchable embraces another religion he immediately becomes touchable.

Patel exhorted the high castes to treat Harijans as equals and eradicate untouchability from their minds:

> I advise you to abolish untouchability which is a curse to the Hindu community of India. You cannot discard your own brother. According to the Hindu philosophy it is a sin to discard anyone who is living. Soul is God and even an untouchable has soul in him. You therefore cannot discard God-Soul.

He believed that along with achieving swarajya it was equally essential for the upper caste ego to attain sublimity by shedding their caste arrogance and accepting untouchables in their fold. He castigated upper castes for not giving proper respect to Dr. Ambedkar:

> Dr. Ambedkar studied with you and also took up employment along with you. However you behaved with him in such a manner that he has nurtured nothing but hatred for you. If a Harijan converts himself into Christianity, the orthodox would push him out, but if he remains a Harijan, people treat him as if he were not a human being. Gandhiji undertook fast to prevent division of the Hindu community and forced changes in the Communal Award but no purpose would be served if untouchability is not eradicated from your mind.

Patel was perturbed that untouchability made the position of national leaders like him morally weak in the eyes of the British who exploited the situation to argue that the Indians were incapable of ruling themselves. He did not want conversions to be used by the British to show to the outside world how retrogressive, backward and inhuman Indian society was. He rebuked the high castes, "If a Dhod becomes a Christian or a Mussalman he can go where he likes. The Sanatan religion has come to such a low degree that a man of other religion came to defend it." Using social issues as a tool to explain the political situation Patel used opportunities to create awareness against divisive elements in the society on the one hand to highlight how it could be exploited by Britishers to enslave India to their interests on the other. Referring to Communal Award and how it was used as a bait to divide the Indians, Patel said:

> The British Empire feels that we have been defeated or are reeling under fear of the authority which has been puffed up with violence...We have to continue and strengthen the struggle through self-purification.... We are not strong enough to protect our own religion. So if our traditional religion may have reached a stage where a foreigner has to search we should perform the shradh ceremony so as to attain emancipation. In the new reforms a plan was put forth to divide the Hindu community into two divisions. The larger division may be amalgamated with such other castes and other co-religionists in such a way as would result in suffocating the so-called high caste Hindus. But I had a companion in Yeravada Jail, who was clad only in loins. He had given a notice to the Government that he would not allow them to interfere in our established religion. If they were trying to segregate the untouchables permanently, he would lay down his life by fasting unto death.
>
> You may perhaps be aware what the leaders of the Sanatan traditional religion were doing at that moment? Where had they gone? Does the traditional religion belong to the present

> age? It is current since the time of the Vedas. How many have been converted to Christianity? How many have become Muslims? Who are these traditionalists? They are converting only Hindus into their religious fold. Who are these Missionaries? If you had not treated the untouchables inferior even to dogs, would there have been so many Christians?

Patel empathized with Ambedkar and acknowledged how difficult his task was, but he also requested him not to be too harsh on the high caste Hindus. With reference to the Kavitha episode, where upper castes boycotted Harijans over the issue of permitting Harijan students to study together with the upper caste students in the same school, Patel said that "voice of change will seep in slowly as upper castes are 'backward and roll in ignorance', but conversion is not the answer." In his reply to Ambedkar over conversion he wrote,

> You have stated that untouchability is like a disease in the stomach. It is not going to be cured by applying oil on the stomach; it should be cured by surgery only. You are now prepared to tender advice to the people about conversion. It appears impossible to concur with your surgery on the stomach, you are now telling people to apply knife on the throat and chop off head from the body for getting rid of the stomach disease. Therefore, in spite of having extreme regard and sympathy for you, I am forced to disagree with you. The path you have chosen is quite hazardous. I am fully aware that you are in such adverse circumstances that I would hesitate to criticize you, even if you commit mistakes.

The traditionalist in Patel revolted against conversion but the reformer in him opposed Brahmanism and its perpetuation of untouchability, and thus he favoured temple entry and common school for Harijan and upper caste students.

Patel had deep-rooted abhorrence for untouchability. He not only sat amidst the untouchables but also spoke from within their enclosure. With this one significant gesture Patel publicly cemented the wide gulf between 'touchability and untouchability' and left a deep impact on the Kisans of Kathiawad.

Patel, Prasad and Rajaji were ardent supporters of temple entry programme of the Congress meant for the untouchables. Patel favoured opening of the Somnath temple to Harijans. When Rajaji was facing difficulty in getting the law passed on temple entry during his tenure as premier of Madras Presidency in 1939, Patel stood like a rock behind him and gave full support both moral as well as organizational.

The most significant aspect of Patel's attempt at social reform was the vigorous attack he launched against the servile status of women. He attributed the backwardness of the nation to men, who had not given equal rights and responsibilities to women. Addressing the women members of Jyotisangh at Ahmedabad on 2 October 1934 he said,

> The country is treading in darkness on one foot and that too of a male. They are being constantly hammered that they have to shoulder the burden of the house as far as possible. He has not been taught to accept that. In social and national spheres women have some rights and responsibilities. That is why we are lagging behind. Women in one way are extremely courageous. Men do not endure the miseries to the extent women do. In India misery is destined in women's fate and she smilingly endures them. She is not aware of her rights. The society fears that if she is educated she would have knowledge of her rights and will shake off the privations. But that fear is uncalled for. What is good for man is good for women also. The society adopts a partisan attitude between a male and a female. It pardons a male but a woman is permanently censured and disgraced, if she commits a blunder. So long as women are not sufficiently educated and inculcated with national spirit, till then there will be no prosperity.

The unique mix of tradition and modernity in Patel's thinking can easily be traced. While admiring institutions like Jyotisangh he said, 'we are still entertaining the belief that women have to look after their home and hearth only. Such ignorance can be removed by these types of institutions.' His modernity is quite conspicuous in his advocacy for women's education and branching out of their areas of operation from the confines of homes and hearth while his deep-rooted traditionalism was reflected in his statement like, 'future depends on the chastity of girl students'.

There was a curious amalgamation of traditionalism with modernity in the approaches of all the three 'Right' leaders to various social issues. It would not be appropriate to regard them as socially regressive and conservative leaders. If Patel laid emphasis on the chastity of girl students, he also favoured co-education for the girls,

> Experiments of co-education are rare in schools, but what I have heard and witnessed is that nowhere else I have come across such blind trust and confidence reposed by parents of pupils as is witnessed here in this institution. It is very difficult at least in our country to take care of girl students. It is considered very dangerous, causing constant anxiety, but the fact that they have accepted this challenge is a matter of great pleasure to me.

Sensitive to social issues and concerns, Patel attacked child marriage. Advising the villagers of Gujarat against child marriage he told them,

> If you do not stop child marriage you will degenerate and the progeny will be very weak. Why should the government frame laws and tell you that there should be no child marriage? You should understand your welfare of what use the progeny of such weaklings will be to the country? Weak persons can never take or retain swarajya.

In all his speeches Patel consistently attacked the prevalence of early marriage among the farmers,

> One social evil, one finds among the farmers, is that they marry their children at an early age. Burdening young children with family responsibilities at such a tender age is akin to murdering them...it is a matter of shame for us that the government had to pass a bill to prohibit child marriages. This is cited as a reason for our being unfit for swarajya.

Patel was equally perturbed at the status of the widows in the Indian society. Writing to Manibehn about Sukanya, sister of Gandhian Worker Usha Mehta, who had become a widow at an early age, Patel highlighted,

> The one who experiences this sorrow does not wish a rebirth. Now they will shave her head and keep her confined in a dark room for six or twelve months. The society is replete with people who view widows as carrier of curse and bad omen. That is why she has to live in perpetual fear. The relatives would make a claim to whatever property her husband had left behind and this would further bring misery in her life. Nobody else in the world has as difficult a life as the Hindu widow. The social taboos and the society's behaviour towards her tend to be so wicked that even for her to survive becomes impossible. She is educated and today there are institutions, which sympathize with the problems of widows. Therefore she can lead a comfortable life by entering into one of these institutions and by doing some good work for the society.

Patel empathized with the pitiable existence of the widowed women. However, he did not see their redemption in re-marriage. He preferred for them a life-long engagement in a career of social welfare and social service. He wrote,

> In Europe such widows remarry after a year or two after their husband's death. Such instances are on the increase even in our society these days. But their number however is still very small. Who can say as to how much comfort a remarriage brings? In Europe lakhs of such women spend their whole life helping the sick people through training as nurse. In our

country there are few girls from the upper sections of the society who will take to this path. Otherwise there could not be a better vocation for a widow than this one.

Thus while the analysis of the condition of widows in India was objective and rational, the solution Patel suggested remained confined within the matrix of tradition. Therefore, nuances of this kind made Patel appear a 'rightist' to the westernised intellectuals in the country. His ideas are to be understood in totality of the context, and not in fragments.

Patel stood for liberation of women from the yoke of ignorance, illiteracy and superstition. He wanted women to achieve freedom with a sense of responsibility and participate along with men in the struggle for swarajya. "The brave women of Mansa stood side by side with men and showed marvellous courage, strength of will and purpose. They ungrudgingly suffered all hardships, insult and even physical injury."

Patel exhorted men not to keep their women in Purdah. To him keeping them in Purdah was like keeping them away from knowledge and enlightenment. He wanted women to come out from the shackles of illiteracy and acquire knowledge to know what was happening in the world as well as her duties towards her motherland and to provide courage, support and sustenance to the struggle for swarajya. He said,

> You must discard the purdah. You must allow women to see the world outside so that they will realize their duties to the motherland. They must be made literate and acquainted with India's affairs. Without it, they will not be able to play their proper role in shaping the destiny of the country; it would be like a cart going on one wheel?

Patel's strong sense of justice made him protest against any kind of exploitation of women. He even stood for divorce for women, if the situation was not compatible for them. However, he was sensitive enough to visualize the problem divorce might give rise to. Therefore, he reprimanded men to change their ways and atone for their sins if they wanted their wives to be with them. He expressed these views in a letter to Jayantilal Patel, dated 3 June 1949,

> You have yourself committed such grave sins that you will have to do Herculean efforts to mitigate their effects. It is futile on your part to seek divorce from your wife. You have absolutely no right to do so as you have done her a great injustice. On the other hand if she herself decides to seek divorce from you, she is fully justified in doing so. So if you wish to undergo penance for your sins, being in the prime of life, you have yet time to alter the course of your life. So instead of craving for the parental property, you must make a resolve to lead a life of purity and service. If you would succeed in this attempt, may be your wife too would like to re-join you in your changed course of life.

Keeping this aspect of Patel in view it appears that the branding of Patel as a rightist is more political and ideological than historical. Patel aimed at healthy, vibrant, and full of life 'Swarajya' and not pale, diseased, poverty-stricken 'swarajya'. Therefore he often not only inspired the villagers to give up social evils like untouchability, child marriage, but also encouraged them to go for education, give up drinking, opium eating, keep the village and themselves clean, curtail expenses on marriage and 'PreetiBhojan' (meal after death). He advised the peasants not to incur debt and fall into the trap of the moneylenders. If need be they should borrow from one another. He also advised them to spend on the education, clothing and food for their children. He also advised them to build dispensaries and schools.

Speaking at PrantejMunicipality on 22 October 1935 he expressed anguish at the lack of basic medical facilities to take care of delivery cases.

> How much disgusting it is that in such a big town there is not a single maternity home for attending to delivery cases? These are bare necessities of the present times and we have ourselves

> to solve these problems. We are not weak so as to beg from government for help on each and every occasion. We should understand our own responsibilities.

Drinking being common among the tribal and lower castes, Patel saw it as another major social evil in the path of reform of these sections of the society and major obstruction in their participation in the struggle for swarajya.

> I tell the Bhils, Gamits and Chodrabreathen to be bold. God has bestowed hands, eyes and ears equitably to all. As you are ignorant you are consuming liquor and behaving like beasts. I advise you to abstain from these vices.

Patel was perturbed that evil influence of drinking was leading the farmers into the clutches of moneylenders and sending them further into the deep pit of poverty. Broken in spirit and morale they could never become the pillars of strength for the struggle for swarajya. Speaking at the Eight Raniparaj Conference at Baroda he said,

> We are losing our bread in two ways. One is the consumption of liquor. Those who are addicted to it might as well not earn, because what they produce during the day, they spend it in the evening at the liquor or the toddy shop. A person who is addicted to liquor does not have intelligence. Sometimes we hear complaints that if there is prohibition people will produce their own liquor in their homes. This would be a double sin because, on the one hand, it is an offence against the law, and on the other, a sin against God because by doing this you would be destroying the beautiful body God has given you. If God had intended your body to be receptacle for liquor he might as well have made a cask.

The evil of drinking had permeated so deeply among the lower castes that Patel favoured prohibition and along with other Congress leaders like Prasad and Rajaji made it one of the central social issues to be dealt with firmly by the Congress ministries.

> It is not correct to say that the Congress ministers are more anxious to introduce prohibition than to do anything of the removal of untouchability and uplift of the oppressed and depressed. Both these problems are equally important and all Congress ministries have to give priority to both prohibition and removal of untouchability. I do not agree at all with your views about prohibition. India is not Britain, America or France. Its culture and civilization is entirely different from the Western countries. In their civilization prohibition has no place. In India both Hindus and Muslims consider intoxication as a loathsome vice and drink is forbidden by religion. Half of the untouchability problem will be solved by successful prohibition, as it is largely amongst the so-called untouchables and the oppressed and depressed where this evil has played havoc.

To carry out the programme of social reform, Patel supervised establishment of Ashrams all over Gujarat *e.g.*, Bedchchi Ashram where young men were taught to weave. They were told to use Charkha as it would lead them to freedom from Sahukar as well as from the British. Harijan Ashram carried out significant work among the untouchables, under the charge of Narharibhai Parikh. He also looked after the education of village boys at Ras. Ashrams like Satyagraha Ashram, Sabarmati Ashram, Kasturba Seva Ashram, Morali Ashram, Kathiawar Harijan Sevak Sangh, Surat Patidar Ashram, Bhil SevaMandal, Poona Mahua Ashram, Navsari Ashram, Kidhwa Ashram etc. played a significant role in the spread of education of both boys and girls, in educating the people to give up oppressive customs and social evils like untouchability, drinking and 'preetibhoj'.

Speaking at the Harijan Ashram, Ahmedabad on 3 October, 1934 Patel reminded the inmates of the Ashram of what should be the role of the Ashram in the struggle for Swarajya, 'to cultivate strength so that they could overcome severe tests and to inculcate in them national spirit and build up character.

Patel laid great emphasis on the spread of education. He viewed it as the only means to remove backwardness, superstition, illiteracy, ritualism and poverty. However, he stressed on 'Swadeshi' education,

> It is really shameful, if a missionary school is functioning here. They educate our children by fathoming a distance of 5,000 miles and we do not teach our children.

According to him 'swadeshi' education should aim at training the children to remain loyal as well as courteous towards parents, their motherland and religion. Their character, courage and heroism should also be built up. In his view, "The greatest defect of modern education is that children are neither loyal to their motherland nor behave like Indians. Their life is in doldrums. So weak are they rendered, as if they are devoured by white ants and they roam helterskelterin search of jobs. They turn averse to their family, country as well as parents. The chief malady is the foreign power and unstable politics."

CONCLUSIONS

Besides untouchability, prohibition and education, another major focus of Patel's social criticism was of peasants' indebtedness to moneylenders and their indifference towards village industries. Revitalization of the village industries through khadi and charkha, in his view, could lead to removal of poverty. He, therefore, advised the peasantry to use Charkha as it would not only make them self-reliant in their need for cloth, but also restore their self-respect and spirit for freedom, besides providing employment to the lakhs of carpenters and blacksmiths. He denounced excessive mechanization, "people who are engrossed with the ideas of western civilization may think that only the machine would solve the problem of Indian poverty by a process ofmechanization. But it is evident that the machine cannot put all the unemployed to work." Patel reiterated that, "True socialism lies in the development of the village industries. We do not want to reproduce in our country the chaotic conditions prevalent in the western countries consequent on mass production."

REFERENCES

Chopra, The Collected Works, Vol. IV(21).
Nandurkar, Sardar Patel: *In*: Tune with the Millions, Vol. II(56).
Parikh, (1956 reprint, 1971). Sardar Vallabh Bhai Patel, Vol. II, Ahmedabad.
Patel's Presidential Address at the Allahabad Kisan Conference on 28 April 1935.
Patel's Speech at Ernakulum on 13 May 1949.
Patel's Speech at Jyoti Sangh, Ahmedabad, (2 October, 1934) in Chopra, The Collected Works, Vol. IV, 214.
Sardar Patel's Speech at Jodhpur on 25 January 1949.

Chapter 11

Circles of Gender Liberation

Ananta Kumar Giri

Gender is an important fact and challenge of human existence and it calls for creative efforts in understanding its reality, constitution and liberative transformation as much of humankind suffers from varieties of structures, discourses and practices of gender domination which inhibit fuller self-realization and co-realization of constitutive beings of gender such as male, female and trans-genders. Gender identities have complex relationships to biology, societies, cultures and histories. Though gender identities are related to biological categories such as male and female, they are not necessarily fixed. One may be born into a male body but that does not mean that one cannot experience what it means to be a woman which is not just dependent upon sex change. Even as biological categories males and females exhibit hermaphrodite characteristics as there are aspects of female biological characteristics in a male body as there are aspects of male biological characteristics in female bodies.

Though males and females are not just social and cultural constructs, the biological boundaries between them are fluid (see Paglia, 2017). But even though our biological identities are fluid, our gender identities become fixed and essentialized through the workings of society, culture and power. Power and cultural constructions of meaning play an important role in the constitution, structuration and ongoing dynamics of gender identities. Our gender identities become part of varieties of structures of gender domination and in most of the cases in societies and histories it becomes one of male domination. Male domination in gender identities and gender relations leads to subordination of woman but it also leads to suppression and annihilation of feminine aspects within males themselves. This is sometimes reinforced by a bio-cultural logic that men are more rational and aggressive and women are more passive and emotional. Male domination in gender relations leads to such an erroneous construction and self-making that men should be more rational and aggressive and women should be more submissive and emotional. Such a logic of male domination does not challenge men to discover their own soft and emotional dimensions including the vulnerability to weep. Similarly such a logic of male domination does not allow women to realize their own strength and capacity to reason.

Power and existing cultural logics constitute gender identities and gender relations. Most of the time it leads to inequality, subordination and domination. The discourse of empowerment, especially women's empowerment, is a response to inequality of power in gender relations. But while struggle for empowerment is important and crucial for transforming gender domination and for creating transformational gender relations based upon beauty, dignity and dialogues, it nonetheless challenges us to rethink, reconstitute and realize power itself differently in self, society and the world. Usually we look at power, as articulated by Weber, as one's ability to exercise one's power over the will of the others. This leads to a zero-sum approach to and reality of power. In this place we can have a different approach to and realization of power. As Hannah Arendt suggests, to have power is to have the ability to work in concert with each other. Such an approach to power is also reflected in Gandhian approach to power where power is characterized not only by domination but by the desire for communication and suffering in spite of closed walls and stones falling from all sides. Habermasian approach to power and discourse in his project of discourse ethics also shares aspects of such an approach to power (Habermas, 1990). In discourses and practices of women's empowerment we can embody such approaches to power as the ability to work in concert with each other with love, co-suffering, joy and communication with a spirit of both resistance and co-creation.

There have been varieties of ways of realizing empowerment in human history including in gender relations and it has included both violent and non-violent struggles. In this changes in law and consciousness have also played an important role. In transforming gender domination, we can have varieties of creative resistance and movements of co-creation. Here we can bring a spirit of creative and critical resistance to power and a performative approach to transforming gender domination as suggested by Judith Butler. We can perform gender relations differently as relations of beauty, dignity and dialogues instead of relations of domination and annihilation. The performative here creates conditions of realization of potential—suppressed and unrealized —for all.

Satyagraha is one such method, practice and approach of resistance and engagement with performative as creation of new possibilities. Gandhi had envisioned it and put it in practice but some of the basic aspects of Satyagraha have much deeper genealogies sometimes as old as humanity. In *Satyagraha*, we do not construct the other as an enemy. Because of centuries of burdens of gender domination, it is easy to perceive men as permanent enemies on the part of those who are suppressed, oppressed and annihilated (Giri, 2017b). But at the same time there is a challenge for us to go beyond a construction of any gender whether male or female as a permanent enemy to cultivate vision and practices of friendship. *Satyagraha* against gender domination and for creative gender relations embodying beauty, dignity and dialogues moves towards this. *Satyagraha* works and meditates with love and *ahimsa*—non-violence but when necessary it is not afraid to follow the course of violence if pushed to a limit. A true spirit of *Satyagraha* would understand the violence that becomes indispensable to protect one's beauty, dignity and dialogue if pushed to a limit. Selfless suffering is one of the important ways of *Satyagraha* but it is different from masochism and inflicting injury on oneself. If needs be for example if a woman is subjected to violence in struggling for gender liberation then *satyagraha* understands the limits of non-violence in specific circumstance and the need for violent resistance as well. But while engaged in violent resistance, one can still not construct the other as a permanent enemy and move towards reconciliation and construction of an emergent wholeness and oneness (Datta-Ray, 2015).[1]

Satyagraha is a process and works in the field of self, culture and society consisting of *Trigunas-Sattva, Rajas and Tamas*. We can conceptualize fields of gender relations as consisting of *Sattva, Rajas and Tamas. Sattva* refers to dimension of Truth, *Rajas* power and *Tamas* darkness. So far we look at fields of gender relations mainly through the lenses of power and forces of darkness consisting of destructive desire such as a desire to enjoy others sexually or otherwise without mutual agreement and dignity. But beings and fields of gender relations also have a dimension of Truth or truthfulness. This is an ideal in friendship and other circles of intimate relations such as marriage and relations of love.[1] For realizing creative gender relations consisting of beauty, dignity and dialogues we need to mobilize the dimension of Truth hidden in all of us that we are part of a larger whole and we are all connected through multiplex relations of non-duality or *Advaita*. An *Advaitic* consciousness of non-duality would help us realize the truth that the other in gender relations is not totally different from the self and as part of a relationship we should not do anything that would harm the other physically, mentally and spiritually. This Truth about our connected self is hidden from us and varieties of creative processes of self and social development can help us realize this Truth. Truth work and truth meditation as aspect of *Satyagraha* can help us transform the ravages done by forces of *Rajas* and *Tamas.* With creative works and meditation we can also transform *Rajas*—the field of power—to one of *sahashakti* or mutual power. We can transform the fields of *Tamas*—darkness—to fields of light. This requires creative efforts in walking, meditating and dancing with our desire through art and spirituality. For example, with deep friendship and sharing of creative pursuits such as poetry and drama, we can transform our rapacious desire which constitutes *Tamas* to a desire of light and joy of mutual presence and dance.

This requires movement. If we continue to be bound to fixed positions of gender identity then we become prisoners of a logic of domination. The mutual dance of Radha and Krishna constitutes here an inspiring way of dancing with our gender identities. As gifted to us in the immortal poetry of Jayadev's *Gita Govinda*, while dancing together Krishna touches the feet of Radha going beyond the logic of male domination. Radha here embodies eternal *Shakti*, feminine energy and realizing this calls for creative works of mutual love and care which is practiced in traditions of *Tantra*. In the Bible one woman washed the feet of Lord Jesus Christ but in a spirit of mutual movement Lord Jesus Christ now can wash the feet of this waiting woman. This can fully realize the creative feminine in Lord Jesus Christ who embodied kindness and compassion and related to women with respect, care and love going beyond the logic of patriarchal male domination in existing Jewish religion and society.[2]

Movements of gender liberation calls for creative movements of travel. Transcending gender domination calls for moving from fixed positions. In societies of male domination, women have limited access to travel. But while travelling from positions to positions, places to places, we need to learn new languages of bodies and cultures. It is said that female bodies speak in a different language compared to male bodies. So for realization of beauty of our bodies and our desires we need to feel and understand the languages of our bodies including the integral sacredness of our bodies even when engaged in relations of desires. Translation of language of our bodies including bodily desires is also accompanied by learning and translation of other languages of our life world. Most of the time the languages of our life world are dominated by power and desire and both of these are often colonized by the language of a colonized life world. Here we can go beyond the colonization of the language of our life world by languages and forces of market, money, power and state and bring other languages such as languages of Truth, Love and *Ahimsa* to interact with colonized languages of our life world which many a time is a language of violence.

Travel across life worlds from one position to other helps us go beyond the traps of fixed and sometimes inconsiderate positionality and creates possibilities of trans-positional movements. Travel and translation helps us in going beyond the traps of subjectivity and objectivity in our fixed positionality and create possibility for transpositional subjectobjectivity. Such transpostional subject-objectivity which goes beyond the opposition between subjectivity and objectivity helps us in realizing gender liberation (see Giri, 2017).[1] Many a time positions of both men and women become locked in fixity and this is not helpful for realizing creative gender relations characterized by beauty, dignity and dialogues. This is true of women's positions including feminist standpoints or feminist epistemological standpoint. Travel, translation and accompanying transpositional subject to objectivity can help us overcome such limitations and be part of border-crossing transmutation of positions and identities.[3]

Movements for gender liberation is a multi-dimensional movement for realization of wholeness out of our existence of fragments including broken fragments. This wholeness—aspired for and realized to the extent possible—embodies a spirit of *lokasamgraha. Lokasamgraha* is a very important invitation for self, social and cosmic transformation from the Indic tradition and it appears in Srimad Bhagbad Gita, a key text in spiritual quest of humanity from India. It is usually translated as well-being of all but it also refers to the process of gathering—gathering or collecting of *loka*—people. It is creative gathering of people and the accompanying process of mutual care that leads to well-being of people. As a process of gathering it is not just confined to the public, the public sphere—or public political processes. It also involves in an integrally inter-linked manner gathering of soul—*atmasamgraha*. *Lokasamgraha* and *atmasamgraha*—gathering of soul and people—leads to a creative gathering of society not just as a mechanical entity but also as a living process of critique, creativity and transformation. It also leads to creative regeneration of commons and a cosmic mobilization of energy. *Lokasamgraha* challenges us to realize that our life, self, society and the world have a cosmic dimension and our cosmos is not just a dead entity but a living evolving process. *Lokasamgraha* challenges us for a transformation of our cosmology from a mechanical one to a living and a spiritual one.

Lokasamgraha challenges us to realize well-being and happiness for all but for this we are all invited to be creative in our strivings and struggles and it cannot be left to the others, society and state. At the heart of *Lokasamgraha* is care and responsibility which connects the vision and practice to *Lokasamgraha* in the Western political traditions such as in the works of Hannah Arendt and in the Chinese philosophy of *Tian-Xia*—All Under Heaven.[4]

We can bring the vision and practice of *Lokasamgraha* to our fields and circles of gender relations and make it an integral part of struggle for gender liberation. *Lokasamgraha* is related to generation of well-being and thus is at the root of this heart-touching aspiration and prayer: *Lokah Samastah Sukhino Bhavantu* which means let all people and all being be happy. But how can we be happy? What is the meaning of happiness when it becomes a slave of quick satisfaction and consumption *Lokasamgraha* and when we are chained by gender domination. Can we be happy without being creative? And can we be creative when we are chained to structures and discourses of domination? Creativity may be the foundation of well-being, creative self and creative society. Thus along with the familiar prayer *Lokah Samastah Sukhino Bhavantu* we can strive and pray new prayers: *Lokah Samastah Srujana Bhavantu*—let all people be creativity, *Lokah Samastah SrastaBhavantu*—let all people be creators,

Lokah Samastah Saha Srasta Bhavantu—let all people be co-creators. For creating circles of gender libration we need to bring this prayer and practice of self and co-creation which challenge us to realize that we are primarily beings of creativity and not just salves of routine practices of gender domination.[5]

Our fields of gender relations also can be circles of gender liberation. We need to create circles of gender liberation in various domains of our individual and collective lives such as family, friendship circles and institutional domains such as schools, colleges, universities and offices. These fields today are characterized by varieties of threats of violence. Sexual harassment and violence is a challenge in India, USA and many parts of the world. To face this challenge we have sexual harassment laws in many places. But just having sexual harassment law in place is not enough. We need creative inter-gender relations of care, communication and sharing. When we become swayed by dark desires such relations of care, communication and sharing can help us overcome this to some the extent.

There have been varieties of efforts in our contemporary world for gender liberation. Self help groups and micro-finance groups are hailed as harbingers of women's economic empowerment. But there is a foundational problem in the language of self help. We need to transform this into mutual help groups. And help here lies not only in earning profit but being co-travelers in fields of creativity. Our SHG groups are mostly and exclusively busy in only giving and receiving loans. Nothing much happens outside this logic of stock taking. Even in the much celebrated case of Grameen Bank in Bangladesh the meetings of women do not have other related activities such as reading some life-elevating books together. So in meetings of self help groups with a spirit of gender liberation we can have varieties of learning and creative activities involving both the genders. Some of the books to be read here can involve new ways of envisioning and creating gender just relations drawing on the best practices and possibilities both from tradition and modernity. Our Self-help groups as mutual help groups can be circles of co-learning and creativity where not only women but men and women together can read together and also do artistic works together. They can also sing and dance together.

Learning involves love and labor. It is an epistemic work and meditation. Learning involves self, other and the world in complex ways as it is not confined only to the double contingency of self and other. Learning as involving self, other and the world involves what social theorist Piet Strydom (2009) calls triple contingency learning. Triple contingency learning involves ethics, aesthetics and responsibility. We need to bring this trigonometry of ethics, aesthetics and responsibility to our circles of gender liberation. Learning involves epistemic works and meditations but it also involves ontological works and meditations. As participants in circles of gender liberation, we are engaged in creative epistemological works and meditations. One aspect of this work and meditation is to realize how struggle for gender liberation is related to other challenges of liberation such as caste, race and class. Knowing about such interlinked constitution of our gender identity and struggle for liberation calls for creative knowledge works. But our epistemological work also involves going beyond dominant epistemology of the modern world what Boaventuara de Sousa Santos (2014) calls epistemology of the North. We need to learn from multiple epistemological traditions of gender liberation, for example, simultaneously from modern struggles of feminism as well as traditions such as *Tantra* which challenges us for new ways of realizing gender emancipation including the beauty and dignity of our bodies (see Giri, 2016).

Feminist movement has been an important movement in our modern world which has helped us to go beyond the limits of modern construction of knowledge especially positivism. According to the great Indian philosopher R. Sunder Rajan (1998), feminist turn has helped us realize post-positivist modes of knowing but feminist movement has been primarily epistemic. Feminist knowledge has been primarily epistemological and despite its critique of male exclusion and domination is still within the limits of the modernist primacy of the epistemic. Modernity gives primacy to epistemology to the neglect of the ontological. Feminism unfortunately suffers from this modernist limits of the epistemic and neglect of the ontological. But today we need to relate the epistemological and ontological together in creative and transformative ways. Transformational feminist knowledge can involve both epistemology and ontology in creative ways embodying what we have explored as ontological epistemology of participation (Giri, 2017). It can also become a part of an ontological epistemology of transmutation.

Our conventional models of emancipation including gender emancipation suffers from a logic of linearity. One aspect of linearity is a binary approach—either you are on our side or the other side of line. But gender relations defy this logic of linearity as the logic of entwinement of Ying and Yang from the Chinese tradition and aspects of Tantra from Indic traditions suggest. For realizing gender liberation we need to go beyond a lines and cultivate circles of creative gathering of self, other, society, world and cosmos. Circles of gender liberation as part of inter-linked other circles of liberation such as caste, class, race and liberation from one's ego thus becomes part of spirals of liberation dancing with love, care, courage, *chung* (right mind) and *karuna* (compassion) in the midst of violence and communication gaps of many kinds.

REFERENCES CITED

Butler, Judith (1996). "Performative Acts and Gender Constitution: An Essay in Phenomenology and Feminist Theory." *In*: Twentieth Century Performance Reader. London: Routledge.

Dallmayr, Fred (2015). *Against Apocalypse: Recovering Humanity's Wholeness*. Lexington Books.

Datta-Ray, Deep K. (2015). *The Making of Indian Diplomacy*. Oxford: Oxford U. Press.

Giri, Ananta Kumar (*ed.*) (2017). *Pathways of Creative Research: Towards a Festival of Dialogues*. Delhi: Primus.

Giri, Ananta Kumar (2017a). "Transforming the Subjective and Objective:

Transpositional Subjectobjectivity." Chennai: Madras Institute of Development Studies, Paper.
2017b. "Swaraj as Blossoming and Satyagraha as Co-Realizations." Paper.
2016. "With and Beyond Epistemologies from the South: Ontological Epistemology of Participation, Multitopial Hermeneutics and the Challenges of Planetary Realizations." Paper.
Giddens, Anthony (1992). *Transformation of Intimacy*. Cambridge: Polity Press.
Habermas, Jurgen (1990). *Moral Consciousness and Communicative Action*. Cambridge: Polity Press.
Irigary, Luc (2002). *Between East and West: From Singularity to Community*. New York: Columbia U. Press.
Miri, Mrinal (2009). "Gandhi and Empowerment." *In:The Modern Prince and Modern Sage: Transforming Power and Freedom*, (ed.), Giri, Ananta Kumar. Delhi: Sage.
Menon, Nivedita (2010). *Seeing Like a Feminist*. Delhi: Penguin.
Paglia, Camille (2017). *Free Women, Free Men: Sex, Gender, Feminism*. New York: Pantheon.
Pande, G.C. *Bharatiya Samaj Eitihasik Aur Tattwik Bibechan*.
Santos, Boaventuara de Sousa (2014). *Epistemologies from the South*. Boulder, CO: Paradigm Publishers.
Strydom, Piet. 2008. *New Horizons of Critical Theory: Collective Learning and Triple Contingency*. Delhi: Shipra.
Sunder, Rajan R. (1998). *Beyond the Crises of European Sciences: New Beginnings*. Shimla: Indian Institute of Advanced Studies.

ENDNOTES

This is also true of the so-called most characteristic index of one's biological identity such as male and female sex organs which have aspects of both male and female biological characteristics.

Camille Paglia critiques constructivist approaches to gender identity but we must not fall prey to a reverse biological determinism. Paglia writes:

> We must remedy social injustice whenever we can. But there are something we cannot change. There are sexual differences that are based in biology. Academic feminism is lost in a fog of social constructivism. It believes that we are totally the product of our environment.

> [..] Neither militant feminism, which is obsessed with politically correct language, nor academic feminism, which believes that knowledge and experience are constituted by language, can understand pre-verbal or non-verbal communication. Feminism, focusing on sexual politics, cannot see that sex exists in and through the body. Sexual desire and arousal cannot be fully translated into verbal terms. This is why men and women misunderstand each other (Paglia, 2017: 55).

But what Paglia may consider that even though sex exists with our body but our body itself is much more an open journey then a fixed and essentialized either or identity. Men and women misunderstand their bodily desires including facts and experiences of orgasm but they also understand each other through evolving communication which is a journey.

Mrinal Miri (2009) suggests that this is different from Foucauldian approach to power.

Datta-Ray argues that in case of Kashmir, Gandhi's support for military response to aggression from outside forces is within the framework of non-violence.

In their works Anthony Giddens and Luce Irigaray point to the challenge of honesty and integrity in sexual relations in the midst of dishonesty of many kinds.

Here the relationship between Maria Magdelana, the inspiring spiritual co-traveler of Lord Jesus Christ, and Lord Jesus Christ calls for deeper realization. For many their relationship was one of deep love and respect. According to some sources, Maria Magdelan was a priestess in a temple which imparted deep feminine knowledge like Tantra and she imparted such knowledge to Lord Jesus Christ.

I have explored this in my paper in my paper on transpositional subject objectivity.

Nivedita Menon suggests limitations of such essential standpoints in her *Seeing Like a Feminist* (Menon, 2010).

As Fred Dallmyar, the deep seeker and thinker of our times, writes:

> As an antidote to the spread of "worldlessness" in our time, Hannah Arendt recommended the restoration of a "public realm" in which people would actively participate and be mutually connected. Digging beneath this public forum, Heidegger unearthed the deeper source of connectedness in the experience of "care" (*Sorge, c ura*) in its different dimensions. From the angle of human "being-in-the world," care penetrates into all dimensions of this correlation—in the sense that existence is called upon to care about "world" and its constituent features (fellow-beings, nature, cosmos). Differently put: There cannot be, for Heidegger, an isolated "self-care" (*c ura sui*) without care for the world—that includes care for world maintenance (without which *Dasein* cannot exist). In this latter concern, is work does not stand alone. In the Indian tradition, especially the *Bhagavad Gita*, we find an emphasis on a basic ethical and ontological obligation: the caring attention to "world maintenance" or loka-samgraha. According to the Gita, such attention needs to be cultivated, nurtured and practiced in order for human life to be sustainable and meaningful (Dallmayr, 2015: 51-52).

In his work on Indian society and tradition, philosopher and historian G.C. Pande challenges us to realize that society consists of not only *bidhi* but also *sadhana*. Sadhana is a field of creative works and meditations. Sadhana also involves struggles and what Sankar Singh Niyogi used to call sangharha aur nirman.

LIST OF CONTRIBUTORS

1. Mohammad Akram, Professor, Department of Sociology, Aligarh Muslim University, Aligarh
2. Nadiya Muzaffar, Research Scholar, Department of Sociology, Aligarh Muslim University, Aligarh
3. Madhu Nagla, Professor, Department of Sociology, M.D. University, Rohtak. Email: bnagla@yahoo.com
4. Poornima Jain, Professor and Head, Department of Sociology and Political Science, DEI (Deemed University), Agra
5. Tarun Joshi, Research Scholar, Dept. of Sociology and Political Science, DEI (Deemed University), Agra
6. Julie M. Geredien, Artist and educator, Maryland, U.S.A., engaged in independent research. Organized a template for World Citizen Learning Groups and taught a full-year course at Anne Arundel Community College, called *The Axial Moment: An Integrated Approach to Human Transformation through Education.* Has written *Toward a Cosmopolitan World Social Body: a Treatise on Harmony* (to be published in 2018 by Cambridge Scholars Publishing); and *Practical Spirituality and the Transformation of Power* (published in anthologies). Julie has taught for 15 years in mostly public school settings. She has an MFA in Classical Theater and an MA in Elementary Education. E-mail: jgeredien@gmail.com.
7. Deepti Priya Mehrotra, Associate Professor, Department of Sociology and Political Science, DEI (Deemed University), Agra
8. Abdulrahim P. Vijapur, Professor, Political Science, Aligarh Muslim University, Aligarh
9. Abha Chauhan, Professor, Department of Sociology, University of Jammu, Jammu
10. B.K. Nagla, Politicizing the Feminine: Sociological Analysis of Gender Issues, Former Professor of Sociology, M.D. University, Rohtak. Email bnagla@yahoo.com
11. Ashish Saxena, Professor & Head, Department of Sociology, University of Allahabad, Allahabad. His research interest includes – Agrarian studies, Development studies and Subaltern. Email: ashish.ju@gmail.com
12. Vijaylaxmi Saxena is faculty in Sociology and presently teaching at C.M.P. Degree College, Allahabad. Her research interest includes, Women empowerment, Sociology of Law, Child labour, Indian sociology. Email: vijaylaxmisaxena73@gmail.com
13. Nandini Singh, Associate Professor, Department of History, Satyavati College
14. Anant Giri, Professor, Madras Institute of Development Studies, Chennai